Roses Down the Barrel of a Gun

Georgia: Love and Revolution

For Dave with thanks

Jo Seaman

Grosvenor House
Publishing Limited

This book is published by
Grosvenor House Publishing Ltd
Link House
140 The Broadway, Tolworth, Surrey, KT6 7HT.
www.grosvenorhousepublishing.co.uk

A CIP record for this book
is available from the British Library

ISBN 978-1-78623-592-3

"Wow, what a story!

Roses down the Barrel of a Gun is an incredible memoir of one British woman's experience working and living in a tumultuous Georgia.

I have learned so much about this country, its culture and its history by reading this wonderful book and the author's love of Georgia really shone through as I read. This book manages to convey the warmth and welcoming nature of the people Jo met as well as more difficult living and working conditions as Jo arrived at the British Council in Tbilisi. As well as giving insight into life before, during and after the Rose Revolution in 2003, which I found incredibly interesting in itself, the author manages to include a more personal narrative filled with the difficulties of transferring to an overseas role, the culture and warmth of the new country and the development of new friendships and relationships. I like the descriptions of the meals, and the toasting and felt as though I had a seat at the table as I read.

In addition to not knowing much about Georgia, I'm also unfamiliar with the work carried out by foreign embassies and initiatives like the British Council. I enjoyed finding out about the exhibitions and performances and I think that this book highlights the vital importance of the arts to society.

Roses Down the Barrel of a Gun is a fascinating insight into a country that I knew little about and I highly recommend this book."

LoveReading (the UK's leading book recommendation website)

"I absolutely loved reading this book! It was fascinating to hear of Jo's arrival in Tbilisi, the challenges she faced and overcame in setting up the new British Council office and expanding their activities: her role in the Rose Revolution, and just how life was in general at that time. It made a huge impression on me, because Tbilisi was such a different place when I worked there - it is hard to believe that so much had changed in such a short time. I also loved the anecdotes, which had me laughing out loud." **Alexandra Hall Hall, former British Ambassador to Georgia**

"Roses Down the Barrel of a Gun is an amazing book. Jo Seaman goes to Georgia to set up a British Council office. Which might be a challenge - she's into challenges - but the challenge, presumably, would be bureaucratic and administrative. It's not. Georgia - just shaking free from the Soviet yoke and its legacy - is at a cross-roads in the country's history; the whiff of revolution and change is on the streets, the old guard is being threatened, and reacting. The skills needed to set up the British Council against this background are immense - finding and persuading key politicians, identifying and recruiting the right staff - some of whom will rise to prominence in the new Georgia - and playing the diplomatic game. Even finding a safe office. Not to mention getting stuck in snow storms, armed guards on trips to the mountains (complete with bullet holes in the windscreen of their jeep) and guards at the office. All against the backdrop of immense political change, which Jo not only witnesses but is part of. (Jo is there when women start placing roses in the barrels of guns). But Roses Down The Barrel of a Gun is more than that; it is also a highly personal story. It is beautifully written, by someone who came to love the country, and is told with the most delicate of touches and the most subtle and telling pay-off lines. I read Roses Down The Barrel of a Gun in two really enjoyable sittings. It's a must-read book." **Gordon Stevens, Author**

"A vivid account which will draw the reader into the sometimes little-known but culturally rich country of Georgia. Jo describes the parlous state of things before Georgia's Rose Revolution and the courage of the Georgian people with sympathy and emotion." **Chris Nunn**

"Her enthusiasm and love for the country combine with deep insights that she gained about the movement for change by being closely connected to young Georgians through her work there, as well as to her diplomatic and other connections. It's a fast paced and vivid account of the early days of the revolution, alongside an intriguing glimpse into the life of a diplomat, written with flair by someone whose personality and affection for Georgia shine through every page." **N McBain**

"I stumbled upon this book not really knowing anything about it but was gripped from the first page. It was fascinating. As I read this book I was fascinated by the details of life in this area and the political changes and events that took place while Jo was out there. The details of both everyday life and the work of the British Council are really interesting and to present that alongside significant danger and political turmoil makes for a cracking read. So much so that I consumed this book over two days!" **Sarah Lingard**

"Written in the style of a novel, I found this account so gripping that I read it from cover to cover in one sitting. Draughty corridors of military academies and journeys by road and train between the three capitals; the amazing food wine and friendly people, historic buildings and bustling markets, but also the challenges of setting up a new British Council office, recruiting and retaining staff, upgrading premises, organising VIP visits, scholarship schemes and arts events, fending off persistent requests for funding and at the same time trying to keep a bored spouse happy. And alongside all of this, revolution was in the air.... with the electoral reform Projects Jo had set in motion helping to fan the flames." **Paul Woods**

"Thoroughly enjoyed this book and couldn't recommend it highly enough. The author paints such a beautifully vivid and colourful picture of this country and its warm, courageous and hospitable people that it is now very firmly at the top of my travelling bucket list!" **Jo Chatters**

"What a beautiful, uplifting and easy to read book! I really enjoyed it. It gives a fascinating insight into the workings of overseas British Government operations, and the links with other Governments and players in a country. The book was very romantic too and it often felt I was reading a novel! **Ian Livy**

"This is a beautifully written, informative book which was so easy to read. It contains lots of historical facts as well as great descriptions of Georgian culture and political change and keeps you hooked wanting to read more." **R. Gourley**

"A beautifully crafted tale that intertwines the true story of a little reported revolution, the workings of British diplomacy, and a good old-fashioned love story. A great read, that keeps you enthralled to the end." **Adrian Paul**

"I relished every single word of this book. This was not only a colourful, vivid, real-life, hands-on history lesson, but a glimpse through a window into a very personal journey, full of the trials and tribulations of living, loving and leaving.

Roses Down the Barrel of a Gun is a banquet for the senses: I can taste the honey and the sparkling wine, feel the earth shake and the bombs boom, the pangs of heartbreak. I can smell the velvety roses and the smoky goulash, see the crumbling balconies of the houses, and the women selling exquisite silk paintings on trestle tables. I sense the fear and the despair, but more importantly the hope that shines through for both Jo and Georgia. This is a beautiful book inside and out, dotted with authentic photographs, and to be enjoyed by everyone." **Caroline**.

"Are you looking for a masterclass in running an office in a foreign country with 18 hour-per-day power cuts and random gunfire in the street; or a love story with tears and laughter; or tales of a Revolution which might have ended in a bloodbath - but didn't? If so, read this book! It's not fiction. It all happened!!!" **Chris Lakeman Fraser**

"This is a fabulous book! It's a great (true!) story, told with genuine warmth, humour and intelligence, against an interesting political and cultural landscape. I loved reading the beautifully recorded detail of how the author's days, months and years evolved during a fascinating time in the history of Georgia. I very much enjoyed learning about a country that I previously knew little about, whilst also being given a generous glimpse into the life and mind of an intriguing person - with a love story to boot! This book has a bit of everything to highly recommend it." **JBW**

"I found the combination of personal story with the backdrop of the revolution in Georgia made for a fascinating and entertaining read. The writer makes the historical events of the time come alive with her down to earth observations and experiences of setting up the British council office. I particularly enjoyed how the friendships and relationships shaped such a rich, informative tale. I would thoroughly recommend this book." **Nancy Sayles**

"I spent several years in Tbilisi and know several of the people mentioned in the book. It is a great read and really captures the essence of the country as it was at that time. Jo has managed to capture the true character and personality of the Georgians and their unique culture." **Therev**

"This is a fascinating read and gave me an intriguing insight into life in Georgia. I had never considered visiting the country - now I can't wait to book a trip! Jo's book is a joy, easy to read and full of wonderfully descriptive adventures. Be warned if you buy it though, you'll be following in her footsteps very soon..." **Lorna Cowan**

"What a thoroughly brilliant, well researched and gripping read." **Lena Milosevic**

A great recount of a very important time in Georgian history, full of vivid stories, characters, warmth and charm. **Ekaterine Gureshidze**

I personally know most of the people mentioned in the book and it warmed my heart and made me feel nostalgic for those times. This book will tell you a lot about Georgia's history and Georgian people. It's beautifully written and I highly recommend it! **Maka G**

This book is a very truthful narrative about the most interesting time in the history of independent Georgia. **Maya D**

Figure 1 Barrie Watson and Rusiko Tkemaladze

This book is dedicated to Barrie Watson who is no longer with us. Barrie was an English language teaching adviser who worked in Georgia and Armenia and before that in West Africa and Algeria. Through his work training trainers, writing textbooks and his help in setting up the English Teachers' Association of Georgia (and many other achievements), he helped change the lives of perhaps millions of people for the better. Barrie was talented, modest, committed, insightful and funny – he is much missed.

Contents

Map

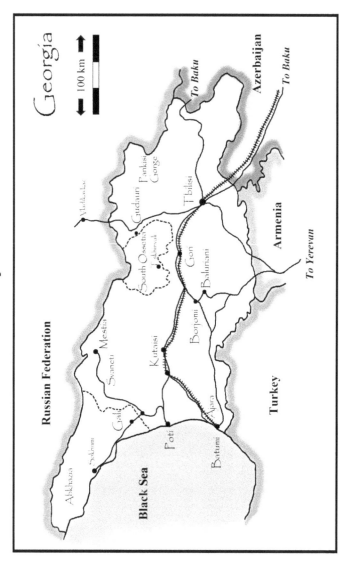

Prologue

Tipping point

November 22 2003, Tbilisi, Georgia.

They came from the streets leading into Freedom Square, from all over the city, all over the country and they were waiting. Strangers standing together in the cold. Some carried children and girls held dark red flowers. Waiting and expectant, they crouched low in their black leather jackets and cheap wool coats, huddled around smoky braziers and muffled against the biting cold.

We were due to launch an art exhibition in the Karvasala Gallery that evening, on one of the streets leading off the square, about 100 metres from the massing demonstrations. My colleague, Irakli, phoned me. 'Jo! I think the revolution is starting!'

Would it be foolhardy, reckless, or just plain pointless to go ahead with the British Council exhibition? Or would it look feeble and fainthearted, and somehow make a political statement, if we cancelled it? What about our colleagues visiting from all over Eastern Europe for a workshop on the Peacekeeping English Project? How safe were they, even more in the dark in this unfamiliar and volatile city than I? I was the director and in charge and I had to decide what to do. I phoned my contact at the British Embassy – he could advise me.

'We think the revolution is starting!' I told him. 'You know how many guns there are in Georgia...We could be in a state of civil war by tonight!'

'Can you give us half an hour? The Rugby World Cup Final is on and England is playing Australia...'

Part 1 The Job

1

Arriving

February 2001, Tbilisi, Georgia

The aeroplane skipped and lunged along the broken slabs of the runway of Tbilisi airport. Looking out with great interest at what I could see of Georgia – to be our new home – I was struck by the dull greyness, the air of neglect, the airport tower that looked drawn from a Tintin cartoon. 'How Soviet it seems,' I said to my husband, Alek. He, being Polish, had some experience of Sovietism.

'Don't judge a book by its cover.'

I was going to Georgia to work as the Director of the British Council. Before I got there people quipped, 'Midnight train to Georgia!', 'The devil went down to Georgia!', 'Rainy night in...' The quips came so often that the gentle humour faded.

'No, not that Georgia!' I had to say.

One friend said, 'I just can't imagine what Georgia can be like. I can only think of old Soviet-style posters of healthy young men and women harvesting fruit.'

Some asked, 'Actually, where *is* Georgia?' Where indeed? On consulting a map of the world I saw that, pleasingly, Georgia seemed tantalisingly remote and exotic, and yet, to be right at the centre of things. East of Istanbul, south of Russia – in fact, hang on, isn't that the border with Chechnya? – west of Azerbaijan and north of Armenia (which two countries, incidentally, have been in a state of frozen conflict over Nagorno Karabakh). Within Georgia's borders – or some would say without – were two disputed territories Abkhazia and South Ossetia, frozen conflicts here too, from time to time spiced up by interventions from Russian parties.

In any case, Alek was right. Georgia's years in the USSR had finished in 1991 and, as he implied, it seemed it had never become truly Soviet. Georgia had flourished as a beautiful playground for Russian Tsars for many centuries. Indeed, under the Soviet Union it became a favoured destination for Moscow-based apparatchiks to holiday. With the collapse of the Soviet Union the money and links were withdrawn – by 2001 Georgia had deteriorated into an unstable and potentially failing state. Many in the West did not want to see a failed state, with its inherent risk to the wider region, on NATO's border – and a number of international organisations, including mine, were opening up or expanding to provide support in this recently independent country.

We were met at the airport by my new colleagues, Katie, the Office Accountant, and Vakho, the Driver. Katie stood holding a bunch of flowers and Vakho had a sign with our names on it. They looked a bit anxious at the arrival of this new boss. Perhaps because jobs were hard to come by and if I turned out to be a difficult, new broom, type of manager I might sweep them away...But we were delighted to meet them and I hugged Katie to thank her for the flowers. Then thought, 'Oh dear, perhaps Georgia is not a hugging kind of place?' Or perhaps Katie herself might not like being hugged? But she smiled and Vakho ushered us to the office car, which turned out to be a worn-out Mitsubishi saloon, low on its springs. It had seen better days.

We piled in and set off towards the city. While there were indeed a few Soviet-era buildings and the ubiquitous grey blocks of flats, there were numerous grand churches and wide tree-lined avenues of beautiful old 19th century terraced houses. There were some impressive palaces – some of these were old but, intriguingly, there were quite a few brash new ones that looked out of place. There were many houses that had balconies overhanging the cobbled streets. It was enchanting. 'The balconies are so beautiful,' I said. They were intricately carved wood or delicate wrought-iron and were wrapped round the pretty, faded houses which layered up into the hills of the little city.

'They're really Turkish,' said my husband.

Figure 2 The House on Dadiani Street

But the city also looked as though it had been trashed. Some of the balconies were lop-sided and creaky. Most of the houses had peeling paint and some were sprayed with bullet holes from the civil war of only a few years earlier. Here and there, street cobbles had lifted up and there were potholes all over the roads. If Tbilisi looked like a beautiful woman, she looked rough. A beautiful woman with a bit of a hangover, perhaps.

We had a good introduction to how things worked in our new home from that drive from the airport to the city. I had noticed, when arriving in a new place, that watching how people drive could tell a lot about how that country is governed. The way people drive tends to show how they obey rules – whether there are rules at all – and how people treat each other. In Tbilisi it was manic...Fast and hair-raising, a battle between clapped-out old cars and a sprinkling of big, shiny, black four-wheel drives with blacked-out windows cutting everyone else up. There appeared to be no working traffic lights as, in fact, there was no power.

It looked on the edge.

2

Briefing

I had applied for a job in a country I hadn't been able to
pinpoint on a map to do a job I wasn't sure I could do. As
with many multi-national organisations it could happen that
you were sent to a country of which you had little or no prior
knowledge and a new posting often meant a steep and rapid
learning curve. I was accompanied by a husband who had
high hopes he would be happier and more settled in Georgia
than he had been in our previous homes in Egypt, Britain
and indeed his birthplace of Poland. We had big expectations
but, deep down, we were both a bit apprehensive.

I had worked for the British Council (the UK's organisation for cultural relations and educational opportunities
between the UK and other countries) for 15 years, mostly in
the contracts wing. I had been working in Cairo for four years
had developed into quite an experienced project manager of
contracts funded by donors such as the European Union, the
World Bank or the UK's Department for International
Development. With my move to Georgia, however, I was
moving into a more mainstream function – I was to be a
Country Director, and, as such, responsible for all the various
activities we could afford to deliver which would enhance cultural relations. 'Cultural relations' can be quite a vague term.
To me the fundamental issue was that the British Council

makes friends for Britain and that this is not one-sided – true friendship is a two-way and mutually beneficial relationship.

While I had some experience in certain areas I didn't have detailed knowledge of the more traditional cultural or English language teaching activities for which the British Council is better known and, at 37, I was relatively young to take up a director position. In Georgia I was to have responsibility for expanding a tiny and apparently somewhat neglected operation into a full office with new projects that made a difference to relationships between our two countries.

Oh, and I also had to open an entirely new operation in Yerevan, the capital of neighbouring Armenia, in readiness for another UK-appointed colleague. He was to arrive some six months after me and take over there. There were a lot of uncertainties and I had much to learn. I felt nervous. A colleague advised, 'Do your best and be yourself'. I would always do that – but would it be enough?

#

Before I got to Tbilisi I had briefings to prepare me for my new post.

'Congratulations on your appointment. I expect you have been busy reading up on where things are heading in Georgia?' I was in the Foreign and Commonwealth Office's flamboyant Victorian Italianate London offices for my briefing with the FCO Desk Officers. I wondered if this was like an interview and I should give them a potted version of my reading. I needn't have worried as I was there to listen and learn and I had my notebook at the ready.

The Desk Officer continued. 'President Shevardnadze is already well known to the West as he was Soviet Party Chief in 1972 and Soviet Foreign Minister under Gorbachev in 1986 – some call him the Silver Fox. He was a key player in opening up the Soviet Union – to be more economically liberal.' He added, 'After the collapse of the Soviet Union Shevardnadze succeeded the first President of Georgia following a brutal civil war in the early 90s. Since then he has been keen to improve Georgia's relations with the West, much to the annoyance of his Russian neighbours – as you will doubtless know, Russia still sees many of the former Soviet countries as part of their sphere of influence. In fact Russian 'peacekeeping' forces occupy two breakaway regions, Abkhazia and South Ossetia. A flare-up between Georgia and Russia over these regions could have serious ramifications.' I nodded and my colleague from the FCO told me more.

'Shevardnadze is an ageing president. The key question for Her Majesty's Government is who will eventually take over from him and what the next government will look like. At present corruption, human rights and poor governance are big issues. This matters to us as Georgia shares a border with Turkey (and is therefore a neighbour of NATO) and moreover BP are putting in a pipeline to connect the Caspian and Mediterranean seas. Any more instability there and Georgia will be increasingly vulnerable to other influences such as organised crime, trafficking and terrorism.' I was nodding and writing hard.

'HMG is not the only player on the block. The European Union and individual EU countries and, in particular, the United States are investing in a number of different projects in Georgia. We have high hopes that your arrival will help beef up UK's presence in Tbilisi and beyond. Russian is the second language but there is a lot of interest in learning English, particularly by the younger, post-Soviet generation, so your organisation will doubtless have much to offer. Don't think you will have a problem with access.' I must have looked puzzled.

'To top politicians.' Of course. 'But personal security is a challenge and the rule of law is weak. It's an exciting place to go to. Good luck!' Almost as an afterthought he added, 'And as for Armenia, we are planning a VIP visit to Yerevan next year – but I can't yet reveal who this will be. Your help in opening up a new British Council operation there as soon as possible will be much appreciated.' I looked expectantly at my colleague. 'Yes, the highlight of the VIP's visit will be to launch your new operation.'

I smiled enthusiastically – no pressure there, then.

#

'I hope you don't mind that you started your briefing at the FCO rather than here with us?' asked my new boss, Rosemary, in the British Council's London office – a modern open-plan building near Trafalgar Square.

'Of course not.' I knew how significant the relationship with the FCO was. After all, some of the British Council's funding – about a third at that time, far less now – came from them and it was important to work closely with them and to understand their priorities. But the British Council has a much wider remit than bilateral government-to-government relations. We were 'arm's length government', raised two-thirds of our funding from clients and customers and could forge much broader relationships with non-governmental organisations and the private sector. With all the issues in Georgia, this promised to make my job an interesting one. 'Do you know who the VIP visiting Armenia will be?' I asked.

'Not yet,' said Rosemary, 'but what a wonderful opportunity for you to showcase what we can do. You will be one of our first British colleagues to go to the South Caucasus. Until now the office has been managed remotely from Russia.' Interesting, I thought, as I knew relations between Georgia and Russia as countries were not especially warm...I learnt that the Moscow and Tbilisi offices had de-linked a year ago. There had been a local Georgian Manager doing a great job heading up the small operation in Tbilisi, but she had resigned six months beforehand. The office now comprised ten Georgian staff, who did a lot with a small grant focusing on English language teacher training, for which there was also a British adviser, and a small library. They also managed scholarships on behalf of the FCO and others, and managed a project called the 'Peacekeeping English Project' (PEP), funded by the UK's Ministry of Defence.

Rosemary told me that the Georgia office had been one of our smallest operations, but following some strategic decisions about our global network of offices, extra funding would be forthcoming. Many of the British Council's operations in Western Europe were being scaled down – a painful process – and those further east, the new Post-soviet countries, were being expanded. Robbing Peter to pay Pavel? I wondered.

'We don't have a high profile in Georgia,' said Rosemary, 'so developing a strategy for arts and cultural work will be a good way to attract public attention. The sooner you can get out to post the better – no time for language training for you, I'm afraid. One vital thing you should know is that we believe the Tbilisi office itself is not up to global standards,' she added, handing me a check-list of what the global standards were. My boss told me that we might need to move office, in which case the new premises would need to reflect modern British architecture; be appealing to young people; have a flexible space to take into account our different projects and activities and be cost-effective. 'Premises projects can be quite time-consuming. It might be quite a challenge as we just don't know what is available in Tbilisi that would be suitable,' said Rosemary.

'And how is your husband? Is Alek looking forward to the move?' It was well known that overseas postings could be challenging for accompanying spouses. It wasn't always easy to find work, paid or unpaid – and it was usually easier for the person being posted to make friends and feel more socially settled through all their various networks. I told her he was delighted. Having grown up in Poland he knew more about Georgia than I did. 'It might be an easier posting for him to get work than in Egypt?' suggested Rosemary. Indeed. He spoke Russian fluently; as that was the second language in Georgia that would come in handy. He also had an MBA.

'He is better qualified than I am,' I told her. It all augured well.

#

Before I left London, Rosemary and I paid a call on the Georgian Ambassador to the UK. He was charm itself and flung out his hands in a welcoming way, immediately asking, 'Why is there no BBC transmission in Tbilisi?' I said I would try to find out, but reminded him we were from the British Council not the BBC and that we covered English language, education and culture, that sort of thing. 'Ah yes, British Council, yes. Yes, Georgians are highly educated, but there is high unemployment particularly amongst the youth – it is a big challenge for us. Anything you can do to give more access to English language learning for business and jobs, to the internet via computers, would be most welcome.' I said we would be re-doubling our efforts to help. The Ambassador graciously presented me with a copy of the Georgian National Epic Poem, *The Knight in the Panther's Skin* by Shota Rustaveli. It is a beautiful medieval work, and was translated in 1912 by a British woman, Marjorie Wardrop, who was a polyglot, scholar and sister of the first British diplomat to be posted to Georgia, Oliver Wardrop.

The Ambassador told me there were some good contacts between Bristol and Tbilisi which were twinned cities and that Newport had good links with Kutaisi, the second city. 'But on the whole we simply don't have enough contact between Britain and my country.'

#

I was also in touch with Katie, the Office Accountant in Tbilisi. She had sent me useful emails on logistical things for our forthcoming arrival. She had added to her latest message, 'Finally I would like to send you my best regards and to say that I (and all the staff) can hardly wait till we meet you. We are like lost chickens.'

I couldn't wait to get there.

First night

February 2001, Tbilisi

Here we were, some months later, in Tbilisi, struggling up the stairs with our heavy suitcases to the apartment which accountant, Katie, and driver, Vakho, had found for us. It was a light, fully-furnished flat on one of the main avenues not far from the British Council.

'Can I walk to the office?' I asked. I wasn't keen on driving and it would be wonderful to be independent and be able to come and go as I pleased.

'Oh yes, you can walk, it isn't far,' said Katie, 'but just take care – it can be dangerous. You know – muggings. Definitely don't walk alone after dark.' Alek looked unhappy. Katie showed us around the flat.

'It reminds me of Warsaw apartments,' said Alek. 'I know this smell of varnish.' He had grown up in Poland and had escaped to the West in the late 1980s, before the Iron Curtain had been drawn away so spectacularly. By 2001 Poland was a country transformed but here in Tbilisi we were seeing echoes of a Soviet era long since passed.

The apartment had parquet flooring throughout and a mixture of flimsy 50s furniture alongside some darker, more solid pieces. I loved the retro lampshades. It had a spacious living room, a neat bedroom and a small library stuffed with books in Georgian and Russian and a number in English.

Our landlords were clearly well-read. There was a small kitchen bursting with cooking equipment and a compact bathroom dominated by an elderly washing machine. Vakho showed us a formidable-looking little generator on the balcony and told Alek, in Russian, how to operate it, in case we had a power cut. Alek translated for me. This time I didn't look happy. I hoped I wouldn't have to struggle with it personally.

Katie had brought us some food and told us that our colleague Barrie, the English Language Adviser, would show us round the market the following day. Vakho said to Alek, 'Let me know if you need anything – I am not only a driver, I am office handyman too.' With lots of thank-yous and good-nights and pleased to meet yous, he and Katie departed.

Alek and I set about unpacking all the paraphernalia we had been able to squeeze into our suitcases to last us our first couple of months in Georgia. We were also expecting a consignment of 'heavy baggage' with less immediately important stuff to follow some months later and this was due to come by the cheapest possible route – in this case from Cairo to the port of Alexandria and from then on by sea across the Mediterranean, through the Straits of Bosphorus across the Black Sea, to the Georgian port of Poti, then overland again to Tbilisi. Such an exotic route.

It could be a lottery travelling between countries as you were never entirely sure what to take on the aeroplane and what to pack into the heavy baggage. Depending on issues with customs clearance at both ends it was entirely possible you might not see your things again. I had heard many stories of colleagues' possessions being broken, broken into or incomprehensibly stuck somewhere through corruption, incompetence or issues with the weather, or a combination of all these. I knew of one such consignment which arrived in India just before the onset of a monsoon season and which got stuck for six months, while the office management team jumped over seemingly endless bureaucratic hurdles. When the heavy baggage was eventually cleared, almost everything in it was completely destroyed – damp, mildewed or rusted away.

We were happy to make the most of what had arrived with us. With a flourish Alek produced a bottle of Brandy he had bought at Vienna airport, where we had changed planes. I unpacked two expensive and heavily scented candles I had bought there too, to grace our new home. I put the flowers Katie had given me and the fancy candles on the coffee table.

'I thought our flat would be more up-market than this,' said Alek. 'Aren't you supposed to be a director now?' And as such he thought I should have a more 'presentable' apartment, suitable for entertaining significant official contacts. Outside the watery February sun had set and it was getting cold. 'Bacon and eggs?' We went off to rustle up a simple supper when –! Power cut.

We stood in the dark for a moment. I stumbled in the unfamiliar and now completely black apartment to find the candles on the coffee table – I could smell their sweet, heavy scent in the chilly gloom. I fumbled to find some matches. 'Have no fear – we Poles are resourceful. I have a torch on my keyring,' said Alek.

'Should we get the generator going?' I asked. We squeezed out on to the freezing balcony; me pointing the torch at the generator, as it was also entirely dark on the street outside, and Alek trying to remember which bit to pull and which bit to push and in what order, and swearing at it in Polish. In spite of all his efforts it didn't work. We had to admit defeat and called Vakho, apologising for calling him out so soon. He also apologised as neither could he coax the generator into life. 'It was working when we tested it yesterday...' he said mournfully. Vakho called out a mechanic – who couldn't fix it either.

I said I was sure we'd be fine. 'We have torches and candles and we'll just keep our coats on...' It was bitterly cold. Alek and I felt it all the more as we had just come from Egypt.

'You should still have some hot water in the tank though, and you still have gas,' said Vakho and again we said goodnight.

Alek and I bickered in the icy kitchen as we learnt how to use the unfamiliar cooker. Alek held the little torch while I managed to cook bacon and eggs. We ate it by candlelight – expensive Austrian candles – in our coats, hats and scarves at a little formica-topped table in the cramped space. It transpired that we didn't have any hot water, after all.

'Fancy a cup of tea?' asked Alek adding a glug of Brandy to each cup. It tasted vile but it was warming. We spent the first evening squabbling in the dark. While I was excited to get started on my new job, perhaps Alek's challenges would be different. Perhaps what he had seen reminded him too much of what he had left behind in Poland. To bed with so much to think about...Before being lulled into a deep and dream-free sleep by the chugging generators in the dark, diesel-fumed city outside.

#

The next morning was sunny and bright and we had power back on. I was excited to see the flat properly. I found numerous candles and boxes of matches dotted around in strategic locations. Alek was like a bear with a sore head after the Brandy and tea cocktails. 'Pain-killers – where are the pain-killers?' he grumbled as we were still in a state of unpacking disarray. He fiddled with the TV and found CNN so we had some sense of what was going on out there. 'It's 20 degrees in Cairo,' he said gloomily.

There was a knock at the door and there stood Barrie, the British Council's English Language Adviser. 'Got over the culture shock yet? Fancy a walk around Tbilisi market?'

We were joined by Martine, Barrie's French wife, and they took us to shops and the market and pointed out places of particular importance and interest to foreigners. The market was huge and bursting with agricultural produce – row upon row of different meats – all the different bits of a cow, or a sheep, or a goat you can imagine, and some perhaps you can't. And – oh my. Rows of piglets lying on their backs, tiny trotters aloft…There were piles of persimmons and pomegranates, heaps of dried apricots, dates and plums; potatoes and onions, parsley and carrots, and jars of pickled vegetables. Enticing heaps of walnuts and almonds and mounds of colourful spices. All laid out in a pleasingly colour co-ordinated array. Alek and I debated what to buy and eventually decided we should be able to cook a chicken in our somewhat daunting kitchen.

In addition to the market there were little local provisions stores that stocked groceries and packaged food. 'Don't count on things always being available,' said Martine. 'If you see something and want it, buy it. It might not be there again.' I asked her how frequent the power cuts would be and she said, 'All the time. You will get into a routine of knowing when you can use your washing machine. If there is a power cut, it won't work, even with a generator – as soon as the power goes on put your washing in.'

Barrie and Martine took us home to their flat for dinner and while we relaxed we asked them about living in Tbilisi. Barrie had worked as an English Language Teaching (ELT) Adviser for many years, including in West Africa and Algeria. He looked laid-back and unflappable. He appeared to like Georgia very much. 'It's a compelling place. Wait and see for yourself. There aren't that many 'Western' foreigners here,' he added, 'maybe a few hundred – some North Americans, French, Dutch, Danish. Maybe about a hundred British. Lots of Turkish truck drivers though and Russian and Armenian business people. It's quite a fluid place, people are in and out of Tbilisi all the time.'

As we were leaving, Barrie handed me a copy of a Georgian English language newspaper. I thanked him and looked down at it. The headline on the front page said, 'Beating of foreigners continues.'

4

First day

I got up early the following morning to gear up for walking to work. It was only about fifteen minutes away, but I couldn't shake off the 'foreigners being beaten up' newspaper headline and I wanted to memorise my route. It would be all too easy to get lost in this unfamiliar city. In fact I had been up for hours getting ready for the day ahead. From my briefings in London I had summarised my 'to do list':

- With my colleagues, develop a strategy for the British Council in Georgia
- Develop new, and expand existing, programmes that make a positive difference to cultural relations
- Overhaul office financial systems and manage resources effectively
- Assess team capabilities – recruit new staff where appropriate and arrange training
- Check the office premises are 'fit-for-purpose'
- And open a completely new office in Armenia. From a distance – with the clock ticking for the visit of an as yet un-named VIP who would officially declare it open...

Where to start?

Figure 3 Tbilisi balconies

I set off for the office, turning left and walking down the road purposefully, trying not to look like a foreigner. It was a broad street flanked by tall 19th century buildings, elegant but worn, and fringed by high trees either side, still adorned with a few shivering leaves. A brisk wind blew clumps of fallen leaves down the unswept street and curled them around the little Orthodox church.

It all looked so romantic. Run-down, but romantic…

#

Scurrying across the wide Chavchavadze Avenue, one of the main roads in the city, I arrived at the British Council. Scurrying because – although there were traffic lights and a pedestrian crossing – there was no electricity so the traffic lights were not working, and the drivers were haring up and down the road with scant regard for the many pedestrians.

The British Council was situated within the State University of Tbilisi. This was in a row of solid imperial buildings with impressive, enormous, almost Narnian arches. I went into the cavernous entrance hall of the university and up the curving staircase. At the top, at the junction of two long corridors, was a large metal door with a little laminated sign that said 'British Council' on it.

Not the modern, glass and chrome look that most British Council offices had. I pushed open the heavy front door. There was a short corridor leading to a desk that took up most of the width of the corridor. Sitting at the desk, with a huge smile on her movie-star face, was Anka, the receptionist. Beside Anka was a flipchart board and behind her some large cardboard boxes piled high. It looked so grey, so cramped. And, apart from Anka's glowing smile, not the look to welcome visitors to the best of what Britain had to offer.

'Jo, you are here!' said Anka, jumping up to greet me. She opened a door to her left, into 'the office'. This was a small room with three desks crammed into it with little signs perched upon them; one for Katie (Accountant) and one for Barrie (ELT Adviser) and one for me (Director). A tall, wooden sash window let in dusty light from under the arches which faced Chavchavadze Avenue. In the corner was a heavy-looking safe with a kettle on it. Behind each of the desks were shelves, crammed with so many files, so many folders.

Figure 4 Anka in the British Council Reception

To Anka's right was the door to the library. Again, not a big room, the library had four small reading tables, a library reception desk for the librarian and the IT guy, and three mini-desks for the rest of the team squeezed into the corners. Every wall of the library was shelved and these were stuffed full of books. There appeared to be no storage facilities at all – hence all the computer boxes piled high in the corridor.

There was minimal heating by way of rather odorous portable gas fires in each room. As for enabling access for anyone with a disability, well, we were some 100 steps up cracked stairs.

But, overriding all that, members of the public were already sitting and standing at every available space in the library – studying, reading, learning. Immediate physical proof, if I needed it, that what the British Council was offering was in demand.

We stepped back into the office and Katie offered me a cup of coffee. She filled the kettle on the safe with water from a bottle, saying, 'We have had such small budgets but such big demand for what we do – we have been stuck here trying to make the most of it. We're so happy we have a chance now to start to sort it all out.' I learnt that the Georgian Office Manager, who had left some six months before, had learnt how to say 'no' diplomatically a hundred different ways to all the requests for projects and funding and support from Georgian people and organisations.

Luiza, the office cleaner, came in to our office and smiled fulsomely at me. She said hello and asked Katie to apologise that she couldn't say more than that in English. I said I was sorry I couldn't speak Georgian. 'Not many foreigners can master it,' said Katie. I asked how to say hello in Georgian and duly said *gamarjobat* and we all laughed at my terrible pronunciation. Luiza took the empty bottle from Katie – she said something in Georgian and disappeared. She was gone some time then appeared again with the bottle, now full. Hang on – where did Luiza get water from? 'Where is the kitchen?' I asked.

Katie and Anka laughed. 'We don't have a kitchen – we don't have running water in our office.' Oh dear…Katie took me out of the British Council rooms and down a long, chilly corridor with lifting linoleum to the rear of the university building to the university WC. In the corner of the room was a hand basin with cold water. 'This is where we fill up for water for the kettle. It does get a little cold here.' It was glacial in the university building and we still had our coats on.

I thought of the checklist my boss in distant London had given me and our remit to promote the best of British design through our offices. That the operation should offer a flexible, modern office space for people to learn, to network, to access information and ideas. Or even just be healthy and safe. This office must surely fail almost every health and safety directive – there wasn't even a fire escape. It certainly wasn't a place where we might host events for influential decision-makers and Very-Important-People. I knew it was not the fault, in any way, of my colleagues there or those who had been there previously. It was difficult to find appropriate offices in Tbilisi at that time.

In any case I didn't want to look backwards for reasons as to why it was like this but to find a way to get out of this office and into one that would enable us to expand and make a difference. I added 'manage a premises project' to my to-do list. This could be the most time-consuming thing of all. Numerous forms to complete and a lengthy approval process with my HQ colleagues. Consultation over location, architecture, legal and security issues and, of course, cost-effectiveness. Finding appropriate offices in Britain is bad enough but in Georgia I imagined it would be on another plane entirely.

#

Katie gave me a box containing my new business cards which read: *British Council Director, Georgia and Armenia* with all the contact details in English on one side and in Georgian on the other side. What fabulous script! I turned the card over, looking at the fantastic curls and loops. To me it was totally unrecognisable. Even Cyrillic script was more familiar. I bet that is what Narnian script would look like.

Katie smiled and said, 'Yes, it is completely unique and ancient, one of the fourteen scripts in the world. Armenia has its own script too.' I felt these small mountain-fringed countries had somehow carefully guarded their cultures down the centuries. I had the double thrill of seeing my name with 'Director' next to it, also translated into this beautiful ancient language. Katie reminded me gently that I had a schedule and I duly sat down to meet each of my new colleagues officially, starting with Katie herself. 'With the new budgets we will need to be fully functional and manage everything here rather than from the Moscow office,' she told me. 'And we have literally no space at all for all the files. We can't get rid of financial paperwork for five years for audit reasons. As you know,' she said, looking at me to check that I did know.

I nodded. I had been through enough internal and National Audit Office audits to know how essential it was to get your audit trail in place and for records to be kept meticulously. Katie pulled back her chair and showed me boxes of financial papers shoved under her desk. She could hardly move her feet beneath her desk.

'Some training would be good,' said Katie. 'Training is the key to the future. I work out much of what I need to do through guidebooks. Our colleagues in Moscow used to do most transactions and I never got to see the full picture.' Katie gave me an armful of papers on staffing and contracts that needed to be updated. It felt daunting.

I then met Eka, who managed the promotion and invigilation of UK exams, mostly those to help gauge candidates' levels of English language skills. There were also modest numbers of candidates sitting professional exams, international GCSEs, A levels and British university exams done by distance learning. I asked her about her job and the challenges she faced. She gestured, 'As you can see we have nowhere to host the exams. I have to book rooms in hotels and it can be quite stressful – the big hotels, which are reliable, charge a fortune and the smaller, cheaper ones often don't have electricity. I also cover Armenia and getting there and running things from a distance can be trying.'

Before I had a chance to open my mouth to ask a question of my next colleague, Maya Z, she said, flamboyantly,

> *'A thing of beauty is a joy forever*
> *Its loveliness increases; it will never*
> *Pass into nothingness!'*

While I, open-mouthed, thought, A level English, um, um, she continued, 'Don't you just love Keats?' And she told me she helped Georgians get places on courses at UK institutions. 'But as most Georgians are impoverished, not many can afford to go.'

I met Tamuna, the librarian, who told me the library was so much in demand – which I could see for myself – that people would queue to get a seat at one of the tables. 'Everyone wants to learn English. English is the language of the future – but we need more space, more books, more materials.'

Last on the schedule was Nata, who managed 'exchanges'. This meant managing marketing, recruitment and selection procedures for a number of scholarships in the UK, and making arrangements for visitors coming from Britain to Georgia. 'Have you had many visitors to Georgia?' I asked.

'Only one or two colleagues from London and Moscow. We had a party of British MPs hosted by the British Embassy who paid us a call a while back.' I wondered what they made of the office. 'They weren't at all impressed – but I think they saw the value of what we can do,' said Nata. In fact I had heard of that visit and conjectured that it may have contributed to the push to improve the facilities and to expand our budget – and hence our ability to make an impact in Georgia. I asked Nata what she thought I should focus on. 'Tomorrow you will be interviewing candidates for the prestigious John Smith Fellowship Scheme at the Embassy.' Not much time to prepare! 'And on Monday you will do the same for Armenia in Yerevan,' said Nata.

'It takes about five hours to get there,' said Eka, who could hear our conversation as we were all squeezed up together in the corner. 'Vakho will drive us down. I'll be coming with you to invigilate exams on English language levels for the Armenian candidates.'

Bring it on. I logged on to my computer and scanned through all the inevitable emails that had accrued in the few days since I had left my previous job. It was less than a week since I had left Cairo. Strangely, while I felt new here in Tbilisi, my familiar former job already seemed distant. I really wanted to get out there and meet significant Georgians in education, the arts, the government, from non-governmental organisations and civil society, as well as the business community – I would listen to and learn from anyone who would talk to me.

#

After work, kind Katie took Alek and me to her flat for a glass of homemade wine. Her husband produced this, flamboyantly adding, 'My feet have trodden the grapes for you!' I learnt my second Georgian word *gaumajos*, cheers – also *didi madloba*, thank you very much. They turned out to be useful words.

Much fortified, Alek and I went home to our flat. We tried to rustle up a roast chicken in the rickety gas cooker and have a hearty, warming meal. Alas, our chicken turned out to be a hen. With an egg inside it…

'And the generator is still buggering about,' said Alek. Apparently power cuts could last 18 to 23 hours a day.

5

Friends of the family

February 2001, Tbilisi

It was Valentine's Day and the morning felt bright. Colleagues had brought cakes and sparkling wine to the office and our driver, Vakho, presented all the women with bunches of sweet violets. Our drab little office felt transformed.

Vakho and I set off to visit the British Embassy. While the British Council office was right in the centre of Tbilisi, the Embassy was housed in a wing of the Sheraton Metekhi Palace Hotel – on the road to the airport and quite a way from the city centre. Although it purported to be a palace, the hotel was a modern, grey and rather uninspiring building. Her Majesty's Ambassador, Dick Jenkins, welcomed me warmly. 'Welcome to our new 'Cultural Attaché'; in fact the first. It's good to have you on board.'

The British Council does not routinely have diplomatic status and, in general, is proud of its institutional independence and being 'arm's length from government' – but in certain countries, such as Georgia in those days, it could be difficult to work without being under the wing of the FCO – so, with my arrival, our operation was accorded diplomatic status.

'I'm glad to be able to brief you now,' continued Dick, 'as I leave post next week. Deborah Barnes-Jones will be the new ambassador, so you'll be working closely with her.'

He told me the British Embassy had been operating since 1995 and that it was not a big mission, with seven UK-appointed and 20 Georgian colleagues. These included personnel from the Department for International Development, the Ministry of Defence, and staff dealing with consular, political and trade issues. 'As things stand now, we are particularly interested in what might happen after Shevardnadze goes – it is all somewhat uncertain. As you might imagine there is always the fear of political unrest and instability in a region which borders NATO.'

The ambassador told me that there was an oil and gas pipeline due for construction which would take vital natural resources from the Caspian Sea through to Western Europe via Azerbaijan, Georgia and Turkey. BP was leading a consortium working on this. He continued, 'The frozen conflicts in Abkhazia and South Ossetia are potentially a cause for concern. Oh, and there is also Ajara, which is run as a semi-autonomous region under a chap called Aslan Abashidze – the Tbilisi government lets Abashidze get on with it and it's rather an authoritarian and corrupt sort of place. For a country that has a population of less than four and a half million people, there is a lot going on in Georgia.'

Dick said that that there had been high hopes that the post-Soviet years would lead to investment and prosperity, as had happened in the Baltic States. Alas, the general instability caused by a series of internal conflicts, corruption and collapsing government structures meant it had become a risky place for potential investors to do business. Relationships with Russia were strained and – as few Western investors had filled the economic vacuum – the economy was in poor shape. There was high unemployment and a substantial black economy.

The ambassador added, 'However, Georgia has a rich, ancient and unique culture and they see themselves very much in the European tradition. Potentially, if Georgia could ever get its act together, this could really be a thriving tourist destination, as it used to be, and they could export high quality agricultural produce – the wine is rather good! More specific to you, Jo, we're interested in finding out about perceptions of Britain, particularly amongst the younger generation. Anyone over 35 will have grown up in the Soviet era so their world view is likely to be different to that of younger people.'

'Are there any market research companies?' I asked.

It transpired that these were in their infancy. 'Many of the organisations and institutions that many countries take for granted are not yet in place in this one,' said Dick. I felt I could start by asking my own colleagues what they thought. They all seemed young, early or mid-20s perhaps. I asked about the education system.

'I think it is fair to say the education system is in a state of decline and corruption appears to be embedded in the system. One of the challenges in a Soviet-style command economy was that there were a small number of decision-makers who told a large number of decision-followers what to do. There are some bright young stars out there – we just need to find them.' He added with enthusiasm, 'I will be more than happy to pass on all the requests for support for cultural activities and funding to you. You must meet Mr Rukhadze of the Anglo-Georgian Friendship Society…'

As I stood to leave, Dick added, 'There are a lot of guns here, by the way, and not much of a police function – you have arrived at an interesting time.'

#

I met Lali, the Georgian head of the Department for International Development (DFID), in the Embassy meeting room. She gave me a briefing on the work of her department. 'Georgia is, of course, a transitional economy,' she said.

'Transiting from where to where?' I asked.

'From being a poor country to be a middle-income country. And when this happens successfully, and (as we hope) Georgia becomes a stable, prosperous country, then DFID scales back its involvement and eventually should be able to withdraw altogether. At the moment we spend about £3 million per year.' She told me that unfortunately the statistics could be misleading. Having a few exceptionally rich people could skew the figures and make the average income per capita look higher than most ordinary people enjoyed – it could appear that a country was richer than it actually was.

'Georgia seems like that,' I said. 'It seems a very poor country. How many other middle-income countries have 18-hour power cuts a day?'

'Indeed,' said Lali. 'In the meantime we are focusing on poverty reduction programmes.' I told her I hoped the new British Council strategy would be able to contribute to Georgia's development in some way. 'Please don't neglect the arts,' said Lali. 'We love culture here. But we have the clock ticking right now – we have a number of candidates to interview for the John Smith Fellowship Programme.'

This scheme provided three-week programmes to three bright young people per year. It was funded under a trust in the name of John Smith, the former Labour Party leader who died in 1994. The successful JSFP candidates would go to UK together and have introductory seminars and discussions on political processes in UK with other representatives from various countries from the former Soviet Union. Each one would have personalised, tailor-made programmes of attachments to institutions of particular significance to their own professional background – they might have attachments with the BBC, or a devolved parliament, or Amnesty International or similar. At the end of their individual trips, they would get together and discuss action plans, challenges and how they would put their learning into practice.

So we were looking for the new generation of leaders, people who could make a difference. Lali told me they had a real problem getting good candidates from government and the public sector. All the 'good' people gravitated towards Non-Governmental Organisations (NGOs). 'Or are working for foreign organisations?' I suggested, smiling at her.

#

Lali and I agreed who would ask what questions to try to identify the future leaders. The first candidate was from the Liberty Institute. This was a progressive NGO for advocacy and campaigning on human rights. We wrote down our thoughts on the interviewee. I was impressed. If all of Georgia's young people were like him, surely things would get better here soon. The next two candidates weren't so good, however.

After them was a young man from the Government in Exile of Abkhazia. Abkhazia was one of the 'breakaway' regions, a frozen conflict. There were hundreds of thousands of internally displaced persons (IDPs) from there and South Ossetia in and around Tbilisi. Most of the IDPs lived in chronically dilapidated hotels and were terminally unemployed; with high unemployment for Tbilisi residents, this compounded social tensions in the city. There was no freedom of movement for most Georgians in and out of

Abkhazia (and indeed, South Ossetia), but this did not deter criminal gangs who ran car, drugs and other criminal rackets over the unofficial borders. It seemed clear to many that the Russian authorities were turning a blind eye to these activities – Abkhazia and South Ossetia had in effect become puppet states to the Russian Republic and they were potential flashpoints between Georgia and her powerful Northern neighbour. The interviewee from the Government in Exile of Abkhazia was an excellent candidate.

The next candidate was an intense young man, an MP whose passion was taxation. 'One of the big challenges for the Georgian government is that the tax coding system is obsolete. It isn't rational and no-one understands it - and few people pay tax properly,' he said. 'And because no-one pays tax, the government cannot provide public services – and because there are no services people need to pay bribes to get even basic things done.' Lali nodded her agreement. 'Corruption in political life is rampant,' said the candidate.

From all the political briefings I had now had, it was apparent there were huge challenges to confront in Georgia. These were the kind of young people who surely had to be part of Georgia's future – but how easy would it be for them to contribute, given the apparent entrenchment of the ruling elites?

#

When I got back to the British Council Barrie gave me a briefing on his English language teaching projects. 'We are principally working with the English Teachers' Association of Georgia, ETAG – a feisty non-governmental organisation comprised mainly of women. Or perhaps I should say an NGO of feisty women?'

They had chosen to join this NGO to get professional support. ETAG had been set up by the British Council in 1994 and Barrie was carrying forward his predecessor's work to support teacher training, textbook writing and testing. Some ETAG members had been trained in Britain as teacher trainers – opportunities for foreign training and education were not easy to come by, so training teachers offered a potentially powerful way to raise education levels for many more people.

'Our vision is to have regional offices all over Georgia which can provide support for all English teachers, wherever they are – ultimately the aim is that ETAG is entirely self-sustainable, that is, the teachers and those who use its services pay for membership. At present, however, it needs consultancy to get it set up and technological and material support from the British Council – books, computers, tape recorders and so on.'

'Barrie, it sounds brilliant. I'd like to meet the feisty ladies soon.'

'I'm sure you will,' said Barrie. 'In fact I think Madame Mzia is sitting outside in the corridor waiting to meet you.'

Mzia, the Head of ETAG, and I greeted each other expansively. 'We have monthly meetings on Saturday mornings and try to invite native English speakers to come and address us,' Mzia told me. I told her that sounded wonderful. 'Would you please come and give a presentation to us on British culture?' she asked. Oh my. 'For about an hour? Tomorrow morning?'

#

That afternoon I had my last briefing on our existing work as I went to meet my colleagues at the Peacekeeping English Project (PEP) office. This was a project funded by the British Ministry of Defence, with a contribution from the Georgian Ministry of Defence in the form of office space.

It was an English language teaching (ELT) project, one of over 20 at that time which were running in Central and Eastern Europe, the South Caucasus and Central Asia. Colleagues in UK provided overall strategic management and recruited the ELT advisers. In Georgia, it enabled military staff, by being able to speak English more effectively, to take a more effective role in regional and international operations and in humanitarian or disaster-relief activities. The British Council managed a British adviser, Ray, and a team of Georgian teachers and managers who provided specialised intensive classes and management support.

Lia, the Director of Studies, met Vakho and me at the entrance to the Ministry of Defence and helped guide me through the bureaucracy to get into their building. While it was heavily guarded it was a scruffy building that had seen better days. The PEP offices and classrooms were on the top floor and the lifts did not work. We panted up nine flights of dusty stairs. Ray and his colleagues greeted us with big smiles. They did this every day.

There were a few offices headed up by a small team who managed a language laboratory and series of classrooms. Lia showed me into one of their classrooms to reveal Lela teaching a classroom of mostly uniformed men sitting behind battered desks. The soldiers sat up straighter when we walked in.

'We are training a small team in testing English to definable standards,' said Ray. 'It's an important part of reaching NATO membership, one of the objectives of the Georgian government. The testing team are learning about the theory and practice of testing and how to design items and assess testees according to the Council of Europe Framework. Ultimately we want to train the trainers and have the centre completely absorbed into the

Georgian ministry when the UK funding stops.' If it were successful, this would be an excellent example of institutional development. Like many government to government projects, however, its success depended to a large extent on the support and political will from the men at the top, the Georgian Minister of Defence and the British Defence Attaché. In addition, of course, to having the right staff delivering it. I was impressed with my new colleagues.

#

Later at home, Alek had worked out how to use the cranky oven and had cooked a tasty meal. He produced a bottle of Georgian wine. Lovely. But I was feeling low. As well as feeling a bit anxious about having to deliver a one-hour presentation on British culture the following morning (where to start?), I missed the easy familiarity of seeing our friends in Egypt. Even more so, I missed my family. A cousin would be getting married in Scotland the following day. We had been invited, as of course had my much loved (and latterly, little seen) family. I couldn't go, having so recently started my new job. 'Well, you have to take the rough with the smooth,' said Alek. 'You wanted this director job, after all.'

He distracted me by trawling through all the Georgian and Russian TV channels. We found *Who Wants to be a Millionaire* in Russian. Alek translated the questions and even I, with my limited knowledge of Cyrillic script, could anticipate some of the answers. 'Tolstoy!' We found the same programme in Georgian. Neither of us could understand anything at all but we could see the prizes. These were the equivalent in Georgian Lari of £10,000 for the top prize, and only about £4 for the lowest prize. It seemed so little. This was an exceptionally poor country.

6

Cultural exchanges

February 2001, Tbilisi

Madame Mzia, the Head of the English Teachers' Association of Georgia, welcomed me to her office just before 10.00 the following morning. Although I thought I had arrived early I could see behind her a room already packed full to bursting with chairs lined up in rows, and on them the feisty women of ETAG. The room was so full those who couldn't squeeze onto the rows were on easy chairs and sofas around the periphery, and on one of these was Barrie, our English Language Adviser. He greeted me with a cheery wave. It was cold in the room, as there was no heating, and we were all still wearing our overcoats and scarves.

'Madame Mzia,' I said to her confidentially, 'I have to confess I found it a challenge to put together a one hour presentation on British culture at such short notice. With your permission, however, can I suggest an alternative presentation?'

She smiled. 'By all means. We really just want the opportunity to learn from you – we don't have that many opportunities to interact with native English language speakers.' Music to my ears. Mzia introduced me graciously to her colleagues who were looking at me with some curiosity and smiling in a welcoming way.

'Ladies, I am pleased to have this opportunity to meet you, as I have learnt from my colleagues,' I gestured to Barrie at the back of the room, 'how significant ETAG is for the British Council.' They all turned round and smiled and clapped towards him. Evidently he was well regarded.

I carried on, 'Your work in reaching thousands of young people and helping them learn new skills is at the core of what we in the British Council do. I hope my organisation will be able to help expand the resources and methodologies you have available to you. As to the purpose of my visit to you today, I have to start with an apology that I cannot give you a presentation on British culture.' Some of the women looked at each other. 'If I am honest, it is quite difficult to give a presentation on my own culture before I know more about yours as, until then, I don't know what things are similar and what is different.' And they laughed. 'Perhaps we could do this a different way. Please feel free to ask me any question at all and I will answer you as well as I can.'

The audience looked at me, pondering on this. There was a silence, apart from squeaks from a few chair legs as members of the audience shifted in their seats.

One woman cleared her throat and said, 'What do you think is the most significant factor in the Northern Ireland peace process?' Oh my. It was my turn to be silent while I considered this. I had been expecting a question like 'Why do British people like tea with milk?' or something like that.

So I said, 'The importance of communication – and that the various parties have recognised that they need to talk to each other and to be open to learning about a different point of view.'

And we discussed it a little more. Mzia asked for another question and again there was silence until someone said, 'What do you think of essery English?' – or that is what it sounded like.

'I'm sorry, I don't have good hearing,' which was true – I asked her to repeat her question. The ETAG lady said it again, although this time it sounded like, 'What do you think of estuary English?' Others in the room were helping too by saying 'estuary, estuary'.

I was none the wiser. 'I'm still sorry but I have to admit I am not familiar with 'estuary' English…' I knew about contracts, personnel management and development management techniques but I was not an English language teaching expert – and I had been away from Britain for years so things I might have picked up there sometimes passed me by. At the back of the room Barrie smiled at me. 'But I am keen to learn about it.'

The lady explained that the estuary was of the River Thames and that in effect it was a regional accent that had permeated popular speech far beyond its catchment area. 'In other words, is it all right to have regional accents or should we be teaching 'received pronunciation'?' asked another woman, and there was much nodding and discreet discussion.

'I am not an expert, clearly,' and they laughed, 'but if you can make yourself clearly understood then perhaps accent itself doesn't matter too much?'

More discussions and a few more questions, then a silence. 'One final question,' said Madame Mzia, scanning the room and then catching someone's eye.

'Have you noticed any cultural similarities between Georgia and the United Kingdom?'

'I have only been in your country a few days and I am looking forward to finding out more...' I had to stop and think. I thought of the apartment that Alek and I were living in. It was not a large flat but one of its rooms was crammed full of books. The library had Georgian writers but also

Tolstoy, Lermontov, Shakespeare, Dickens, Voltaire, Goethe. It might not be representative but I felt it might be. 'From what I have seen, in Georgia many people love books, reading and literature, as many of us do in Britain – and from what I have heard you treasure your history, as we do in my country. You also have an undeniably popular British cultural export, *Who Wants to be a Millionaire?*'

7

Road trip

February 2001, the road to Yerevan

On Monday Vakho picked us up in the worn, old office car with Eka, the Exams Manager, sitting in the front. It was a cold, dark morning. 'I think it might snow,' said Eka. We drove along the Mtkvari River on the roads out of Tbilisi – Alek and I exclaiming and peering up at the beautiful, balconied pastel-painted houses built into the cliffs on the other side of the river. 'The British ambassador lives in one of those,' said Eka.

'He has a better deal than we have,' said Alek.

As we were driving out of the city, two policemen standing near a shabby Lada police car waved us to the side of the road with a baton. Vakho immediately concurred and slowed to a halt. They questioned him and peered into the car with detached interest at us. Vakho answered their questions, and the only thing I could make out was 'diplomat'. They waved him on without wasting more time on us.

'What was all that about?'

'They wanted money.'

'Why, what have we done? Or not done?'

'Nothing,' said Eka, 'they do that to everyone. They don't get paid salaries, so they wave people down to get money on some pretence. They let us off because you are diplomats and as such are too much hassle.' Vakho added a sentence which Eka translated. 'Our car doesn't have diplomatic number plates – if it did, they wouldn't bother waving us over at all.' It seemed the police were not really there to 'serve the public'.

The road took us across wide, flat plains, past innumerable farms and run-down villages. Vakho dodged sleepy pigs and cows ambling across our path. The road started to climb higher and snaked around the hillsides and through forests, heavy with long-lain snow.

Figure 5 Bridge on the road to Yerevan

We went past a high, curved stone bridge over a steep mountain gorge. It looked like it was in a fantasy, built for giants or centaurs to cross. Past another half-made, decaying metal bridge, which stopped, frozen halfway across the valley. 'Why is it like that?' I asked.

'When the Soviet Union collapsed the men who were building the bridge just stopped. There wasn't any money to pay them to finish it,' said Eka.

We went past a massive skeleton of a building, rusting away, in the middle of nowhere. 'A factory,' said Eka and we peered into its vacant windows as we passed. Everything inside had completely collapsed. It was hard to imagine it when it must have been busy and functional and full of Soviet workers.

All the time snow was falling, getting heavier and heavier as we drove. The road deteriorated the further away from Tbilisi we got. I complimented Eka on her faultless English (she had virtually no accent at all) and asked where she learnt it. 'Here in Georgia – but I spent a long time in Germany. My German is better.' During the Soviet Union era there were many links with East Germany and anyone who could travel evidently tried to go there. She looked a little German as she had blonde hair and blue eyes. Most Georgians had dark hair, pale skin, and dark eyes. It turned out Vakho was half-Georgian, half-Ukrainian; there were also many links between Georgia and Ukraine. Vakho too had blue eyes but, although he was young, he had grey hair.

'I was the driver to a foreign TV crew in Chechnya a few years back,' he told us. 'Several times we were caught between fighters under heavy gunfire. Once we had to get out of the car and hide in trenches in the woods. One of our party got shot and I had to get him to safety.' I was glad we were in safe hands.

Vakho was driving like a slow-motion rally driver, back and fro across the road, dodging potholes filled with snow and ice. As indeed were all the vehicles, including those coming from the opposite direction. They were all negotiating the best possible route and so were on whichever bit of the road they could drive.

We arrived at a collection of sheds and some signs that announced that we were at the border with Armenia. Vakho asked for our passports and residence cards. 'Don't we need to go too?' I asked.

'No, stay here in the car, it is warmer,' and off he went to the Georgian and then the Armenian immigration sheds. We didn't have visas for Armenia as such but had been given two laminated cards from the Armenian Ministry of Foreign

Affairs. They had passport photos of us – one said 'Resident' and the other 'Diplomat' and other important facts in Armenian and English. After twenty minutes or so, Vakho came back and gave us our passports and all our various laminated cards. Sure enough, we had an exit stamp out of Georgia and an entry stamp into Armenia.

We set off again, higher up and higher still into the mountains of Armenia, the Lesser Caucasus. Vakho was struggling with the car and the snow was getting thicker. I asked Vakho, a little nervously, if this was normal? Eka translated, 'No, not normal…' It was a white-out, by now a blizzard, and the car was skidding and sliding over the icy road. We lurched off the road and into deep snow. Actually we didn't know where the road began and ended and we didn't know where we were. What we did know was that there were four of us in a clapped out old Mitsubishi, two women wearing high-heeled work shoes, thin wool work coats and I had a big navy blue felt hat that made me look like Mary Poppins. We had between us some bottles of water, a bar of chocolate and a banana. We pushed open the car doors into the snow and ineffectually tried to dig it out but, where the car was stuck, it was waist-deep. The wind was fierce and shrieking and my Mary Poppins hat flipped off my head and into the blizzard. The snow was so thick we could hardly see each other so we abandoned this and got back, shivering and damp, into the car. We weren't the most conversational group. After a while, Alek said, 'Perhaps we'll be found dead in here when the snow clears...'

We tried to wave down the few vehicles that passed. A couple of clunky old Soviet-era tractors and a four-wheel-drive car with 'Department for International Development' emblazoned across it. They laboured past and didn't stop. The snow was clogging our windows. We were beginning to resemble a lumpy igloo in the howling snowstorm. Perhaps another vehicle could hit us? Then, by some miracle, the driver of a UN vehicle stopped. He guided his impressive 4x4 near our car and he exchanged technical, vehicular words with Vakho. He hitched up his tow rope to our sad, old car and hauled us out, backwards, to thank yous in as many languages as we could muster. When he could, the UN driver released us and went on his way. We limped on to Yerevan and arrived, exhausted, several hours late.

#

Our British Embassy colleagues in Yerevan greeted us warmly. The John Smith Fellowship candidates, whom Eka invigilated for their English tests and whom I interviewed with an Embassy colleague, were not happy at all, however. We did our best to placate them and they turned out to be bright, articulate young people.

'Yes, it can be a sore point having activities managed from Tbilisi,' said Tim Jones, Her Majesty's Ambassador to Armenia. I could see what he meant. 'We need to get cracking to open the new British Council office. Could you come back in a few weeks and we can interview for your new Office Manager?'

I hesitated. The snow, the roads…'Out of interest, are there flights between Tbilisi and Yerevan?' I asked him.

'Yes, there is a UN flight, but if the weather is bad, it is difficult for the planes to land. I wouldn't recommend it at this time of year.' By car it would have to be.

Tim gave me a briefing. 'As you will appreciate, Armenia is a landlocked country whose neighbours are Georgia, Iran, Azerbaijan and Turkey. There is a frozen conflict between Armenia and Azerbaijan over the disputed territory of

Nagorno Karabakh and the border between Turkey and Armenia is technically closed – no diplomatic relations. The Armenian government has good relations with Russia – but no border – and they have an open border with Iran. In many respects the most significant land route to get Armenian goods out is via Georgia to the north. The borders, however, have been described as 'porous' in places.' I agreed the crossing point seemed informal. Who knew what was being smuggled across those borders?

Tim told me that Robert Kocharian was a youngish President and the country was stable and controlled. There weren't the same issues regarding electricity, gas and water cuts as there were in Georgia. There had been a major earthquake in Spitak in 1988 – perhaps 50,000 people had been killed and many more lives devastated. As a result of the earthquake, President Mikhayil Gorbachev had asked for help from countries outside the Soviet Union. Perhaps this had been a sign that things were opening up, or of desperation – the beginning of *Glasnost*. 'There is also an old nuclear power station at Medzamor, about twenty miles from Yerevan.' Oh dear. 'Make sure you have iodine tablets in case it explodes – the tablets are supposed to reduce the effects of radiation,' Tim advised.

He told me that there was a sizeable Armenian diaspora, including in the UK, and that often they were influential and wealthy, especially those in the USA. Much of the Armenian economy relied on remittances from its diaspora. There was enormous interest in learning English and in European culture in all its many forms, so the new British Council would be a welcome addition.

'Do we know who the VIP is yet?' I asked.

'No, but we have been told the visit is likely to be in November. We are keen that the opening of the British

Council will be the highlight.' We had nine months to get the office established. I had no idea how feasible that was. 'You can use a room in the Embassy as your office, to get you up and running.' That was one good thing and I was grateful for that.

The next day our drive back was less hair-raising and we had the reassurance of driving in convoy with the Tbilisi-based British Defence Attaché. We rendezvoused with him outside our hotel and Vakho gave the driver an enthusiastic bearhug. 'This is my brother, Levan!' said Vakho. 'He is a champion motocross driver!' We looked enviously at the Defence Attaché's Landrover Discovery. I hoped Levan wouldn't impress us with his talents – there was no way we could keep up. It had stopped snowing and instead it was a cold, sunny day. The air smelled crisp and clean. Not long after leaving Yerevan as far as the eye could see it looked like the landscape was iced like a wedding cake.

The car tyres still skidded on the icy roads and Vakho put all his own driving skills to good use – we made it back to Tbilisi safely. We could see now how dangerous our journey out must have been. As we drove back I thought through all the things I needed to do. I added:

- Get iodine tablets
- Buy a new office car
- Buy a new fit-for-purpose hat

8

Bank job

Later that week accountant Katie and I sat down to work out our budgets and what we could afford. We needed to compile a financial plan to send off for approval to our London-based colleagues. Getting a new office car was now top of the list and it would be the most expensive thing. 'We haven't been spending any money on anything but essential things,' said Katie. 'We wanted to wait till you got here.'

Here we were in late February. The financial year runs from April to March and we needed to get cracking to get it all sorted to be able to spend any money still unallocated. It couldn't be carried forward – if it wasn't spent in the appropriate financial year, you lost it. Katie pulled out some of the papers we needed for the plans from under her desk. 'Mice! Mice have been eating our accounts,' she said. Sure enough there were tiny teethmarks on the wads of paper. What would the National Audit Office make of that? The mice have eaten my homework...

Getting somewhere to store all our files was pretty much a priority too and a quick-fix solution to that was to get a bigger flat for Alek and me. Katie and I sat with our figures and calculators, checked and re-checked costs, made estimates, did spreadsheets. Some hours later we came up with A Plan. We worked out we could afford:

- To buy a new car
- For Alek and me to move to a bigger flat which could offer overflow office facilities
- To employ a new colleague in the library
- Long overdue pay rises for my Georgian colleagues

Brilliant. After some hurried conversations with colleagues in distant London we had our plans approved.

With advice from a British Embassy colleague, Alek would be looking at potential new flats. Alek's professional background had been management and it would be a good use, temporarily, of his time and experience. I was worried it didn't sound like there were many opportunities for jobs for him.

#

I had no idea how easy it would be to buy an appropriate new car quickly in Tbilisi. I sat down with Katie and Vakho. 'I should explain. I know nothing about cars,' I said.

'Neither do I,' said Katie. But driver, Vakho, of course, knew all about cars – we'd be a good team.

Katie translated for Vakho. He said, 'I have seen one! It's a Landrover Discovery – like the Defence Attaché's car. You know, the one my brother, Levan, drives.'

I said quickly, 'We need to run a tender exercise – we can't just go out and buy that particular car because we like it.' We had to follow UK public sector rules for expensive items – to get at least three quotes and show evidence of market-testing and getting value-for-money. Katie translated and Vakho looked puzzled. This had not been the way things had happened in Soviet times. In a 'command heights' economy you bought what you could, when you could and you did what your boss told you – there was no choice. Even though the Soviet Union had collapsed ten years earlier, Georgia had yet to embrace the culture and institutions of modern business methods.

As our accountant Katie knew the theory of market testing but she said, 'We have never had to do a tender exercise in this office.' She added, 'We have only ever bought shelves and desks. All the books and computers came from the UK.'

'OK, well, what is it about this car that we like, so we can compare it to others?' we asked Vakho.

'It's a Landrover Discovery – and it's available now,' he said. After more discussion, we came up with our criteria for selection:

- Four-wheel drive and must be able to cope with atrocious road and weather conditions for frequent long journeys to Armenia
- Reliable make with spares available locally
- Within the budget we had agreed with London
- Available now

With this Vakho and Katie tested the market and prepared paperwork and reported back their findings. 'Landrover Discovery!' Vakho couldn't wait – this was a proper driver's car.

#

We had to wait a few days for the money for the car to be transferred from HQ to our bank account, before we could sort out the purchase. This was before internet banking and to add to it Georgia was a cash economy – almost all purchases had to be made in cash. The morning we were expecting our bank transfer to arrive Katie burst breathlessly into our office. 'I have heard a rumour that our bank is going bankrupt!'

What? I was shocked. I couldn't imagine a bank going bankrupt. 'How? How do you know?'

'On my way to work I could see lots of people queuing to get their money out but they won't let them in.'

A run on the bank!

'It does happen here from time to time.'

Where I came from, at the time, it was unthinkable. What to do? There was the money for the car and the staff salaries and the rent. It was all earmarked and we couldn't afford to lose it. I couldn't face phoning my UK colleagues to tell them, only weeks into my new job, that we couldn't access our office money. I phoned Peter, the Management Officer at the British Embassy. 'What? Can a bank go bankrupt? We have the Embassy local account with them too! Let me check it out.'

I tried to concentrate on drafting a job description and newspaper advertisements for the new Office Manager for the, as yet, non-existent British Council in Armenia. When the phone rang I snatched it up. It was Peter.

'Yes, the general view is that the bank is indeed collapsing. It's imperative to get the money out immediately. I've pulled the Ambassador out of his meetings and we'll go down to withdraw everything and get down to the Bank of Georgia to open a new account. It's the Ambassador's penultimate day in Georgia! By the way, we're grateful for the tip-off – we had a salary run coming in from London tomorrow.' As they were a bigger operation than our small office they ran the risk of losing far more money. 'If you like, and with your approval, we can withdraw your money and park it temporarily in our new account,' offered Peter.

'I like and I approve,' I said.

'You'll need to come and withdraw it from our new account though.' Peter and the Ambassador hot-footed it to the bankrupt bank, pulled diplomatic rank, withdrew their money and the British Council's, and went on to the open arms of the Bank of Georgia. They had a warm welcome for their new client.

Vakho turned up at our office to drive Katie and me to the bank. He was a tall, broad-shouldered, handsome man and today he was wearing a new, black suit. He looked like a bodyguard. 'Excellent,' I said, 'Wear sunglasses. And don't smile!'

While I had been disappointed that the Sheraton Metekhi Palace Hotel, where the Embassy was located, wasn't much like a palace, I wasn't expecting the Bank of Georgia to look like, well, an *Art Nouveau* opera house. The walls were painted *eau de nil* and there were faces of gods painted atop well-proportioned columns and it was festooned with gold-painted scrolls and curls. The cashier was in the middle of the elegant room in the cash booth which comprised looping, curvy metal tracery. Curiouser and curiouser.

Katie and I signed hundreds of forms with Cyrillic writing on thick, cream paper to open our new bank account. We wanted to keep the money on us as we needed to spend it sooner rather than later. The cashier handed me a large, plump envelope and I stuffed it into my bag. I stepped out on to the main square in Tbilisi. Colleagues had told me I looked like a foreigner as I was taller than most Georgian women and had blue eyes and wavy brown hair. Not only did I feel like I had a beacon shining above my head that said, 'foreigner here, mugging opportunity here…' I could add to that 'foreigner with $15,000 in cash in her handbag... the same as a Georgian Lari millionaire!' But there was Vakho with his sharp suit and black sunglasses and we legged it to our knackered old car – off we sped to the office, to stash the money securely in our safe.

A rumour emerged that the wife of the director of our former bank had withdrawn all the bank's money and run off to Switzerland with her lover.

9

Getting out there

February 2001, Tbilisi

The following day we bought the Landrover and there was more than a tinge of excitement in the office. Not least for Vakho who turned up again in his slick, dark suit to escort Barrie, our English Language Adviser, and me to my first meeting with the Minister of Education.

Barrie and I were shown into a room in the ministry which had the usual broad sash windows, high ceiling and a long table. At one end of which sat the minister, Alexander Kartozia. Dark-eyed and with a luxurious moustache, he rose to greet us warmly, both hands outstretched in welcome. Around the table sat perhaps 20 members of his staff whom he introduced. And sitting on two side tables, or standing in any available space, were another 20 or so people. A keen audience, as only Barrie, the minister and I actually talked at all. What the 40 other people – who observed our conversations with such interest – did was chain-smoke. In fact probably the only people who were not constantly smoking were we three talkers.

It was a long meeting, maybe two hours and – such was the nature of these things – no-one wanted to leave before the minister finished. We discussed how the about-to-be-expanded British Council could help improve the much needed reform of education in Georgia. Barrie updated him on the British Council's existing and expanding English language teaching activities and about the English Teachers' Association of Georgia network of dedicated and talented teachers. Potentially, the pedagogical pilot work they were doing, over time, could be woven into the fabric of education reforms in Georgia and make a deep impact on standards of teaching, textbook writing, testing and examinations. That was easier said than done, however, and there were many, many reasons why green shoots could wither. While we ruminated on the challenges in education, the serious business of chain smoking was ongoing to the point where it was hard to breathe. In fact it was hard to see clearly. The minister eventually wrapped up the meeting and guided Barrie and me into his personal office. He flipped open his packet of fags and turned to us and said, 'Cigarette?'

'Er, thank you, don't mind if I do,' said Barrie.

#

My next 'out there' meeting was with the Minister of Culture, Mrs Sesily Gogiberidze. The minister stood up from behind her imposing desk, greeted me warmly and invited me to sit for coffee with her.

'We are all so pleased the British Council is expanding and we very much hope we can work collaboratively on many new activities.' Her English accent was impeccable. I replied that I hoped so too and how much I was looking forward to learning about Georgian culture. I had to confess I hadn't known much about Georgia before I arrived.

She smiled, 'Many Western Europeans don't seem to know much about us. We are a country at a crossroads, in many ways. We have an ancient culture on one of the main thoroughfares of the Silk Route but we see ourselves as rooted in European traditions. In fact we are one of the world's oldest countries and the second oldest Christian country – we call our country *Sakartvelo*.' The minister said she hoped I would find out for myself that Georgian singing and dancing were unique. 'Modesty aside, we think they are exceptionally beautiful. In fact there will be a performance of Georgian dancing at the Opera House soon so you can see for yourself. The company tours abroad a lot so you need to catch them while you can.'

I said I'd make sure I was in Tbilisi. The minister told me that many forms of culture were much appreciated in Georgia: classical music, theatre, painting, sculpture, literature, film. 'We are proud of our own culture but we thirst to know about others too, classical and contemporary. I don't think you will be bored here,' she smiled again. 'Our challenge, and if you can help with this it would be much appreciated, is to help draw attention to the richness and diversity of Georgian culture. We also have a fabulous material culture, ancient religious sites and artefacts and archaeological sites but again, we have little money to invest in these to present them to international standards. We have high hopes that our economy will improve so that we can improve our infrastructure and get tourists back again.'

I said I hoped we would be able to help – but I thought it seemed a Catch-22 situation. They evidently needed the income from tourism but I couldn't imagine any but the most adventurous of tourists coming to Georgia with the power cuts and the 'beating up of foreigners' branding – and adventurous back-packer tourists don't tend to spend much money.

#

That weekend there was a reception at the Metekhi Palace Hotel to welcome our new Ambassador, Deborah Barnes-Jones. 'Georgia seems to be a lively place – how have you been getting on?' she asked me.

'It's not boring here...'

'It will be good to put our heads together on our Chevening scheme,' said Deborah. The Chevening programme was a global scheme which provided Foreign and Commonwealth Office (FCO) funding for exceptional young people to study at Masters level in UK. As with the DFID-sponsored John Smith scheme, the British Council managed the scheme on FCO's behalf – advertising, shortlisting, interviewing, helping to find appropriate courses in Britain and providing support to the Chevening Fellows during their stay in UK. If we identified the brightest and the best potentially these were important contacts for the Embassy, for the British Council and for British businesses wanting to expand their markets. 'Let's meet soon to discuss our strategy and on which sectors we want to focus in Georgia. We only have three awards a year here so we have to make the most of them.'

We couldn't stand around chatting to each other. This was the moment to dive in and meet people. There were contacts from ministries and business; from cultural organisations and from other diplomatic missions. Deborah was being introduced by members of the Embassy team. For me, too, it was a room full of strangers and I looked around wondering where to start. But, after all, what is a stranger but a friend you haven't made yet? I dived in and started conversing and chatting and networking, and the important business of exchanging business cards and making mental notes of which people to try to meet again in a more formal situation. Many, or at least some, of these people could be just the contacts we needed to start shaping the new British Council strategy in the arts, education and governance.

What wonderful names people had – men with names like Giorgi, Irakli (Hercules, I was told), and Hamlet. Women called Ketevan (Keti/Katie), Ana or Natia and, to my delight, Salome and Medea. While I was in the thick of the networking Deborah turned up at my side and said, 'Jo, excellent, here is someone I would like you to meet.' She introduced Mr Temur Rukhadze from the Anglo-Georgian Friendship Society and promptly disappeared. Mr Rukhadze was quite a short, late middle-aged man and he gave me a warm handshake and started to talk rapidly but quite quietly to me in Russian. I had to bend down to hear him and quickly said, apologetically, that I spoke only a little Russian. He went silent and we looked at each other. We looked somewhat desperately around the room. I recognised someone from the British Embassy and, taking Mr Rukhadze's arm, I made a beeline for her.

'It's Maia, isn't it?' and she turned and smiled at me. Maia was the Embassy's Georgian Press and Public Affairs Officer. 'I'm sorry, but Mr Rukhadze here wants to tell me something but, alas, I don't speak much Russian (and no Georgian), and I think he doesn't speak English.'

'Yes indeed Jo, I often translate for the Embassy. I think I can guess what Mr R. wants to ask you about,' and she turned to Mr Rukhadze. He spoke to her, even more rapidly, in Georgian. Maia turned back to me. 'Mr Rukhadze is happy you are expanding Anglo-Georgian cultural relations and welcomes you to Georgia.' I replied that I was delighted to be here and to be able to expand on what my colleagues had started.

'Yes, yes,' he said warmly, 'we need more, and I have a proposal for you.'

We encouraged him to tell us. 'We need money for our office, the Anglo-Georgian Friendship Society. To buy computers and a fax machine and to employ staff.' Ah.

'And what does your organisation do?' I asked.

'We promote friendly relations between Britain and Georgia...' said Mr Rukhadze.

I told him that was wonderful, but that, alas, the British Council was not a 'donor' and that we could not give money to other organisations in that way. 'And I hope my own office will be doing much to promote British-Georgian friendship – perhaps there is something we can work on together? What kinds of activities does the Anglo-Georgian Friendship Society promote?'

Mr Rukhadze looked disappointed but asked if the British Council could host the Wardrop Exhibition on a tour of the major cities in Georgia. I remembered the Wardrops from my meeting with the Georgian Ambassador; they were the British brother and sister team who had lived in Georgia in 1918 when Georgia was independent from Russia for a few brief years, before it was absorbed into the Soviet Union in 1921. Oliver Wardrop had been the first British diplomat to Georgia and he and his sister, Marjorie, had been keen admirers of Georgian culture. Mr Rukhadze told me that some years back the British Embassy had produced a series of good quality exhibition panels in English and Georgian about the Wardrops. They had only been exhibited once in Tbilisi and were now in storage.

'We will do our best,' I said as encouragingly as I could, 'but I should tell you that our current priorities are to promote the teaching and learning of English and to arrange exhibitions of contemporary arts, alongside helping in some way with some of the many development challenges Georgia faces. We are predominantly looking at what young Georgians want and need.' I didn't want to sound rude and I said this as politely as possible. I couldn't see how hosting the exhibition, no matter how good it was, would contribute to my own organisation's emerging strategy and it would take valuable time and money to put it on. We smiled, shook hands warmly and we agreed to meet again.

'Maia, he seems a lovely man but I don't understand what the Anglo-Georgian Friendship society is all about. Am I wrong or is it left-over as a sort of 'Soviet-style' friendship society?' I had heard that during the Soviet years these types of societies could be a way of the KGB getting close to foreigners to find out what they were up to – surely they were redundant now?

'Mr R is a little hindered in that by not being able to speak English,' said Maia. 'He is also the head of the Georgian-Romanian Friendship Society.'

'I wonder if he has more fruitful conversations with the Romanian Embassy than he did with me?'

10

Bittersweet

March 2001, Tbilisi

After the frenetic first few weeks it was time to relax and not to think about reports and plans and what needed to be done. One night our whole office went to a Georgian restaurant down near the Mtkvari River. At the entrance was a sign saying 'No guns!'

The restaurant was traditional and had high, vaulted ceilings with exposed terracotta bricks. We were shown into a private room on our own and I could see that off the main hall of the restaurant there were similar rooms. There was a long table, punctuated by candles and ashtrays, and on the walls were tapestries showing dancers, hunters and musicians in traditional costume. At the corners of the room were terracotta pots and wooden carvings. We could hear music – the sounds of rhythmic drumming, pipes and an accordion – coming from the main hall. As the restaurant filled up the music was drowned a little by the laughing and chatting and occasional raised voices of our fellow diners and the bustle of the waiters backwards and forwards with dish after dish to each of the tables. The smell of roasting meats, spicy sauces and fresh salads filled the room. It gave me the feeling of being at a medieval banquet – but one where you had to leave your weapons at the door.

Alek and I had no idea what to order. We were keen to see the menu but it was dizzying with so many things from which to choose. I knew my colleagues did not have big salaries and I wanted this to be my treat so I had taken out what seemed to be enough of the currency, *Lari*, to pay for a meal. While I was the host, as we were pausing with indecision, Nata asked, 'Would you like us to order to show you examples of Georgian cuisine?' She and Eka put their heads together and rattled out the order to the waitress. While we were waiting, I looked down the long table and saw that it was in fact four tables placed end to end. Perhaps it would be difficult for us all to talk to each other?

'Why don't we put the tables into a square?' There was a pause and everyone looked puzzled.

'Yes, why not? For a change.'

When the waitress came back we were all busily moving the tables into a square and she looked astonished – but she appraised us with a practised eye as she opened bottles of red and white wine which she placed between groups of us. I noticed my Georgian colleagues were looking quizzically at each other – then Maya Z asked, 'Barrie, are you going to be *tamada*?'

'Er, OK,' he agreed and he raised his glass in a toast. 'Welcome to Georgia, I hope you will enjoy living here as much as I have.'

'We can't imagine you ever leaving Barrie,' chorused my colleagues. I, unsure what to do by way of reply, raised my glass and said how happy we were to be here.

Maya Z explained, 'Toasting is an art form in Georgia. The *tamada* is the toastmaster – we call this type of feasting a *supra*. It means table in Georgian. Eating and drinking together is an important part of our culture.' The food started to arrive: the routine didn't follow the *a la Russe* menu of starter, main course, pudding, but was more like a *tapas* or *mezze* arrangement. First, cold starters were placed before us: crisp salads fragrant with fresh herbs; hard, salty slabs of cheese; tangy walnut dip, aubergine dip, in fact lots of different dips, served in attractive pottery bowls and sprinkled with pomegranate seeds or chopped parsley, along with 'mother's bread'. Then some hot vegetarian dishes: creamy melted cheese, and *lobio*, a kidney-bean stew, dark and rich. Just when we thought we couldn't possibly eat any more they brought succulent grilled meats: chicken, lamb, pork, beef served with sour plum sauce, *tkemali*.

'I love it all but I especially love this,' I said, savouring its bittersweet taste. Then, just in case we were still peckish, came fat, crispy chips and *khachapuri*, circular bread filled with hot, juicy cheese, like an inverted pizza. We ate and we chatted and we ate some more. 'I keep hearing how corrupt things are in Georgia, but what does it mean in everyday life?' I asked one of my colleagues.

She hesitated and said, 'To give you an example, it is difficult for children get into university without their parents either bribing the admissions body or giving payments direct to lecturers – then they get given the questions they would be asked in the exam.'

Alek said, 'That reminds me of Poland in the 1980s. We had a system whereby students were examined together – the examiner would choose one student randomly for oral exams and if he or she failed, the whole group did too. We used to have to take bottles of vodka as thank you presents.' Presumably if one student didn't provide their bribe, and didn't know the questions, they risked failing and the wrath of the whole group.

'Yes, and there are many other problems – people can bribe someone else to take exams for them. The whole system of registration is rotten. Or the exam markers have a system to give special marks to selected candidates. The Ministry of Education has signed up to a World Bank programme to clean up education. It has been going since the late 1990s but nothing seems to have changed.'

'How come you are all so bright and clearly well educated?' I asked.

'Educating their children is a number one priority for Georgian parents – and we do work hard. Lots of people want good qualifications so they can leave and try and get a good job in Western Europe or North America.'

Brain drain. 'You can't lose your best people,' I said.

'It is hard, though. Corruption isn't just in education.'

Other colleagues joined in. 'If I want my rubbish collected, or to see the doctor, or to register for housing and many other transactions, I have to pay the person in front of me but there is no guarantee that what I need will get done.'

'The tax system is terrible, hardly anyone pays it if they can avoid it. It just goes straight into the pockets of the public officials.'

'Does the government deliberately pay lower salaries because they know people will take bribes or do people take bribes because their salaries are so low?' I asked. We laughed as it was indeed complex; we couldn't begin to work out that conundrum.

'It isn't just the government sector. Business deals are about who you know and who owes who a favour. *Obligatsia*. Hardly anyone uses contracts to agree things. Deals are done by men at night in rooms like this, over a good meal and a lot of wine.'

Evidently there was a system – based on relationships not rules, perhaps. 'Yes, it is a sort of a system.' But how sustainable was it? I was wondering how they could reform just the education system, if in fact some of the problems were deeper than education alone. Shevardnadze was at the helm and a lot of people in the West seemed to love him but he seemed remote from the everyday problems ordinary Georgians faced.

'Some say the Russians are behind the instability. They don't want Georgia to be developed or to accept Western help and they are trying to frighten away the foreigners. The Russians want our country to be weak.'

When we asked for the bill to my horror Alek and I realised we didn't have enough cash to pay for our meal! 'This is one of the challenges of living in a cash economy,' said Barrie. I had to ask Anka to reassure the waitress that we would come back the following day with the balance of what we owed. As any project manager knows it is routine to estimate a cash-flow forecast to make sure we had enough money in the bank to pay for project activities – I would need to make sure I had enough real money in my purse to ensure my own flow of cash.

#

Hours later, deeply asleep in our chilly apartment in the wee small hours, Alek and I awoke to sounds of gunshots being fired. Not distant, quite close. Volleys of shots answering each other like a coded conversation, somewhere on the street below. 'What's going on?' I murmured.

'This country is collapsing,' said Alek, jolting awake. 'Even in its worst days, Poland didn't get like this…'

Perhaps this was an accepted way for disputes to be settled? We knew the rule of law was weak. If Tbilisi was a woman, yes she was beautiful. She was unique and compelling – but she seemed fragile and battered. Manipulated.

11

Ballet and brown envelopes

March 2001, Tbilisi

I had managed to get us tickets to see the Georgian National Ballet perform at the Opera House. It was an opera house that looked just as you would hope an opera house would look: ornate, grand and impressive. The house was full. Already Alek and I knew some people and could wave our greetings to people we recognised. 'There's the Ambassador – and there's the Minister of Education!'

'There's the woman from the logistics company who is clearing our stuff through customs!'

The lights dimmed for our night of Georgian dancing. From the darkness came the sounds of ethereal flutes, resonant, rhythmic drums and sinuous piping. The lights softly came into focus drawing us in and here, now, were the dancers. Handsome young men, hands linked across each other's bodies, weaving across the stage diagonally like a slinky snake in perfect time to the drums and flutes. Then leaping and posturing with shields and knives, clashing daggers with razor-sharp accuracy, sparks flying from the colliding blades. They were joined by beautiful, tall girls who floated across the stage with swan-like elegance. The men's dance evolved into one of wooing and strutting their masculine stuff for their stunning female counterparts. The girls played the men off against each other and acknowledged their courtship with elegant nods. Many different dances but the themes were the same: the men were men, warriors and fighters but they could be floored by their beautiful women. The women were women, lovely, remote and perhaps stronger than they knew. It was exquisite. Alek turned to me with shining, happy eyes and said, 'This is what Georgia should be all about!' He was finding other aspects of life here trying.

#

Alek and Katie, the accountant, had found a large, rather lovely new apartment for us which occupied two floors of a larger building. I hoped Alek and I would feel more settled there. The upper floor in the flat had beautiful high-ceilinged rooms with tall windows and metal shutters. There was an expansive reception room with parquet flooring, floor to ceiling cut-glass mirrors and an impressive chandelier. A blousy sofa and chairs and – oh my – a grand piano. The furniture was made of heavy, darkly scented wood with carvings of trees and hunting scenes. It looked like a ballroom. The kitchen was well kitted out and had a pipe for the gas cylinders we would doubtless need. Downstairs was a basement with low ceilings and more modern rooms: a guest room, a kitchenette and a large room – which was perfect for storing all that stuff from the British Council office.

Outside there were vines curled around wires over a garage and a balcony from the kitchen overlooked a small courtyard garden with trees. I had to ask what they were. 'One is a pomegranate and the other is a walnut tree,' said Katie. How exotic.

That night we heard shooting again, from the streets near our new house. We had an electricity cut and ran out of gas. 'At least we've got water,' said Alek.

#

After transferring as much as we could from the office to our new house we rearranged the shelves in the library and freed up just enough space for new desks. We hid the desks behind the shelves to try to make it feel like an office. We put up newly framed British Council posters. We installed a small fridge and Vakho put up wall cabinets in the management office. Luiza, our lively cleaner, was delighted that she now had somewhere to put all sorts of paraphernalia. A while later I opened the wall cupboard to find neatly stacked china teacups and saucers. On tea and coffee canisters were sticky notes saying:

'For visitors'

Next to them, a small bottle of Brandy with a note which said:

'Brandy for staff'

Maybe I should complete the set with a canister labelled:

'Tranquilisers for director'?

#

We wanted our office to be as tidy as possible as the new Ambassador, Deborah, and the Embassy Management

Officer, Peter, were due to visit. I wanted them to be aware of our current operating conditions. Their eyes popped at our office. 'How do you cope without running water? The fainter hearted would have booked a ticket back to London at an early opportunity,' said Deborah.

Leave Georgia, to do a dull job in London? 'We're trying to make the most of what we have. This is better than it has been,' I said. And, in a way, our office was a microcosm of what was going on in Tbilisi itself.

'I can see your little library is clearly well used – keep me posted on how your new projects and activities shape up,' said Deborah. I told her that I had colleagues coming to help us shape our emerging arts and education strategies and to advise on maximising our library resources. 'And you'll be over to interview soon at the Embassy for the next round of Chevening scholarships? I can see you won't be able to host the interviews here.'

'By the way, have you heard that a number of foreigners have been knocked out and robbed on their doorsteps at night over the last few days?' asked Peter. I hadn't heard. 'To be on the safe side you should have security guards stationed outside your house at all times. I can give you the contact details – I think you should get them as soon as possible.' How much do they cost? I wondered, thinking of our stretched budgets.

#

The end of the financial year was looming and an important thing I had to do that week was pay the annual rent for the office. Katie and I had looked high and low and had not found a contract between the British Council and the Tbilisi State University. We had withdrawn $3000 in cash, which was apparently the agreed sum. 'I know our office isn't up to much but that is very low annual rent,' I said as Katie put the dollars in a brown envelope.

I took one of my colleagues with me to meet a chap from the university who was apparently the appropriate contact. His office was a few blocks away from ours and had a rather lavish view over Chavchavadze Avenue, one of the main roads in Tbilisi. The man at the university was a large, portly chap – he looked solid and powerful. He welcomed us in, gesturing in a grand fashion for us to sit.

'Coffee? Tea? Wine? Brandy?' he offered. 'It is wonderful to meet such lovely ladies from the British Council,' he said. 'I hope you are enjoying being here in Georgia.'

I said I was, very much. 'It is a great honour to be working here. I'm sorry to see that there are so many problems though. It seems a struggle for many people in Georgia.'

'Things overall are getting better, but yes, there are problems. We can always do with more help. Do you have any money to help with reform of higher education?' he asked, hopefully.

'Alas, no,' but I told him about the FCO's Chevening scholarships.

'I may suggest some candidates for you,' he said.

'It will be an open competition,' I replied, sounding, doubtless, a little prissy.

'Of course, of course,' he said, sounding, possibly, a shade cynical.

'We are here to pay the rent for our office.'

'Ah yes. The business of business.'

'I'm not sure how we pay our account.'

'I can make sure it gets to the right place.'

We looked at each other, and I slid the brown paper envelope across the table. Without losing eye contact with me he reached out his hand and pulled it towards himself.

12

Green shoots

Vakho and I set off in our new car for our next trip to Yerevan. Alek didn't want to come too so we were on our own this time. I briefly worried that Alek didn't appear to be enjoying our new life as much as I was but I was too busy planning ahead for my job to think more about things at home. Vakho and I pooled all the words of English, Georgian and Russian we knew. I had a vocabulary of useful Polish words and there were many similarities between Polish and Russian. I learnt there were wolves and bears in the forests we were driving through. We saw some enormous, modern houses in the hills overlooking Tbilisi. I asked Vakho if they belonged to gangsters or perhaps politicians. 'Same thing,' said Vakho.

It was not snowing but higher in the mountains, snow lay heavily. This time we were able to stop at a café just over the border into Armenia. Vakho had a smoke – as it was against British Council rules to smoke in

Figure 6 Valley in Armenia

72

the car – and I looked over the wide, spectacular snow-filled valley.

Vakho asked if I wanted coffee. 'Instant or...' and just as I was about to say 'Turkish', he interjected with '*Armenian* coffee.' One of the many conflicts in this part of the world was the serious impasse between Turkey and Armenia.

Travelling on further and higher up we drove through a wide plain, which we hadn't been able to see on our previous blizzard-bound journey a few weeks earlier. The snow had been compressed thickly on the road ahead, like a silver ribbon against the bright snow on the plains either side.

Coming slowly towards us was a little Russian Lada with five big, black leather-jacketed men crammed in. Our tyres skidded. Our Landrover gave a sickening lurch and started to slowly pirouette round and around on the glassy ice towards them. From our slow-motion, circular sweep across the road I could see them looking at us with horrified, open mouths. Vakho somehow maintained control as the heavy car looped before them. We ended on their side of the road gently reversing towards their flimsy bonnet before stopping about a foot from them. Looking down over my shoulder I could see them clapping with relief in their gloves. Vakho turned to me and said hoarsely, 'Jo, may I? Cigarette in car?'

'Yes Vakho!' Office rule broken.

#

On to Yerevan. Impressive neo-classical buildings with enormous arches framed the elegant Republic Square at the heart of the city. It was busy with smoke-puffing Ladas.

In the British Embassy in Yerevan I interviewed for the Armenian Chevening scholarship awards alongside the Deputy

Figure 7 Republic Square Yerevan

Head of Mission. We also discussed the job description and advertisement for the new Office Manager. The Embassy would put the ad in the local press and shortlist candidates and I would come back in three weeks to do the interviews with them. It was ridiculously busy.

'I have news,' said Tim, the Ambassador. 'We know who the VIP who will open the new British Council will be.' I was all ears. I hoped it would be someone young, or appealing to young people. A famous artist perhaps – or a musician – or a sports-personality-of-the-year.

'The Duke of Gloucester,' said Tim.

A Royal VIP!

'The Duke of – which one is he?' I had to ask.

'The Duke is the Queen's cousin,' Tim continued. 'This will be the first time a member of the Royal Family has ever visited this part of the world, so the visit is a big deal.'

'Yes, I can imagine.' And I could. I carried on smiling at Tim but inside I was grimacing with anxiety.

'Security and planning will be tight – and we need something juicier than cutting a ribbon across a doorway.'

It was only six months away. I had been told that my UK-appointed successor to the British Council in Yerevan would not have arrived in his new job by then – and I had discovered that, while we had guides in the British Council to help scale down offices, there was little advice on how to open up a new one. We were starting from scratch.

#

The most pressing thing we had to do in both offices, as part of a 'green shoots' strategy, was to train our existing, young and quite inexperienced team and recruit new staff. For the Georgia team we needed to appoint:

- an Office Manager to help sort out the internal issues and find us a new office
- a Project Manager to help get out there and develop new, impactful projects
- a new Receptionist

In Armenia we could only afford one person, who would need to be able to do everything. It was getting urgent.

It transpired that it was not a straightforward process. Although we had *hundreds* of applicants for each position, few people had the experience and approach for which we were looking.

'I see the corridor is full of models,' said Barrie. Sure enough, a long queue of beautiful girls were lining up to hand in their applications, minutes before the closing deadline for the receptionist position. While beauty might be an asset, they had to demonstrate an extra spark, an ability to make the most of their immediate job, to be a good team player and so on. Reading all the applications taught me a great deal about aspirations and issues for people in Georgia and Armenia. But, just as elsewhere, what someone – or, on occasion, someone else – wrote on paper, did not necessarily manifest in a bright, creative, forward-looking interviewee. We were able to shortlist few of those who applied and only interviewed a small number for each position. It was striking that older applicants struggled more with the process of applications and interviews.

We engaged Anuki as our new Receptionist. She was full of verve and very pretty too. It was more difficult identifying candidates for the two more senior positions. One interviewee for the Office Manager job said, 'I'll do whatever you ask me to.' How Soviet. The last thing I wanted was someone who would wait to be told what to do – we needed self-starters. I was delighted, therefore, to interview Zaza, one of the younger applicants for that position. Someone who would be an asset to any organisation – a self-starter extraordinaire. When I offered Zaza the job his current employer (an Italian agricultural import-export company) immediately offered him a pay rise I could not compete with. I told him he needed to do what was right for him. I was delighted tenfold that Zaza decided to accept our job offer.

When we were interviewing for the Project Manager position we were looking for someone who could either help us shape new projects in education reform or in governance and human rights. Both were evidently areas of huge significance in Georgia and in an ideal world we would have appointed one person for each sector but we couldn't afford that. We needed someone who had a thorough grasp of what was going on in Georgia, who had a finger on the pulse and ideally who also knew the best of what the UK could offer in their area. I asked one interviewee what he knew of education issues in the UK. He said, with enthusiasm, 'I love the UK. In a former life I used to be a little girl in the north of England!' Alas, that hadn't given him much insight into education reform in contemporary Britain.

We had high hopes for our final candidate for the Project Manager job, another young candidate in his late 20s. He said, 'As you will know from my application, I had a joint-funded Chevening scholarship – I have an MSc from Edinburgh University and am enrolled on PhD studies there. The most significant things Georgia can learn or adapt from the UK are broadly on the application of the rule of law, on improving access to justice, adoption of human rights laws, the importance of an independent judiciary and of freedom of the press.'

'Constantine…'

'Call me Kote.'

'Kote. When can you start?'

#

Word was obviously out that the British Council were interviewing for new staff. Nino, our new library assistant, handed me the CV of a young man who was waiting beside the reception desk in the corridor. I glanced at it and saw he was called Jacob Jugashvili. I said I could see him for a few minutes.

'I wondered if you have any jobs in information technology? I have a little company to help set up webpages and other support.' I told him we already had an IT Manager and said that if we had any more vacancies they would be advertised openly and we would have competitive interviews and so on. Jacob was interesting and engaging and he told me he was also an artist. He gave me his website address. 'I'd be pleased to know what you think of my work – I've had a few exhibitions in New York and in Britain,' he said. I love interesting, contemporary art so I said I would check him out and visit his gallery, and off he went. His name seemed familiar. Josef Jugashvili, was, of course, Georgia's most famous, most controversial, most infamous son. The Man of Steel. Jacob was a great-grandson of Stalin.

#

In Yerevan I interviewed for the new Office Manager with the Deputy Head of Mission. When we finished our questions, it seemed to me that one candidate stood out, head and shoulders above the rest. My colleague asked me what I thought.

'Yulia was great, she had it all,' I said. 'Evidently she has good organisational skills and a thorough understanding of cultural issues and dealing with the press; she is familiar with budget management and she has such phenomenally good English skills.'

'We're relieved you agree – we know her well but I wanted to be objective and not influence your decision.'

'Subject to references, I think Yulia will be the face of the British Council in Armenia.' I was relieved.

Excellent references came through after I had gone back to Tbilisi and I phoned Yulia to congratulate her. 'I'm very pleased to offer you this position – it promises to be a lively one. A VIP will be visiting at the beginning of November, to launch the new British Council, and I look forward to working with you on that. We will have a huge amount to do.'

There was a silence and Yulia said, 'Jo, there is something I must share with you.'

What could it possibly be?

'I'm expecting my first baby. I'm so sorry, I will completely understand if you can't offer me the position.' I paused.

'Firstly, congratulations Yulia. That is wonderful news –
but I have to ask, when is your baby due?'

'The end of October.' Another pause.

'How are your interviewing skills?'

13

Sociable networking

Our new team members all needed to work their notice and would be joining us some months later. In the meantime, more colleagues from UK had started to come out to help assess what the issues were in Georgia and how they could help. Someone from the premises and security team in London came to look at possible new premises. One option was in a bank. 'The security of this place looks good,' said my HQ colleague. This was not a pretty, flowery bank like the Bank of Georgia but a severe, tomb-like building in rather a forgotten part of Tbilisi. It was hard to imagine how it could be transformed into a modern, enticing and accessible office. 'However, none of the places you have identified are at all suitable,' he continued. 'In any case, you need to get approval in principle for funding for your premises move. You aren't even at stage one. You need a 'project initiation document'. A 'PID'.' I could add that to the list of acronyms for all the plans and reports I constantly seemed to be compiling.

I had to hurry home. That evening we were hosting a reception at home, in honour of another visitor, Peter, a British Council education specialist. In the afternoon Nata, our Exchanges Officer, was accompanying Peter to a number of meetings with ministry and international contacts to see if there was anything we could do to complement their activities.

When I opened the door Alek announced that he had given our new cleaning lady her notice. My heart sank. 'She spent more time playing the piano than she did cleaning.' He was dragging the vacuum cleaner round with annoyance. It was entirely up to us whether we had cleaning help or not and I couldn't cope with doing it on top of my intense job – and as I wanted to use the house as an overflow for our deeply unsatisfactory office it needed to be presentable. I couldn't face pointing out that while it had proved challenging for my husband to find a job, he wasn't doing much else – but I certainly wouldn't suggest that his role should be tidying our house. The issue of what an 'accompanying spouse' does is a sensitive one. It can seriously affect how a couple adapts and how successful the officer is at doing their job – quite apart from how happy they both are as a couple.

I didn't have time to think about all that. We had caterers coming soon to set up the drinks and canapés and the house was less than ready. I phoned Zaza. He hadn't yet joined the British Council as our new Office Manager but I knew he was well connected. 'Do you know anyone reliable and available who could tidy my house?'

'Of course Jo,' he said. 'When do you need her?' Right now would be good, I told him. Within minutes, Nino turned up to help. From that moment she was an important member of our household. Beautiful still, she must have been stunning in earlier years, when she had run her own business – but the economy had collapsed and many businesses had gone under. Nino didn't speak much English and this ruled her out from a wider span of jobs, particularly in business, as the few new jobs mostly needed English skills. Like many middle class professionals of her generation she was apparently grateful to be cleaning a foreigner's house. She was breadwinner to a family of men who were struggling to find work.

I felt sorry for our earlier cleaning lady. She too was vastly overqualified, as a former research scientist. Seeing that grand piano, neglected by Alek and me, must have been too tempting.

#

With Nino's help, the dust had gone, the house was tidy and we had spare bottles of water in the bathroom in case the water was cut. The caterers had set up their refreshments and two waitresses, snappily turned out in black and white outfits, were good to go. Colleagues from the office were there to help chat to guests and to help introduce guests to our chief guest. Hang on? Where are Peter-the-education-specialist and Nata?

My phone rang and I could make out Nata's indistinct voice. 'Bomb scare...Evacuation...Soon!' Her phone went dead. My front doorbell rang and I ran to open the door. There was the moustachioed Minister of Education standing on the doorstep with an enormous bunch of red roses. Oh my.

'Minister, what an honour!' I ushered him up to the 'ballroom' where we were having our reception. Other guests started to arrive: women from the English Teachers' Association of Georgia, someone from the World Bank – which lends millions of dollars for education reform – and people from the Tbilisi State University (but not the shadowy man to whom I had paid the rent). New contacts from non-governmental organisations such as the Open Society, someone from the European Commission. The room was full and buzzing.

And then, thankfully, there were Peter and Nata. 'What happened?' I asked them.

'There was a bomb scare and they evacuated the Ministry of Education. Somehow we ended up at the centre of a student demonstration.' Evidently many students were getting increasingly disaffected by corruption and poor governance in the ministry.

#

Before too long I was invited out by some of my sociable Georgian contacts as a new person of some interest. There were not that many British people in Tbilisi at the time – perhaps 100. Word was out that the British Council was expanding and people were curious to know more.

To be on the receiving end of Georgian hospitality at a *supra*, a Georgian feast, is a privilege. The informal but elaborate routine involves a long table and as many guests as can be squeezed along it. There were numerous different dishes served in decorated pottery bowls, many in the shape of animals – such as rams or deer. These were placed at strategic locations along the table. Wherever you were sitting you could access any one of many of the wonderful salads, hot and cold cheeses, lightly spiced grilled meats, piquant sauces, creamy dips.

Our own plates were constantly cleared and replaced with clean ones. This meant that people could leave the long table and join at different places as the mood took them. How bossy my colleagues must have thought me, when

I had suggested rearranging the tables into a square at our first team meal – bucking an ancient tradition. I noted that people smoked constantly during the meal – it wasn't even an inter-course cigarette or two. Alongside all the eating and smoking was copious, copious drinking of wine, or *khvino*. A well-known favourite red is *Saperavi*. A good crisp dry white is *Tsinandali*. It was served out of curvy pottery jugs which never seemed to empty.

'Did you know that in Georgia was wine invented?' asked one of my hosts. No, I didn't. 'Yes, they found the oldest wine storage vessels in archaeological digs and they were discovered to be 6000 years old, maybe more. Every family who can has a vine draped over walls, fences, carports.' Wine drinking was a flamboyant opportunity to celebrate all that is lovely, impressive and notable, and to set the world to rights. The *tamada* – toast master – raised his glass what felt like every few minutes.

'To world peace!'

'To friendship!'

'To all the beautiful women in the world!'

And the ladies in the kitchen came out, pushing a stray hair or two back into place and adjusting much used aprons to receive the toast. They hurried back to carry on cooking, grinding and chopping, and cleaning and slaving in the kitchen while the eating and toasting and drinking continued.

'To Anglo-Georgian relations!'

'To education reform!

And so on. Each toast was followed by the *tamada* downing his glass in one and urging the guest of honour to do the same. I quickly learnt it was important to toast in response.

'To everlasting peace and happiness and overcoming poverty in the world! And thank you to my wonderful hosts and the ladies who cooked this exceptional meal!' I probably added in a few too many wishes to my toasts.

#

June was a sociable month and we were also gearing up for the British Embassy's 'Queen's Birthday Party', or QBP. Most diplomatic missions have a national day to celebrate their identity and their presence in the host country. In fact for many they are celebrating independence from a colonial power – such as the UK. In the UK we celebrate the Queen's Birthday. According to where you are in the world, and what the climate is doing, Embassies and High Commissions can choose between celebrating it in April (when the Queen actually has her birthday), or in June, her official birthday.

In Georgia it was celebrated in June and it would be at the Metekhi Palace Hotel, that is, the modern but functional hotel in which the Embassy had its offices. We had already given colleagues in the Embassy the names of all the top contacts we in the British Council wanted to be invited on the education and culture side.

Peter from the Embassy sent over a briefing note for the arrangements. This was a detailed note telling us who should be doing what, at what time and where at the QBP. He added, 'All the British Council staff can come, the more hands to the pump the better.'

I duly briefed colleagues in my office on the contents of his note. Not everyone was around so I asked if the message could be passed on to others in the team.

Peter's note said I would be in the welcome line-up, greeting guests as they arrived and then I would join and mingle after the bulk of guests had arrived. My colleagues meanwhile were to be in the main part of the reception room waiting to chat to guests and make sure they were well looked after. There was also a reminder, should it be needed, that we were not there to chat to each other and have fun.

'LOOK AFTER OUR GUESTS THIS IS NOT OUR PARTY WE ARE HERE TO WORK'

said the note.

\#

Alek had reservations about the party. 'I won't know anyone.'

'I know but you will never meet anyone or stand a chance of getting a job or something interesting to do unless you get out there.' It wasn't easy for him, I appreciated.

For me this QBP was, however, most exciting. In my previous job in Cairo (although I was the same grade as in Georgia) it was a much bigger diplomatic mission and I was relatively junior. There were many of us to share the burden of meeting and greeting duties. The line-up to welcome guests to the Cairo QBP was at the top of the impressive balcony in the Ambassador's palatial residence and comprised all the senior staff – the Ambassador and his wife, the Defence Attaché, the British Council Director and so on. Middle ranking officers like me were dotted about at significant points with specific jobs to do. The head of our English Language Teaching Centre and I had the job of standing at the bottom of the long, red-carpeted stairs which led down into the large, lush garden – a rarity and a treat in dusty Cairo – and saying 'mind the carpet' hundreds of times to the descending dignitaries.

In Tbilisi, by contrast, I was one of the senior staff and as such joined the official line-up. The Ambassador and I had only arrived a few months earlier, and Maia K, as the British Embassy's head of Press and PR, was on hand to make sure Deborah didn't forget the names and designations of the arriving guests. I hoped I would be able to remember the names of my own contacts.

There we were shaking hands and greeting our guests as an orange sun set over the cobblestoned streets and lacy balconies of Tbilisi.

'Minister!' The Minister of Education leant forward to kiss me on both cheeks and then there was my other top contact, the Minister of Culture, who shook my hand with more kissing.

Then I saw, making her way down the line-up, and resplendent in a bronze ballgown, our office cleaner, Luiza. She was shaking hands vigorously with the Ambassador, then the Defence Attaché and the others. She duly arrived in front of me with a beaming smile and gave me a big kiss saying,

'Thank you for invitation!'

I loved all the networking and the collecting and handing out of business cards. It was not just the frivolity of throwing a party. It is a tried and tested way of getting to know the movers and shakers in a more relaxed environment than over a big table in a formal office. It was all part of keeping a finger on the pulse, of learning what was going on. Who turned up could be an indicator of impact and influence and could be a revealing political statement. Many of the foreign missions maintain a gentle competition as to which of the big hitters will turn up at their respective national day events. Would the President turn up? The Prime Minister? Which ministers?

So mingle, chat, introduce. Make sure the guests are having a good time.

'Jo, I have been looking forward to meeting you,' said an English-sounding voice and I turned to meet a petite blonde woman. 'I'm Amy. I've been trying to interview you since you arrived about the new-look British Council we've been hearing about.' Amy worked for one of the English language newspapers, which were invaluable resources for people like me to attempt to keep up with the twists and turns in Georgian political, economic and cultural life. She needed the copy and I needed the coverage and we promised to meet soon.

Although President Shevardnadze hadn't made it to the party, I was pleased to see two of the recently returned John Smith Scholars at the QPB. I asked them about their recent trip to the UK. 'It was brilliant,' said one. 'I was shadowing the First Minister of Wales and helping his chief of staff. Undoubtedly it will help my career.'

The other had had an attachment with the European Children's Fund. 'They organised many meetings with important civil society and media organisations,' he said. 'As a result I am campaigning to reform media legislation in Georgia.' I was delighted.

Other guests milled around us, greeting each other. 'Can I introduce myself? I am Giorgi Margvelashvili. I am the Vice-Rector of the Georgian Institute for Public Affairs – GIPA. We'd like to invite you to come and look at our institute.' I told him I'd love that. His was just the sort of organisation we wanted to work with and I wanted to try to identify significant areas where the UK's experience and expertise could make a difference.

He introduced me to an American, Mark Mullen, from the National Democratic Institute. I said I had noticed there was a large US presence in Tbilisi. Mark agreed – he told me that the US had put in $1billion in aid in a decade. The same per capita after Israel and Egypt which were the highest recipients of US aid at that time. This demonstrated just how significant a country the US deemed Georgia to be.

'I'm still new in Georgia and you are legal experts so it would be good to learn from you. I've noticed that the concept of a 'contract' is rather vague here,' I said.

'Many people are scared of contracts,' said Mark. 'They don't trust the whole system of governance as the rule of law is shaky here. Sometimes it is easier to trust a real person standing in front of you, or at least to take notice of them. Many of the laws here are totally out of date and open to manipulation.'

'Reform of the law, protection of human rights, nurturing freedom of the press, ensuring that the rule of law works. These are vital to our country's development,' added Giorgi. 'It is a huge task but we have to start somewhere. We want to learn from as many other countries as we can – Germany, France, the UK, the US, Japan.'

At my shoulder, interrupting this fascinating conversation, was a familiar looking man. Shortish and with a big smile on his face. 'Madame,' he said and politely asked Giorgi Margvelashvili to translate. 'What about the Wardrop exhibition?' It was Mr Rukhadze from the Anglo-Georgian Friendship Society and he still wanted me to host his exhibition about historic ties between Georgia and Britain.

I confess I had forgotten about him.

14

Up and down the Silk Route

July 2001, Baku, Azerbaijan

I looked round with admiration and a shade of envy at the British Council in bustling Baku. I had gone to meet Margaret, Director Azerbaijan, and her team to learn from their set-up and to do a peer review of some of their services.

There were many light and airy offices and classrooms, painted cheerful colours and built around a central atrium. This was more like it. Margaret had been in her job since a short while before I started in mine. It was good to have a colleague in a neighbouring country who understood some of the issues I faced. The office in Baku had been operating almost entirely as a centre for English teaching – they had a number of significant English language teaching contracts and there were highly professional teachers and busy classrooms full of students. Like my office, however, the British Council in Baku had never hosted any high profile arts events nor had they managed projects on education and other reform issues. We were learning together as both our operations were set to expand.

Unlike Georgia, which had few natural resources other than soft fruits and wine, Azerbaijan is one of the world's oldest oil producers. On my way back to my hotel, driving past the broad boulevards that looked fabulously Austro-Hungarian – that powerful, imperial look with solid, multi-storied white buildings and big statues dotted about – I saw the shoreline of the Caspian Sea crowded with oil derricks. Hundreds of them. It was quite a sight – not a pretty sight perhaps. It did mean, though, that Azerbaijan had been better able to weather the storms after the collapse of the Soviet Union. As often happens, however, there were big income disparities between those who controlled this black gold wealth and the many more who didn't.

The British Council office in Baku was in the old town and was a large, pretty, white building with oriental touches. Margaret gave me a tour of the building and introduced me to her team. I sat down with two newly appointed colleagues, Nigar and Irina, to go through the checklists we had to complete about financial systems, public relations, new projects and so on – all the things I was trying to put in place in my own office. Margaret and I agreed to work together on joint training for our colleagues and on joint projects for the South Caucasus region, to try to make the most of our budgets.

It wasn't just about the money though. It was also because Azerbaijan and Armenia were technically still at war. Anything we could do to bring people together from those countries on collaborative projects or to share positive experiences was, indisputably, a good thing.

That evening Margaret and her husband took me to a *caravanserai* restaurant. Silk Route traders had used it since the 14th century as a stop-over on their journeys from East to West and vice versa. We loafed on colourful woven cushions at low, dark wood carved tables and tucked in to tasty meats and salads. 'Even though it is separated from Turkey by Georgia, Azerbaijan has some cultural similarities to Turkey,' said Margaret's husband, Kemal, who was Turkish himself. 'Which is handy for me, as the language is similar to Turkish and I can get along quite well.'

The restaurant had arched doorways leading off a gardened courtyard. I was intrigued to see that while there were low arches for people to go through, there were also taller, wider arches for camels. As I was leaving, I thanked Margaret for her hospitality. She gave me a little tin of caviar saying, 'One of the Caspian Sea's other big products.'

I had brought a present for her – a bottle of Georgian wine. 'In Georgia was wine invented!'

#

I travelled back from Baku to Tbilisi overnight on the Silk Route Express train. This was a new service, advertised as faster, more luxurious and more reliable than the ordinary train which apparently took about 20 hours and stopped frequently. The journey by road took about eight hours and the overnight train seemed a suitably novel way to travel without losing a valuable day's work. Although a new service, it already had a suitably faded elegance to it and I was pleased with my own *luxe* couchette. I settled in and got ready for the journey across the plains of Azerbaijan and through the valleys between the mountains towards the Georgian capital.

As well as a fold-down bed, already made up, there was a dainty reading light over the pillow. I had lacy curtains looped either side of my window, a little desk under the window, and a tinny washbasin in a corner. I had already eaten so I read in my room and gazed out of the window, daydreaming, as the sun set.

The compartment guard knocked on my door and explained that he would need to take my passport to show the immigration authorities at the border, along with those of the other first class passengers. 'We will reach the border in the early morning. We don't want to wake you, Madame,' he said in an avuncular way. I gave him my passport, feeling anxious about handing it over to this unknown man. I got ready for bed and tried to get to sleep in the swaying train as it made clunky progress towards Tbilisi. In fact the couchette was stuffy, wildly overheated and I couldn't open the window. I felt dehydrated and was running low on bottled water. I unlocked my door and slid it open to let in some cooler air. My security-conscious husband would have gone berserk had he known. At home he had taken to keeping the metal shutters on all our windows bolted closed at all times. While safe it meant the house was constantly in darkness.

I eventually fell asleep. But awoke with a shake – where was I? What the…? Men were thundering down the corridor. The train was stationary and entirely dark. I pulled the door shut and locked myself in. I squinted out of my window into the darkness but couldn't make out much. We appeared to be in the middle of nowhere. Somewhere flat and featureless in the middle of Azerbaijan. There were dark figures outside – men were out with torches, yelling and banging around under the train.

I worried that if the passengers were required to disembark – oh no – a nightdress and hotel slippers wouldn't be the best attire. My time in Tbilisi had taught me the valuable lesson of never being without a torch so I shone my little light and rummaged around pulling out appropriate clothes and footwear – but I only had high-heeled shoes. I hadn't packed for the eventuality of jumping off a train at dead of night. I sat there in the darkness.

The clanking around and shouting subsided after about an hour and the train, thank God, started to move.

At breakfast some hours later the three of us travelling in the *luxe* class emerged to the restaurant car. All of us looking a little haggard, I have to say – I hadn't gone back to sleep. 'I thought it was Chechen rebels, or illegal immigrants being offloaded from under our carriage,' said one of the other passengers. 'Or bandits – I hear the slow train sometimes gets held up for bribes to be paid.'

'No, the bribes are included in our tickets,' said the other passenger. 'They just keep some money on one side to pay off the customs officials.'

'It was just mechanical failure,' said the guard as he returned our passports.

#

I just had enough time to write up a visit report back in my office in Tbilisi before Vakho and I headed off for Yerevan. As it seemed pointless just two of us travelling down in our spacious car, I now always asked around if anyone wanted a lift down or back. This time, Sandro, our IT guy, was coming with us to help set up the computer in Yerevan. We also took a colleague, Andrew, from our Drama and Dance team in London, who was doing a recce to work out what exciting new events and acts we could bring out. He was finding out what worked, or what didn't, in each of the three South Caucasus countries and what the local arts scenes were like. One thing he learnt was that it was not possible to travel from Armenia to Azerbaijan, as those countries had no diplomatic relations. Any touring acts would have to travel through Georgia.

It was a full car and our final passenger was a rather elderly UK academic. This chap wasn't there under British Council auspices but, in return for the free ride, he had graciously agreed to meet some students and lecturers in Tbilisi and lead some discussion groups. He had never been on this particular journey and I was a little worried it might be quite tough for him in places. 'I've been on atrocious roads all over Africa. I can't imagine it could be worse than that,' he said. Off we set.

I had come to love the journey between Tbilisi and Yerevan with its stunning scenery shifts of pastures, meadows, hills, bare plains then verdant mountains. One thing I didn't love was driving past poverty. There was a lot of it about. Wherever we were on the road, invariably there were people with skinny horses or donkeys dragging wooden carts alongside lumbering, big trucks, struggling around the steep mountain passes; also *mashrutkas*, minibuses crammed full of passengers and laden with luggage and furniture strapped on top. Ladas full of whatever was in season – the back seat might be packed high to the windows with apples, or bits of metal, or mysterious and tightly packed sacks.

As we drew closer to the border it would have been quicker to walk the two miles of mud track. Vakho had a relaxed but confident way of driving to and fro across this heavily pitted stretch of road with ruts and trenches, some almost a foot deep. We passengers, meanwhile, had to grip on to whatever handles we could reach in the car. It wasn't a passive sitting experience. Our academic was gripping on for dear life and he concurred, 'Yes that is indeed one of the worst roads I have ever been on.'

We reached the border crossing. My colleagues in the British Embassy had described these borders as 'porous'. The border guards just seemed to glance into the various packed vehicles. I could imagine someone hiding deep within a car packed with fruit; the guards were hardly going to ask the driver to unpack them all. While all the vehicles queued up for passports to be checked, little old ladies with heavily laden donkeys slowly made their way, unheeded, backwards and forwards across the border. Various agencies, such as the Institute of Migration, had been trying to help crack down on smuggling of guns, narcotics and people.

As soon as we were in Armenia the road improved dramatically. It was smooth and freshly tarmacked. I asked Vakho why the Georgian bit of the road was so bad while the Armenian side was well maintained.

'It doesn't matter to the Georgian government. They care about trade with Turkey to the west, so that is a better road but not about this road to the south. The Armenians, however, cannot officially travel west to Turkey (no diplomatic relations), or east to Azerbaijan (as you know they are at war, no borders are open). They can only go south to Iran which they do, but trade possibilities there are more limited; or north via Georgia into Turkey and Western Europe – it makes sense to maintain this road. Armenians are resourceful. They find a way to trade in spite of all the challenges.'

#

The reason for going to Yerevan this time was to open the new British Council office, a room within the British Embassy. Yulia had recently started to work for us and I had brought a kit of things to start her off – checklists and folders. I had a piece of A4 card which I had typed and had laminated in Tbilisi. It had a logo and details of opening hours and read:

British Council Armenia

Yulia stuck the little laminated sign on the door of her compact little office. 'It's not much, but it's a start.' Her computer was installed and she had already bought a number of essential things locally, like a photocopier. The Ambassador, Tim, came to have a look and said how pleased he was that things were taking shape – he asked us to join him in his office. I was also there to meet the advance planning party for the Royal Visit – which was only three months away.

There were two people; one to talk security and the other protocol and public relations. 'We understand you will be using this visit as an opportunity to launch your new British Council operation,' said the PR woman. Yulia and I nodded. So far the new British Council in Armenia comprised Yulia, a room, a photocopier, a computer, a kettle and a laminated sign. To be fair, the British Council in Tbilisi had been managing scholarships, exams and the Peacekeeping English Project (PEP) in Armenia on behalf of the UK's Ministry of Defence for some years. Barrie had also recently started to set up an Armenian English Teachers' Association, along the lines of the English Teachers' Association of Georgia – but it was far from a full operation.

'We will need something high-profile and punchy. The Duke and Duchess will have a three-day programme in Armenia and we can give the British Council two evenings. The royal couple will be visiting sites of historical significance in Armenia – they will also visit the Military Academy to meet people involved in the Ministry of Defence's Peacekeeping English Project.' So we couldn't use the PEP project as a showcase for the British Council. The MoD had nabbed it first. Fair enough – although we managed it, they funded it.

'As you will be aware, due to security reasons, the visit must remain secret until just before the visit occurs so please bear this in mind in your planning. The events will need to be timed to the minute and all of your staff will need to be well co-ordinated. We will need senior staff to introduce Their Royal Highnesses to significant people. It is imperative to avoid any public relations mishaps as the visit will be held in the glare of press and media.' We nodded some more.

'We'll meet again in September to review your progress and to make sure the whole programme fits together smoothly.'

'Leave it with us,' I said, confidently.

#

Back in our office. 'All of our staff!' said Yulia.

'That's you and me, Yulia! And 'senior staff to introduce key people'...I don't know any of the key people and you will be on maternity leave when they are here.' We fell about laughing at the craziness of it. 'This needs to be a wider team effort – your new Director will be able to take time out from his language training to come for a few days and I will ask Georgian colleagues to help,' I said. 'I will investigate if we can get some additional money to recruit an office assistant to take things forward from you – but we need to start now to think of big events and they need to be 'cultural'.'

Yulia suggested the excellent National Art Gallery could be the backdrop for the official launch party. 'Wonderful idea. We can pack it full of VIPs – between you and the Embassy I am sure we can get a full house of important guests. But we need another event for the other evening. What cultural forms are particularly popular?' I asked.

'Classical music, singing, ballet – and film. Have you heard of Sergey Parajanov?' asked Yulia. '*The Colour of Pomegranates* and *Shadows of our Forgotten Ancestors.*'

Amongst my favourite films. 'I confess I hadn't realised Parajanov was Armenian,' I told her. Yulia decided she should take me to the Parajanov Museum as part of my cultural education. It turned out to be quirky, artistic, thought-provoking and accessible – a great museum. We decided we should show a new British film as one of our two showcase events.

That evening Yulia took me out for a delicious traditional Armenian meal in a restaurant with painted flowers and animals on the walls. She produced a gift – a little bottle of Armenian Brandy. 'Apparently Churchill was fond of it.' I gave her a bottle of Georgian wine.

#

We set off for Tbilisi the next morning, taking Yulia back with us as she was coming to attend some training I had organised. Yulia was some six months pregnant and on the way back Vakho drove gently, almost tenderly, carrying us all safely across the mountains. As ever, the drive was an opportunity for me to reflect on all the things that needed to be done.

• Royal visit, royal visit, royal visit.

15

Training is the key

July 2001, Tbilisi

The next morning I was back in my office in Tbilisi getting ready before the training events which we were about to host. I could hear members of the team arriving by the clunk of the heavy front door. When Katie arrived I could see she was upset – very upset. I asked if she was all right.

'Not really Jo. I'm sad, so very sad. The journalist, Giorgi Sanaia, has been found dead. We all loved him. He tried to expose corruption and all these terrible deals that go on in government – he worked for the Rustavi 2 TV station.' He had been found dead in his apartment. Even investigating the circumstances of his death might be dangerous. 'He was so young...So brave,' added Katie.

'I'm sure this training course is the last thing you need,' I said.

'You know, Jo, we need distractions here,' and she gave me a small smile. 'And we certainly welcome training.'

I had arranged for two training courses – events management and finances. It was a young office (only Katie and I were even in our 30s) and training and learning on the job would be an important part of helping to professionalise us all. No-one in the office had ever had to arrange any

Figure 8 Team training – Tamuna, Nino, Kote, Anuki, Zaza

high-profile projects and, as our office activities would be expanding, we would be arranging and hosting more and more prominent events. We needed to be confident and polished in what we did. We couldn't afford to make mistakes in a glare of publicity – and we had a Royal Visit to get right.

#

The trainers had variously arrived from Britain full of excitement about visiting a new and – within the British Council – little visited country. As we had no meeting room in our office, and it seemed wasteful to hire a hotel room, we ran one course in the library at the weekend, and the other in the basement of my house.

The two women running the events management course knew their stuff. How to host a high-profile reception or arrange an arts event to make every participant or audience member or guest feel 'that was special' so that the event itself reflected excellence of the British Council and of the UK. They were both elegantly turned out, beautifully coiffed, manicured and *macquillaged*. The trainers took their trainees through discussions and exercises on the importance of detailed planning – how to focus on the needs of diverse customers/clients/guests; contingency planning and impact assessment. 'You just can't throw it together at the last minute – planning and communicating effectively within your team is vital. You must be as calm as a swan on the surface but paddling like mad behind the scenes!' A chap from the Press and Public Relations Department told us how to deal with the media, how to write press releases and so on. I am sure many colleagues were thinking with sadness, during the sessions on media relations, of the young journalist who had died in mysterious circumstances.

Meanwhile the power was off and, in spite of ministrations and cajoling from Vakho and an engineer, my generator failed. It was July and the heat in the room rose gradually. Even with the windows and doors open it was exceptionally warm – makeup-meltingly hot. My trainer colleagues were feeling the heat.

'Even with all the planning in the world, there are some things we can't control,' observed Eka. 'Maybe we should have paper fans with British Council logos printed on them in summer?'

'And in winter, scarves?' suggested Nata.

Or wait till we can afford a proper generator – but waiting wasn't an option.

\#

We had a spare day before the trainers were due to fly back to UK – that rare and precious thing, a day off. It was a hot summer and we thought it

Figure 9 Ananuri fortress

102

would be good to get out of the frenetic, diesel-choked little city. We set off for the Ananuri fortress, about an hour's drive north of Tbilisi on the Georgian Military Highway. 'If you carry on driving you get to the mountains to the north and the border with Russia – this road eventually goes to Vladikavkaz, the capital of North Ossetia,' Nata told us. 'Mount Kazbegi is near this road. It is where Prometheus, from the myths, was chained up for stealing fire from the gods to give to the people.'

Driving past hairy hogs and people with donkeys, and dodging slower cars and speeding 4x4 vehicles, we reached the fortress. Our guests, and indeed Alek and I, were impressed. Ananuri fortress sits alongside a broad aquamarine reservoir which lends it a Mediterranean air. Ancient and intriguing carvings of trees, vines and pomegranates adorn its golden stone crenellated walls – the swirly carvings were very early Christian. Dotted about were knee-high statues of rams and horses also decorated with mysterious and beautiful etchings.

#

On our way back to Tbilisi we stopped to show our visitors the ancient capital of Georgia, Mtskheta. 'We want to show our main cathedral, Sveti-Tskhoveli,' said Tamuna. It was built in the 12th century on the site of a church built in the fourth century where a tree of life grew, it is said, out of Christ's robe.

'This is wonderful,' said Alek as we stepped inside. We weren't churchgoers but we could appreciate the musky ambiance of the incense inside the dark, high-domed church. Sweet straw was strewn over the wide flagstones and there were ancient paintings over the walls including, I was intrigued to see, one with astrological figures. One of our women trainers was wearing a clingy top with 'spaghetti straps' and a miniskirt. Colleagues gently asked her to respect the customs of the church, which she did, by covering what she could of her hair and shoulders and legs in light scarves. Another of our visitors, a middle-aged male colleague, needed no such advice. He was evidently quite a High Church Anglican – he looked like 'Our Man in Africa' in a crumpled pale linen suit and a straw panama hat. By way of accessory he was clasping a newly bought Georgian souvenir, an inlaid metal dagger. On entering the church he looked solemnly to the front, then knelt down and kissed the ground, still holding his dagger.

The church was bustling. Half a dozen men dressed in black appeared from the throng and pulled together into a huddle. Heads together and unsmiling they discussed something, nodding and frowning while Alek regarded them with some concern. They looked like gangsters. Then they burst into pure, effortless, polyphonic singing – they were the choir. No weedy hymns by little old ladies, this was gutsy, barrelling stuff. Their singing ballooned out and filled the church, smoky from sweet incense and the thin yellow candles in the big braziers. There were no pews, no seats in the cathedral and the congregation, priests and singers came and went. It looked chaotic – but pure – beautiful.

#

That evening I hosted a party under the walnut and pomegranate trees in the courtyard of our garden. We invited many of our colleagues from the Embassy, all of the Tbilisi British Council office, Yulia from Yerevan and Nigar and Irina from Baku, who had joined us for the training. Kote, Zaza and Anuki, our new colleagues-to-be were there too.

One thing I had learnt from the events management trainers is that for official British Council events, guests needed to know why they are there. Just turning up and milling around is not enough – they have to be parties with a purpose. I made a little speech. I thanked them all for coming and I turned to my new colleagues, who were standing in a little row beside me.

I welcomed them to the British Council and then said, 'Your mission, should you choose to accept it, Kote, will be to find out what the issues are governance and societal reform, find out what the big donors and non-governmental organisations are doing, to develop partnerships, to write proposals and to help us run meaningful projects.' It was a big mission.

'Zaza, your mission as Office Manager is to *please, please* find us a new office, sort out our office contracts and manage our office effectively and efficiently.' No small challenge here either.

I finished by saying, 'Anuki, your mission on reception is to learn how to use the telephone exchange – I would struggle, myself – and for you, and for all of us – to learn everything, take every advantage to learn new skills and be the best we can be!'

16

Things will never be the same again

September 2001, Manchester

In September I had to go on a training course myself, back in the British Council in Manchester. We broke for lunch and emerged from the closeted training room to see colleagues in the open plan office standing staring at their computers. No-one appeared to be working.

They were all watching BBC news footage of two planes flying into the Twin Towers in New York and another into the Pentagon. 'What does it mean?' we whispered to each other, profoundly shocked. How could this happen?

There was so little 'new' news about the atrocities but much speculation. Journalists talked endlessly over looped repeats of the footage. They showed more and more films, taken by those who were there, that have since entered global consciousness like scenes from a much shown disaster film. That night in my hotel room I was on the phone to everyone and anyone and we babbled together our shock and grief.

News emerged of the heroism of passengers on flight UA93 which failed to hit a target. And how – when it was surely obvious to those people that they had only minutes to live – that they could spend that precious time making just one, heart-rending, mobile phone call to a loved one.

I realised, with utter clarity, that the one person I would call would not be my husband but my mother. Which was quite a revelation.

#

I didn't have time to ponder the evils and problems of the world. I had to focus on our Very Very Important Person (VVIP) visit. I had to get back to Armenia to discuss how our programme was shaping up with the official visit co-ordinators.

This time I flew to Yerevan from London and Vakho meanwhile had driven down from Tbilisi to meet me. It was the first time I had arrived at Yerevan airport. I gave my passport and my laminated cards from the Armenian Ministry of Foreign Affairs which said 'Diplomat' and 'Resident' to the immigration official. He looked at them in a bored way, flicking through the passport, while I smiled and waited. Then waited a bit more. And a bit longer. 'Problem,' he said, shoving the passport back at me.

What? 'I beg your pardon?' I squeaked. 'What is the problem?'

'No visa. You don't have a visa to enter this country.' The people in the queue behind me were getting restless.

'That can't be right. I have been coming and going countless times to and from Armenia for over six months,' I protested. 'You can see all the entry and exit stamps.' I showed him examples.

'You came overland. The guards at the land borders do not interpret the rules correctly,' he added in, frankly, a surly way. He didn't have an Armenian accent – he sounded Russian.

'What about these cards from the Armenian Ministry of Foreign Affairs? These give me the right to live here!'

'They are just plastic cards,' he said, shrugging. He motioned to me to step out of the queue to let other passengers get processed.

What on earth could I do? Perhaps I could get my non-diplomatic, normal passport, from Georgia somehow? I knew it was possible to get a tourist visa in an ordinary passport on arrival at the airport. I had a frantic phone call with the Defence Attaché, who was then in Tbilisi and whom I knew was due to come down to Yerevan the following day. He agreed to bring down my other passport. I wondered if I would have to spend 24 hours at Yerevan airport.

When all the passengers were cleared the border guard gestured for me to come back. I opened my mouth but he said, 'Before you think of it, if you are here to work, you cannot get a visa at the border. You cannot pretend you are a tourist. That would be illegal. I am keeping your passport.'

'You can't do that – this is crazy! That is my passport!'

'Your papers are not in order. You must get it back from the Ministry of Foreign Affairs.' And he put my passport in his pocket and walked off leaving me open-mouthed at the desk.

I ran through the deserted airport. My solitary suitcase was going round and round the small carousel on its own. Pushing through the doors to the car park, I saw Vakho, looking astonished that I was so far behind all the other passengers.

'This is not right,' said Vakho after, breathless, I had explained. He threw my suitcase in the car and marched forcefully back into the empty airport, with me trotting behind. I noted, having been through airports many, many times, how *wrong* it felt to go 'backwards'. Vakho tracked down the immigration officials who were smoking in a small room and he harangued them in Russian, demanding the return of my passport.

I only wanted to be in Armenia two days and then I had to get back to Georgia for another important visit. We just didn't have time for this – but they were enjoying their power and the guards were adamant they would not give it back.

'Bastards,' said Vakho emphatically as we walked to the carpark, defeated.

'Vakho, I am an illegal immigrant in Armenia!'

'Don't worry, Jo, we can put you in the back of the Landrover and throw a blanket over you and get you back to Tbilisi.'

I laughed. I wouldn't have considered it but with my luck that would be the day the border guards were trying out their new anti-trafficking sniffer dogs donated by international organisations.

#

In the office heavily-pregnant Yulia and I got on with all the detailed preparations for the VIP visit. It was only weeks away and there was still so much to do.

Meanwhile our Ambassador intervened and got my passport, complete with visa, released from the Ministry of Foreign Affairs. It transpired that the border guards at the airport that day were indeed Russian, brought in to ensure tight security as Vladimir Putin had just visited Armenia.

17

The biggest fief in the fiefdom

September 2001, Batumi, Ajara

I had a quick turn around after our journey back from Yerevan. The following morning, Stuart – the Deputy Head of Mission at the British Embassy in Georgia – had arranged an early morning departure in convoy for a visit to the Semi-Autonomous Region of Ajara.

It was some seven or eight hours' drive to the west and was on the Black Sea coast. Although technically part of Georgia, it was apparently not an easy place to visit and had its own tightly controlled borders. I took both my diplomatic and my normal passports and all the laminated cards I could find. Representatives of several British and other European companies were coming to explore whether there were business opportunities under the auspices of the British Embassy mission. This was a trade mission to a 'state within a state'.

Vakho picked me up and then Nata, our Exchanges Officer, who was coming to investigate whether we could interest potential candidates for the Chevening and John Smith scholarship programmes. We set off to rendezvous with the rest of the convoy.

In the car park at the Embassy Stuart greeted us warmly and said, 'Jo, glad you made it. We need you there.

Apparently the top chap in Ajara, Aslan Abashidze, is keen on education and culture and we want you in the spotlight.' I felt weary.

As I'd been in Armenia I had missed the Embassy briefing on Ajara. I did what all intrepid travellers do and took my Lonely Planet and Bradt guides and read appropriate bits in the car. I knew key things and the books were not bang up to date but they were better than nothing.

So, why was it a state within a state? The region of Ajara was significantly different to other parts of Georgia. It shared a substantial border with Turkey and its capital, Batumi, had been an important port for many centuries. Although apparently one of the first parts of Georgia to be Christianised – in the first century no less – it had been invaded by Turkey in the 16th century. Many inhabitants had converted to Islam although they retained their distinctive Georgian identity. The Russians took over where the Turks left off as victors in the Russo-Turkish war of 1877-78; they established tea plantations, an oil refinery and they built Batumi into an elegant resort.

Ajara became a powerful and influential place but swapped hands again during the First World War, back to Turkey and then – hang on? I didn't realise this – to Britain which made it a Protectorate from 1918 to 1920. There were oil interests and it was an attempt to stop the spread of the Red Army – but the Russians completely overran it in 1920 and from that point Ajara, and indeed Georgia, were annexed to the Soviet Union.

The story didn't stop there. Ajara was given its status of Semi-Autonomous Republic in 1921, perhaps in recognition that there were many Muslim believers bordering Turkey. By the time the Soviet Union crumbled in Georgia in 1991, Aslan Abashidze – a powerful member of a princely Ajaran family – had risen to prominence.

A short, sharp and violent coup d'état in Tbilisi ousted the first democratically elected Georgian President, Zviad Gamsarkhurdia in January 1992. In March that year Eduard Shevardnadze – then Soviet Minister for Foreign Affairs in the Russian Federation – returned from Moscow and was elected Georgian Head of State and Chair of Parliament. Evidently Abashidze, by now Chairman of the Supreme Council of the S.A.R of Ajara, was displeased with this turn of events and closed Ajara's borders to the rest of Georgia. Georgia proper was fragile, with fighting and the attempted secession of South Ossetia and Abkhazia in 1992 and 93 and a brutal civil war in Georgia in 1993.

The relationship between Shevardnadze and the Georgian authorities in Tbilisi and Abashidze evolved into an uncomfortable acceptance of the status quo. Abashidze did not aim for independence but ran Ajara like a feudal lord, playing the big hitters in the region off against each other, building up his own army and entirely controlling borders and revenues from the important port in Batumi. He was elected as President of Ajara in 1998 with 93 per cent of the vote.

Which seemed unlikely.

#

We were met at the border by a smartly suited young man, Zurab, who briefed us on the programme ahead. He told us that our group – which included representatives from freight and logistics companies, a medical services company and so on, plus colleagues from the British Embassy – would have a full programme. We were required to remain in convoy from the moment we entered Ajara and to remain together for the entire programme, until we left. Arrangements had been made for us to stay in a hotel that evening and he would be back to collect us after breakfast the following day.

The hotel was in the middle of a wood evidently miles from anywhere. It was new, clean, rather sterile and apparently our rooms were – almost definitely – bugged.

#

As promised, Zurab turned up the next morning and invited us to follow his car. As our British Council car had diplomatic number plates it was deemed important that while Stuart, as the visit coordinator from the British Embassy, should lead the convoy in the Embassy car, our car would bring up the rear. We noted that we had police outriders at the front and end of our convoy.

Off we set, feeling a little amused and a bit uncomfortable at this display. People we passed looked at us with curiosity. Batumi was a pretty place, a seaside resort, and nowhere near as shabby as Tbilisi.

We were first shown to Batumi Duty Free Port and were encouraged to buy the Dior scarves or Gucci handbags or expensive Scotch. It was well stocked. 'Batumi seems a wealthy place,' said one of our party.

'We have some of the world's finest hazelnuts,' said our guide, Zurab, 'We do a good trade in them.'

We were taken to a huge hangar. We were greeted fulsomely and treated to coffee, cakes and sweet, pink, sparkling wine. Our group was shown around the hangar – there were miniature one-person helicopters, apparently made in Ajara, and shiny, black speedboats on display for our viewing pleasure – the gadgets were sinister and the hangar looked like something from a James Bond film set.

Our tour guide told us facts and figures and Stuart said admirably diplomatic things in response. There was a full media presence. Our group, about twelve of us in all, was being filmed by TV cameras – the company, I learnt, was Ajara TV and was owned by Mr Abashidze himself.

'Our Chairman of the Supreme Council takes a keen personal interest in this factory – but it is not all fun,' announced our guide. 'Now we will take you to a kindergarten.'

This time, because education was my thing, Stuart gestured, with a broad smile, that I should take centre stage. I put on my most diplomatic face. The school was unlike any school I had seen in Georgia. It was sparklingly new. We looked at classrooms with tiny desks and chairs, an impressive array of teaching materials, games, toys and lively pictures plastered on the walls. We were shown around the blocks with miniature, pristine WCs for little girls and little boys.

'Our Chairman is committed to excellence in education.'

'It is impressive. But where are the children?' I asked. For it was entirely empty – a ghostly little school.

'The school is not yet open. We hope it will be within the next few weeks. Perhaps months.'

Off we set to visit the university, again accompanied by the TV cameras and journalists. It was quite a cavalcade. We piled out and our entourage arranged themselves behind Stuart and me. The TV crew adjusted their equipment and followed our every step.

Our guide led us up broad and impressive white marble stairs and along cool, sweeping corridors. Stuart and I nodded a measure of appreciation as we learnt facts and figures about the university. 'The Chairman himself designed the layout of the building – it was recently finished. The Chairman also personally designed this chandelier.' We saw in front of us an enormous chandelier, heavy with sparkling crystals.

Our tour continued. 'There are 50 brand new computers.' We looked to the right to see the computer laboratory. 'The Chairman himself chose the books.' We looked to the left to see that the library was impressively full of leather-bound tomes along with many contemporary texts. And on and on. We walked through room after room kitted out in high quality furnishings and equipment and personally selected desk lamps.

'It isn't much like the Tbilisi State University,' I remarked in an aside to Stuart. Out loud I said, 'Yes, you are right. It is unlike any university I have ever seen – you have wonderful facilities. But where are the students?' For, again, it was completely empty apart from our own group.

'We can't let them in just yet,' said our guide. 'They might damage things. We want to keep it perfect for as long as we can.'

'I'd like to meet some students. If possible,' I said.

'I'm not sure there will be time on this occasion,' replied Zurab.

As we continued our tour I glanced out of a window and saw hundreds of young people in the courtyard of a neighbouring building. They were standing around chatting and laughing and smoking, or playing basketball. They looked like students anywhere. 'The real university,' whispered Nata. They were coming and going from an ordinary, rather shabby building. Although we didn't meet any students, we were introduced briefly to the head of the English Department at the university. Just long enough to say we would keep in touch and that we would try to share materials and training with them. It would be something.

#

Zurab informed us, 'And now, our Chairman is graciously hosting a lunch for your group followed by a performance of Ajaran music, song and dance at the Ilia Chavchavadze State Theatre at about 3 pm. The lunch is not for Georgians, however; just the British.'

'Actually I'm Irish,' said Dr Mike.

'And I'm Danish,' said Charlotte, who worked in the Tbilisi office of a British electrical engineering firm. 'But more importantly, can we go back to the hotel to get changed?' she asked. Charlotte was a tall, beautiful woman with long red hair. Today she was wearing a cream jacket and top and striking pair of black leather trousers and high-heeled boots. Fine for walking around looking at things but not for a theatre outing perhaps. One of the men in our party was wearing a brightly coloured short-sleeved shirt.

'No. We can't possibly keep the Chairman waiting and we are already behind schedule.' The convoy got back on its wheels and we belted over to the lunch, which was held in the neo-classical Ajaran Assembly building.

Zurab briefed us on what to do when meeting Mr Abashidze. For the ladies a discreet curtsy was appropriate. It was important not to turn your back on him when the audience with him was over but to walk slowly backwards until you were out of the room – he was, after all, a prince from an ancient family. We all met him individually feeling, for some reason, a little nervous. He presented all the women with Gucci scarves and the men with silk ties. I absolutely did not want the Gucci scarf. But equally I couldn't find a way to say I didn't want it. I later gave the scarf to Nino, our cleaner at home.

We sat down to lunch. Abashidze gestured where he wanted the various guests to sit. Stuart was opposite him, I was a little further down. Our translator Maia C from the

Commercial Section of the Embassy was on one side of him. Susanne, who was working on a customs reform project, was instructed to sit on the other side. When she sat down it was as if she was sitting on drawing pins.

It was a long and elaborate lunch not at all like the relaxed and informal ones I had experienced in Tbilisi. There were lots of toasts though and Stuart was coping well with the responses. At one point Abashidze said, with translation, 'You English left us in the lurch in 1921. Abandoning us to the Red Army.'

We all looked down the table at Stuart. 'Actually I myself am Scottish,' said Stuart, 'but I believe there were few British soldiers ever in this part of the world. I don't think they would have made much difference against the considerable might of the Red Army.'

'If you British had succeeded in colonising Batumi, it might have been like Hong Kong,' said Abashidze.

The meal appeared to be drawing to an end and it was nearing 3 pm, when we were supposed to be at the theatre. But the Chairman then announced, 'And now I want to show you our promotional film!' – and we watched a film about Ajara, showing the speedboats and helicopters in action.

#

We eventually finished our lunch and our party made our way on foot across a pretty square, fringed with palm trees, between the Assembly building and the theatre. For our walk Abashidze, a diminutive man, gestured to Charlotte and to me to accompany him as he led the way. He looked up at us both walking either side of him and said, in English, 'What tall girls you are.' We glanced at each other over his head.

We arrived at the superb theatre at least an hour after the performance was due to start. It was a full house. The audience must have been waiting, unable to leave. Our group huffed and puffed getting settled into our seats, with 600 pairs of eyes looking at us in our unusual array of work clothing. The performances were exceptionally polished, whether singers or dancers. They included children who looked like they were about four years old.

'So bad for children this young,' whispered Nata. 'My mother is an opera singer and singing teacher and she says it damages their vocal cords.'

When they came to take their bows, the performers looked nervous and exhausted.

#

After the performance and many polite thank yous to our hosts, our group readied itself to depart for Tbilisi.

'But no,' said Zurab, 'it is far too late for you to go back to Tbilisi. We have arranged for you to stay at your hotel again.' We looked at each other aghast and protested that we really did need to get back. 'No, no, driving after dark is never a good idea. Please stay and enjoy our hospitality one night longer.'

Off we went to the hotel where we had a disgruntled drink in the bar. We had no choice; unless they allowed us through the border we couldn't leave. 'Have we been taken hostage?' I asked. It had been a trying week.

'We don't have enough cash to pay for this extra night,' said someone.

'It's like Pyongyang-on-Sea,' said someone else. 'Run by the biggest fief in the fiefdom.'

#

Arriving back at home, I climbed down from the car, weary after all the long journeys.

'Maia from the Embassy phoned last night to encourage me to watch Ajara TV,' said Alek. 'Your group were on the news for ten solid minutes and eight of those were of you going 'um' and 'ah' at the university. What was Ajara like?'

'Totalitarian.'

18

Dramatic happenings every week

October 2001, Tbilisi

Although I had wanted to get the British Council and our activities in the media, the experience in Ajara wasn't what I had had in mind. I was finally able to meet Amy, the journalist from one of the English language newspapers. We wanted to get into Georgian language press and TV too, but this was a first step and would be an important way of reaching Georgians who could already speak English.

Amy was chatty and interested and had an easy, informal style of interviewing. I told her new colleagues had recently started and that we had started to host visits from colleagues from Britain who were helping review how we could expand and improve the library and the premises, and that we were developing a strategy for arts and cultural events. I told her I loved being in this part of the world and that dramatic things seemed to happen every week. She nodded and scribbled and questioned. She eventually closed her notebook.

#

Sure enough, Amy's article on the interview was published. It was almost a full page. Colleagues crowded round to read it.

It was entitled:

Dramatic Happenings Every Week

The article opened, 'Since the British government has now realised Georgia is important, the new director of the British Council explains the enlarged brief of her operation.' So far so good. 'The British Council, which promotes education and cultural relations in 111 countries, could do with making more of an impact in this one.' OK, fair point.

She wrote about our little library being warm, clean and small with excellent resources. Then there was a whole column about where I grew up and my brother's love of cricket. Was this interesting, I wondered, good copy? Maybe I had chatted too much?

There was also mention of our scholarships programmes where I said we were looking to send the brightest young people for studies in law, international relations, management and journalism. 'It is hoped that the successful applicants, some of whom are newscasters, will help forge the country's future,' I had said.

'If they don't get shot,' Amy commented, presumably referring to Giorgi Sanaia, the young journalist who had worked at the Rustavi 2 TV station and who had been killed a few months earlier.

'Yes...They have to stick their necks out,' I apparently replied, although I didn't remember saying those words precisely.

The article mentioned our planned expansions into human rights, education, anti-corruption, journalism and so on, through awareness-raising events such as workshops, study tours and regional exchanges. 'But how practical are workshops and conferences when Georgians find they have nowhere to apply their new skills?' asked Amy.

'We can only help in facilitating, providing a support network. It might sound frivolous, but we can be like a 'dating agency'. Britain has one of the most developed civil societies in the world and the British Council can introduce like-minded people to each other,' I had replied.

'What about some theatre? As London is the theatre capital of the world and neither is Tbilisi lacking in that department?' enquired Amy. I said that I didn't rule it out – watch this space...

Anka pulled the newspaper toward herself and pointed at another headline.

Thank you to foreigners for not packing up and leaving at this desperate time.

In fact it was a desperate time for most Georgians. Most families had not had a formal salary for months and those who did have jobs that paid were supporting wide networks of family. The black economy was rumoured to account for 50 per cent of transactions.

On the global stage, the US and allies had bombed Afghanistan in October in 'retaliation' for the September 11 attacks against New York and Washington. 'Apparently some Western European musicians refused to come to perform at the jazz festival because Tbilisi is too close to Afghanistan,' said Eka. 'It's crazy. That's like the distance between Paris and Istanbul.'

'It's more likely they have confused the fighting in Abkhazia.' There had been bombing and fighting on the so-called border of this separatist region in the northwest of Georgia some weeks earlier. The situation there was tense.

Closer to home there had been a raid by the Ministry of National Security on the Rustavi 2 TV station. Rustavi 2 was an independent TV company which was trying to expose corruption in public life. The Ministry had raided them as apparently they had not been paying taxes. I thought the raid was rather ironic, to say the least. From what I understood there was no clear system of taxation and hardly anyone paid taxes.

'The Liberty Institute and other NGOs have been encouraging students to protest about the raid on Rustavi 2,' said Kote, our new Governance Project Manager. The papers were full of pictures of students with banners saying things like, 'This is a threat to democracy and free speech'.

After the raids and protests President Shevardnadze had sacked his cabinet. 'There are new opposition parties proliferating,' Kote told me. 'Mikhayil Saakashvili, who was Minister of Justice, has set up the National Movement and Zurab Zhvania, who was the Speaker of the House, has set up the United Democrats.'

Was this political fragmentation an opportunity? Or would things get worse? Altogether it was a risk-filled time. I pulled out our office Business Risk Assessment document to update it – not for the first time.

#

Our heating was erratic and the power cuts at that time were hitting on a daily basis. The following week we were sitting huddled in our coats at our desks and in the library. Most of our library users were women, deep in concentration at their English language studies. We had candles on each table to make it easier to see. I said to librarians, Tamuna and Nino, 'These are terrible conditions.'

But they said, 'Probably better than they have at home. Hardly any of us have a generator.'

I phoned Marina, our new British Council assistant in Yerevan, about the VV Important Visit arrangements. It was almost upon us.

Marina and I hadn't even met, as she had only just started work, after a day of hand-over from Yulia who was now on maternity leave. We were engrossed in discussions about caterers and venues, invitation lists and our minute-by-minute plan. She was having the most rapid induction imaginable. 'The British Embassy have confirmed that the Duke has to give nine speeches in the three days he will be in Armenia,' said Marina. 'And Jo, two of these are for the British Council. You will need to prepare them for him – and also the response speeches.'

I heard shouting and a commotion outside our clunky front door and cut short my phonecall. Our new Office Manager, Zaza, and I scuttled to the door. Zaza peered out through the spyhole to see our security guard, Giorgi, shouting and fighting with a wild-looking man. 'Look, look,' said Zaza.

I squinted out and could see that they were ramming into the plastic chair and the little table at which the guard usually checked the handbags of our library users in a routine sort of way. As the two men were near the wide stairwell in the cavernous corridor of the university their shouts and yells, and the scraping of the furniture, echoed into the building. They were both large, strong-looking men. Zaza and I looked at each other and quickly decided not to try to intervene – neither of us were large, strong-looking men.

'Should we call the police?' I asked.

No!' said Zaza, horrified, and this was backed up by other colleagues. They all agreed the LAST thing we should do was call the police. 'Definitely not.'

'Why not?' I asked, puzzled and worried.

'Because they will beat both of them to a pulp and put them both in prison – and we'll have to pay to get Giorgi out,' said Zaza.

One of my other colleagues peeped out and said, 'It's my ex-husband – he wants me back.'

'He's not going about it in a particularly persuasive way.'

'He's always doing things like this.'

'Does he have a gun?' I asked tentatively.

'I don't know if he will have one with him...' she said.

The ex-husband had started to bellow at our front door. Anka quietly closed the door between the corridor and the library. Our customers carried on studying evidently unaware or unconcerned about the ruckus beyond.

We considered options and there weren't many of them – quite apart from being unable to help Georgi, we were stuck inside our own office with no means of leaving apart from through that doorway, on the other side of which there was a crazed man who may or may not have a gun. I can't phone the Embassy...

Vakho, who would have been an asset, was out but in any case I wouldn't have condoned throwing him in the way of this crazy estranged husband. 'I have a contact in the Ministry of the Interior,' said Zaza and he phoned him, barking requests and instructions. Some 'heavies' turned up shortly but in any case the ex-husband had exhausted himself and vanished. We opened the door and got some of the 'Brandy for staff' from the cupboard for Georgi, who was panting.

I was worried about my colleague and her daughter. 'I have somewhere we can go,' she said and we arranged for Vakho to drive her there after work for some days.

'It could have been worse,' said Tamuna. 'Did you hear that the Goethe Institut staff were held up at gunpoint and robbed in their office?' Dear God.

'I suppose our low-profile office is less likely to attract attention,' I said.

Joking aside, I bleated to colleagues in London, 'We need to fast-track this premises project – we can't stay working in these conditions!' I was told there were lots of requests for money to improve other British Council premises. We in Georgia would have to wait our turn – and if Georgia were so unstable maybe it wasn't worth the investment at all.

#

'You might as well pack up and go home,' said Alek. 'I don't know why you bother. You are obsessed with all this planning and strategising. Your colleagues in London are right, Georgia is clearly not top of their list for investment. Maybe it isn't worth all the effort to get this new office and all these new projects off the ground but potentially a huge waste of time and money if Georgia is so shaky??'

'I can't give up. There is so much we need to do, so much that we can do – but we can't do it without a proper office!'

Maybe Alek was right. Perhaps I was too deeply engrossed in my immediate job and I wasn't seeing the wood for the trees? Maybe my priorities were all wrong? But by now I was hooked on Georgia and her people and on trying to find a way we could help.

19

VIP visit

November 2001, Yerevan

'Pull the British Council banner up higher,' instructed Marina. 'And move the flags to frame where the speeches will be made.' At last. The Royal Visit was almost upon us. The clock was ticking till Their Royal Highnesses would arrive and we were busy putting the finishing touches to the reception area in Yerevan's splendid Moscow Cinema. Marina had only been working for the British Council for a few weeks but we had had so many intensive phonecalls before I could get down to Yerevan that we felt we had known each other for years. She turned out to be a beautiful young woman with long, curly blonde hair. When we met, we gave each other a big hug and immediately got on with the planning.

#

It was all hands to the pump. Yulia's baby had been born the week before and she was phoning in advice and instructions. Nata and Eka had come down from Tbilisi with me and colleagues from the British Embassy in Yerevan were helping too. My boss, Rosemary, had come from London and the new Director Designate, Roger, was taking time out from language learning. Barrie was also here from

Tbilisi – he was vital as he actually knew some of the important contacts we wanted to introduce to the royal couple, as he had been setting up the Armenian English Teachers' Association.

I was fretting a little. That the arrangements would go smoothly, that I would remember who the various people were, that I wouldn't freeze in the middle of my speech. I had written five speeches – two for the Duke, two for the new Director, Roger, and one for me. It was quite hard thinking of different things to say.

The Royal Visit Team had given us not one but two evenings. For the first evening we were showing a film at the Moscow Cinema, Kenneth Brannagh's *Love's Labour's Lost*. Everyone loves Shakespeare and – according to my colleague in the Film Department in London – this production had a 'modern twist'. We weren't expecting the Duke and Duchess to attend the showing of the film. They had a packed three-day programme of people to meet, flesh to press and places to visit. They would join our reception before the film and then go and get some downtime to get ready for the next day, when they would be off again, out and about. We would see them at the National Gallery in the evening to see a different group of people and do the same thing all over again – but this time the British Council in Armenia would be officially declared open.

The film had arrived from the UK. The caterers and flowers and British Council sign were all in place; the Union and Armenian flags were displayed. The security guards had been briefed and double-briefed about the arrangements and had taken their dogs around the cinema to clear it of any uninvited guests. The speeches I had written were all with the appropriate people.

Hang on. I couldn't find my own speech, which I was going to give to introduce the *Love's Labour's Lost* film.

Dammit. I told my colleagues I was nervous about giving this particular address. Somehow it seemed impersonal, standing in front of a massive film screen in front of a cinema audience. 'Someone told me to imagine your audience with no clothes on – it helps to calm the nerves,' said Roger.

'Just relax and be yourself,' said Rosemary.

#

Meanwhile Marina taped discreet arrows on the floor in the entrance to the reception area. The Duke would circulate in one direction, accompanied by me and Missak from the Embassy for translation and we would introduce him to various important contacts. The Duchess would go counter-clockwise accompanied by Barrie and another Armenian colleague.

We had to group all our Armenian VIP guests and to colour code their badges. This would make it easier to introduce the various groups and would give the royal pair a little hook upon which to hang their small-talk. We had lined up all the name badges with different coloured spots for arts and culture; government; NGOs and international agencies. Nata taped corresponding green, orange, red and yellow squares at intervals around the periphery of the room.

The VIP Armenian guests had to be *in situ* before the Royal VIPs made their entrance – as guests started to arrive we had to ask them to 'cluster' around a coloured piece of paper that matched their badge. As in Georgia, people did not always confirm if they were or weren't coming to receptions and we were unsure what the final composition of the groups would look like. Marina checked the colour of one guest's badge and guided her to the 'NGOs' orange piece of paper and asked her politely to stand near it. The guest looked down at it and followed the instructions. Others started to arrive and to cluster around their pieces of paper, getting animated about the imminent arrival of the royal couple. It transpired that the NGO woman was the only guest in her category to turn up. She stood there frowning. 'I'm not standing here on this piece of paper!' she said with annoyance and she broke ranks and joined friends in the group of government invitees.

Various journalists and cameramen were dotted about the room and we were buzzing with activity, checking and re-checking Marina's minute-by-minute plan, paddling away like swans, until, finally, everything was in place. Apart from Barrie. Where was Barrie? He had to accompany the Duchess.

Where was Barrie?

Where on earth was Barrie?

Thank God!

There was Barrie.

Dashing up the stairs clutching his satchel and hastily smoothing his hair.

'Sorry about that.'

We shuffled into our receiving line, as Their Royal Highnesses arrived to shake our hands and be introduced to a room full of eager guests standing around coloured squares of paper.

Roger gave an enthusiastic speech and invited the Duke to do the same. It did feel odd hearing the words I had written being read out by a Duke. I felt a little sorry for the VVIP. Nine speeches in three days and always in the spotlight.

#

'Well done Marina – arranging all this was a huge achievement,' I said. 'Same thing again tomorrow!'

'Can I get back to my real job now please?' asked Barrie.

#

It was almost my turn to be on show as the cinema hall filled with guests. Some were from the VIP party but most were students and younger people. I scribbled down on the back of the Embassy invitation card an impromptu speech.

- Delighted to welcome you to Yerevan's Moscow Cinema, etc. *Love's Labour's Lost.* etc
- Glamorous romantic comedy, etc
- Traditional with a modern twist
- Themes of love, war, tradition and modernity and the distractions that have faced students through the ages, etc
- Etc, etc

The stage suddenly seemed vast, with only a lonely microphone on its stand. I stepped out and the room fell silent. I dismissed the brief thought, 'imagine your audience are naked' and instead could see a number of young people smiling up at me. OK, about 600 of them but actually it was just a room of individuals. I smiled back at them.

'I'm delighted to welcome you to the Moscow Cinema.'

And I found I didn't need to look at my little bit of card after all.

Part 2 The Heart of the Matter

20

The Devil went down to Georgia

April 2002, Tbilisi

After all the excitement and build-up to the VIP visit to
Armenia and getting the office there launched, I was hoping
2002 would bring some calm and peace and an opportunity
to start to feel more settled in Georgia. However, the country
was anything but settled. Someone mentioned to me that the
Georgian government was a 'kleptarchy'. It was a new word
to me. It meant Georgia was ruled by politicians who were
criminals, gangsters. It did feel that ordinary people didn't
seem to matter.

The newspapers mentioned a place called the Pankisi
Gorge. I learnt that Pankisi was some 80 km from Tbilisi in
North East Georgia but that it could take hours to reach on
the rough roads. It was a broad valley some 30 km long
surrounded by mountains and at its northern tip it was near
the border with Chechnya in the Russian Republic. It was
the home of the Kists, who were predominantly Muslim and
within the same ethnic family as their Chechen neighbours.
The general crisis of governance in Tbilisi manifested itself
in the Pankisi region with a paralysis of local government
structures and a complete absence of law enforcement – this,
as well as its remoteness, rugged geography and deep rural

poverty had contributed to the Pankisi Gorge becoming a refuge for criminals and terrorists in recent years.

The region was also a flashpoint between Russia and the USA. The Russian State had long had issues about the lawlessness of the Pankisi Gorge – since the 90's Moscow had blamed the Georgians for not doing enough to stop Chechen rebels entering Pankisi, getting patched up, rearmed and then resuming their insurgency in Russia. By the early 2000s other Islamic fighters also washed up there – from North Africa, the Middle East, Western Europe and other places – wanting to join their Muslim brethren in Chechnya in their fight against the Russians.

The West, and in particular the US, were also concerned that Al Qaeda and its affiliates would take advantage of the complete lack of governance in the area to gain a foothold on the edge of Europe. This was a twitchy, post-9/11 world. Allied forces were in Afghanistan and Bush's War on Terror was at the top of the agenda. As a result, in 2002 the Americans had pledged to send 200 military trainers to 'train and equip' the woefully inept and under-resourced Georgian army to clear the Pankisi Gorge of insurgents. While some in Russia were doubtless unhappy at this development, there was general agreement between many there and in western countries that the Pankisi was out of control and that this threatened security and stability beyond Georgia's borders.

It all seemed so uncertain.

#

I had uncertainties to confront closer to home. By Easter Alek and I had our own crisis unfolding – simply put, we had failed to make each other happy. Living away from immediate family and friends presented more challenges in our circumstances – and we were breaking up. Alek packed his bags and left.

#

The evening he left there was the inevitable power cut, my generator did not cut in and I had no water. The gas cooker was working though, so that was something.

I sat outside on the balcony next to the pomegranate tree, its leaves rustling in the dark night. Otherwise it was quiet. I took my torch and went back into the kitchen and opened a bottle of Saperavi red wine. Not a great idea on my own, but...I was, as you can imagine, low of spirit.

What a terrible mess I had made of my life. My good friend Jane and I had charted the ups and downs of life and decided much of human existence revolves around 'love and furniture', or the pursuit of either of these. It was often such a struggle. Why was it, we wondered, that if one's material life, or job, was ticking over nicely, it seemed to be at the expense of emotional security? We knew that money didn't buy love. Or, conversely, how often are couples desperately, hopelessly in love but without the means to sustain their relationship? It was a puzzle.

I started to sing to myself. Those sad, melodic 'break-up' songs. If I had electricity I would have put on a CD but this was the next best thing and maybe I needed to warble away my sadness. From the balcony of the apartment upstairs came another song, deep and strong into the dusky night. I shut up straightaway. It must have been the builders who had started working on the floor above my apartment – perhaps they had heard my terrible singing? There were maybe three of them singing a Georgian song, and another, and another, polyphonically. It felt like a serenade, from these invisible singers.

How sad – how lovely – and how much better singers they were than I was.

#

The day after Alek left I had to make a trip to Armenia to do the next round of scholarship and staff interviews in Yerevan. I felt raw. Vakho, gentle giant, arrived at my house with the car. He knew about my estranged husband's departure, as he had taken Alek to the airport. Vakho helped me into the car. 'You need time, Jo...' And offered me one of his throaty Georgian cigarettes.

I did what I had to do in Yerevan and in fact it was great to see Yulia, Marina and our new Finance Manager colleague there, Mikhayil. Our tiny operation there was expanding. It was a welcome distraction to do something I enjoyed doing.

As we drove back I realised that, outside my immediate office, I didn't have many friends in Georgia. I had been working hard, travelling backwards and forwards to Armenia and other places so often, I didn't have much of a life left over. Maybe my priorities really were all wrong?

#

Going into work, I pushed open the heavy door of my office with a leaden heart and geared up to meet my colleagues. What I met with was overwhelming sympathy and support. In Georgia many people had been through far worse and everyone had their own domestic issues and circumstances to deal with – many of the women in the office were single mothers who had separated from difficult husbands. On my desk was a little parcel of chocolate and biscuits and a bunch of violets. I never found out who left them.

#

The next day Maia, the Embassy's Press and Public Relations Officer, phoned me to ask if we could meet to talk about the proposed UK-Georgian alumni association. I had regularly worked with her over the past year and she was a fount of knowledge on who was doing what in the complex world of Georgian politics. She and I had occasionally allowed ourselves to chat in the margins of functions but one way or another we had not been out on a personal basis.

We met to talk about the creation of the alumni association, something we had wanted to launch for ages. The various schemes for scholarships in the UK had deliberately targeted bright young people from the non-governmental sector and from business and – more of a challenge – from the Georgian public sector. While not a huge number (some 50 or so at the time), returnees from the UK came back with increased skills, knowledge and confidence. It was hoped they would be leaders in their fields and would continue to be friends of the UK. An association would enable an easier route to gain access to these clever and forward-thinking young people, and for them, as like-minded UK-trained scholars, to be able to contact each other easily. Maia was herself a Chevening alumna in British Studies from the University of Warwick, in fact the first Georgian to receive the scholarship.

We talked about the challenges of setting up the association. We wanted to facilitate it but not to lead it and we needed the alumni themselves to be proactive. If the association was to be a legal entity it would become an NGO in its own right. As I stood to leave she asked if I was OK. 'You don't look yourself, Jo,' she said with concern. I told her that Alek and I had broken up and she stood up and put her arms around me. 'Let's not talk about anything now... Would you like to go out for a meal?

We went out the following evening and hardly ate. We talked and talked. Listening to some of the things I learnt from Maia about her life and the struggles of everyday life in Tbilisi put my own miseries in perspective.

#

My boss in London, Rosemary, phoned me to offer support. We both knew examples of 'UK appointed' couples who had separated. This way of working could put exceptional strain on relationships, particularly if the accompanying spouse was unhappy. It wasn't always easy to find a raison d'etre, a job, a social network of friends.

'We would completely understand it if you needed to come back to Britain for a breather – or if you wanted to consider short-touring.'

In general, difficult postings could last one or two years but, ideally, a posting lasted three or four years. Post-holders would be more effective the more they knew about the country in which they worked and the better networked and informed they became. Also, having longer postings kept the costs of moving between countries as low as possible. I had only been in Georgia a year but Rosemary had given me the option to throw my hat into the internal recruitment ring and apply for another post much earlier than I should have done. This could mean that potentially I would move on and be replaced perhaps as early as September, some five months hence.

I was grateful that I had this fall back. I considered this option – and I rejected it almost instantly. Although I had lost my husband, I loved this job. I loved Georgia, in spite of all the uncertainty and tension and intrigue. I loved my colleagues at the British Council, as colleagues and as friends – and I knew we had only just begun. In Maia, too, I knew I had found a friend.

21

Plate tectonics

Late April 2002, Tbilisi

It now seemed an utterly crazy thing to have undertaken but on top of everything else I had started my second course towards my MSc with the Open University. I had been plugging away at it from late 2001. All those weekends devoted to writing up assignments, all those projects, all that reading. It was on 'Change, Innovation and Creativity'.

My marriage had broken up in mid-April, I had gone to Armenia and since then I had been juggling marital breakdown with keeping my job going. Now, at the end of April, I had an exam. I had done absolutely nothing to revise towards it. I wrote to my tutor and asked if there was any way I could get out of doing it – he said I could postpone it till October. I just couldn't face wading through this course again. It wasn't cheap and I couldn't afford to re-sit.

I did three solid, intensive, gruelling days of revision. The only way I could tackle it was to break-it-down-into-achievable-chunks. I tried to memorise as much as I could about 'Change'.

I took the exam in the gloomy basement of my apartment, sitting at a solitary desk and surrounded by old British Council materials and exhibitions, old posters and paraphernalia. At the appointed time my Exams Manager colleague, Anuki, unwrapped the exam paper and handed it to me. I launched into three exhausting hours. When I could write no more, Anuki put all my scruffy essays in her plastic folder. She sealed it and she said she would send it off to the OU in Britain on the British Airways flight the following day. 'Are you OK?' she asked, touching my arm solicitously.

'Nothing an early night won't help with.'

#

I couldn't face much to eat but I did open a present from my sister-in-law, Karen, a small bottle of sloe gin. I took a glass to bed. I was sitting in bed feeling whacked, when my room started to shake, accompanied by an eerie high-pitched screaming noise that seemed to be coming through the windows.

Oh my dear God...

I looked at the chandelier – it was rather a fancy house – trembling and jingling and swaying.

Earthquake.

My first thought was, 'If it is time for me to go, please make it quick...'

Then, 'I hope everyone else is OK out there.'

Then, *'Fucking hell*, what if my exam paper never makes it to the UK?'

And then, thank God, the shaking stopped. I got dressed and ran out to check the guards were OK. My mobile phone wasn't working and neither were theirs but we were all fine. Shaken but not stirred. I gave them the rest of the bottle of sloe gin and went back to bed.

Two hours later Zaza was able to phone to check I was OK.

'Zaza, never a dull moment!'

'We've never had one like that!'

In the small hours of the morning we phoned round all our colleagues to check how everyone was. It transpired that the earthquake had been 6 on the Richter scale, apparently the worst for 40 years, and a number of people had died – some when crumbling balconies fell on passers-by in the street.

The next morning in the State University there was rubble and plaster in the corridors and new, alarming cracks in the tall walls near our office. When could we get out of this building? We were still stuck in planning approval hell.

In the office we babbled about what we had been doing when the earthquake struck: 'I was driving and I thought my car was bouncing around!'

'Not just because of the potholes?'

'I fell over in the shower.'

'All the books on my shelves fell off!'

It transpired that Zaza had been in the office and had dived underneath his desk. 'At 10pm? Zaza – you work too hard!'

'There is a lot to do…'

Then Tamuna said, 'Jo – Happy Birthday!'

I had forgotten! When the library closed – as our library users still came in spite of yesterday's earthquake – we ate cakes in the office. Doubtless watched closely by our resident mice. In the evening the whole office went out dancing.

22

I get by with a little help

May 2002, Tbilisi

I checked in the mirror: dress OK, matching shoes, favourite earrings. Plenty of business cards in evening bag. Off I went to the Metekhi Palace Hotel reception to celebrate Europe Day, hosted, of course, by the European Commission. I was geared up to catch up with existing contacts and make some new ones. To find out what was going on, who was 'in' or 'out', what the key issues of the day were, and to try to move along some of our burgeoning new projects.

In the throng of guests chatting and snacking and drinking I saw Amy, the British journalist who worked on the Georgian English language newspaper, the *Georgian Times*. We talked about the earthquake and she told me she had been showing some newly arrived Americans around the city. They exclaimed when they saw the dilapidated state of some of the aged buildings in the city centre. 'My God, I can see how much damage the earthquake did!' one had said to her.

'No, these buildings have been like that for years...None of this is earthquake damage,' she told him. We had heard that some in Georgia thought the earthquake had been caused by the Russians doing underground explosive tests – there were many conspiracy theories. Amy drily added,

'Anyway, have you heard about the latest bout of rapes of foreign women?' How dreadful! 'I fear it's starting again…' While broader geopolitical issues were tense in everyday terms they still felt remote, whereas the fragile state of law and order closer to home potentially affected us more. As it was, I was in the exceptionally fortunate situation of having Vakho to collect and deliver me from work. 'But Jo, you look down. Are you OK?' I explained about my separation from Alek. Amy looked at me sympathetically. 'Emotional hassles do tend to sap one's energy. You could try Tchaikovsky – I find his violin parts help. Perhaps we could find you a Georgian boyfriend?'

I laughed. 'It's a kind thought and I can see there are lots of attractive Georgian men around, but no...I can't face any new relationship right now. Not for a long time – I need to sort myself out. I'll stick to Tchaikovsky.'

We both went off to network. I bumped into Georgi Margvelashvili from the Georgian Institute for Public Affairs. My new colleague Kote (our Governance Project Manager), had been working hard and he had great connections with bright, young, forward-looking people such as him. We had started to run human rights training and curriculum development with GIPA, using British expertise, a perfect project.

I saw David Lordkipanidze the charismatic and handsome director of the Georgian National Museum. He asked if the British Council could participate in helping to renovate the museum or to contribute to an exhibition. 'Did you know that Georgia is the Land of the Golden Fleece?' he added. 'Jason and the Argonauts were said to have landed on the shores of Colchis, on the Black Sea coast, where Georgia is today – in the Greek myths, Colchis was a fabulously wealthy place, dripping with gold, silver, copper and other desirable things, not least the Golden Fleece itself. Jason was on a quest to find the fleece in order to retrieve his usurped throne in distant Iolkos.' I loved the Greek myths. I was all ears. 'He and the Argonauts met the ruler of Colchis, King Aeetes and his beautiful daughter, Medea. At a banquet, King Aeetes agreed to relinquish the fleece if Jason could achieve the unachievable, you know the sort of thing – ploughing a field with fire-breathing oxen, sowing dragon's teeth into a field, fighting off a waking dragon.'

'My job sometimes feels like that...' I said.

'Mine too! But Aeetes told his daughter that he would rather kill his guests than surrender the Golden Fleece – it was too potent a symbol of kingship. Under Aphrodite's spell Medea had been bewitched by Jason and she helped him in his tasks in return for marrying him and they sailed off together. He got the fleece, but they didn't live happily ever after.' David told me there really were golden fleeces. There was gold in the rivers in the mountains and as they used to use sheep fleeces for panning, these would end up glistening with gold. 'Please come to the museum and see our exhibits or, if you like, you could come out to the archaeological digs at Dmanisi. We have been excavating with German, US and French archaeologists for years – we have unearthed some important and unique humanid bones,' said David.

I told him I would love to come and that I was sorry I couldn't contribute to the exhibition – small-overcommitted-office-budgets, have-to-be-focused-on-how-we-spend-our-money. I hated having to say it to him. I could see that if Georgia were a less troubled place, it could be a tourist paradise. Tbilisi could be a jewel, a new Prague with its ancient churches and historical sites. Beyond the city were breath-taking mountains and beautiful countryside. The singing, the dancing, the wine, the food! If Georgia had high quality museums it would open a window to her many treasures – that seemed a distant dream but it was good to talk to someone who, while looking back into layers of pre-history, was also looking forwards to a brighter future for his country. We moved on.

'Hello Minister!'

'Professor, how good to see you!'

After chatting to other guests at the reception, I eventually caught up with the head of the EC Delegation, Torben. We talked about new EU-funded projects. I was keen to establish if there might be any projects which would be competitively tendered for which the British Council might eventually bid. The EC was a big donor and I was pleased to learn that they had projects to support institutional and legal reform, health care and social assistance.

'I know you don't celebrate 'Europe Day' much in the UK,' said Torben.

'Yes, true, but we don't actually celebrate our Queen's Birthday either.' Our UK national day was only marked overseas by the Queen's Birthday Party, an event virtually unheard of in UK itself – only a few people associated it with Trooping of the Colour.

'What do you celebrate?' he asked.

'Bank holidays are popular,' I told him.

#

At home, I was running up enormous phone bills phoning family and friends in Britain and beyond. My family were worried about me. I was trying to put up a brave front at work but I was miserable and moping at home in the few weeks since my marital meltdown. My colleague, Roger, had by now started as the new British Council director in Yerevan so at least I wasn't spending so long away from home. In some respects, though, having more time to myself compounded my loneliness. One good thing was that I got a bare pass in my OU exam – it was the worst exam result I had ever had but I was jubilant.

After some discussion within my family, my brother Martin came to visit me for a long weekend. He had rarely left his own much loved young family and I was grateful to him for taking time out. In celebration of Martin's visit and as spring was in the air, I offered to pay for petrol and a picnic for the whole office to go on a day trip somewhere. Few of my colleagues could afford to take trips out of Tbilisi. Although their salaries were reasonable, many were supporting wider networks of unemployed family members – every *Lari* counted.

Figure 10 Carving on the 12th century Gelati Monastery

'Where would you like to go?' I asked.

'Shall we vote?' suggested Nata. Voting was unusual in this post-Soviet society. In general, you went where your boss told you – but we could do things in a different way.

Everyone made suggestions and we settled on a trip to the 12th century monastery of Gelati. We crammed into the Landrover and the Mitsubishi and it took many hours to get there over the dreadful roads. The cathedral was situated, as they often seemed to be, in the middle of nowhere, accessed over a rickety bridge across a verdant valley. It was spectacular and was a religious site of considerable importance. I was again struck at how spiritual many of my young colleagues were.

#

Martin and I also went for a walk through Tbilisi on another sunny, easy day. We strolled together past flower stalls selling dusty roses and looked up at the elegant, old, neo-classical buildings along the wide streets. If you squinted it might look like Paris on a spring day. We took photos of the Orthodox churches and statues of great kings long gone, nestling in the sweeping valley. Had coffee together in a café down by the river, lazily making its way through the city.

'This is the first time I have been for a proper walk in Tbilisi,' I told him. When I had been with my security-conscious ex-husband, we never felt we could relax for fear of muggings – but now it was springtime and I felt more optimistic, somehow.

Figure 11 Narikala Fortress Tbilisi

#

My dear friend Helen also came to visit. I showed her round my huge apartment, leaving till last the huge, sunny room that looked like a mini-ballroom. The one with the chandeliers dripping with crystal, the four-metre high etched and gold-framed mirrors and the pale parquet floors. It was quite a spectacular room anyway and she was wide-eyed and open-mouthed at the opulence of it – when she saw the grand piano she gave a happy squeak and sat down at it. In the piano seat were some scores and she flipped through them and started to tinkle the piano keys with delight. I lay on the sofa beside her and talked, and talked and talked. Helen, concentrating, said, 'Uh huh, uh huh, oh dear, yes, I see.' In exactly the right places. She was always good at saying the right things.

'Sorry we haven't got any water,' I apologised. But the generator was working and I did have gas so I could at least cook my guest a meal.

'What an apartment, though,' said Helen.

'I know – but it is just not me. Too big and too full of angst,' I said.

#

I took Helen out to the Ethnographic Museum set high up in the hills behind Tbilisi. It was a glorious sunny day and the sky was high above us. On the way there she said, 'Where are all the rosy-cheeked young people picking fruit on collective farms?' She had been the friend who had said, all that time ago, that she couldn't picture what Georgia was like but only as if from a Soviet poster. 'It is so lovely here though, isn't it?' she added, happily gazing out from the car at fields full of wildflowers. It was a joy to be able to walk around at the museum in the bright sunshine, away from the tangled, tense little city.

The museum was not one building, but 18 houses set amongst sprawling grounds with fruit trees, flowers and butterflies. These were traditional, wooden houses representing different regional styles. Many had wide balconies and carved decorations and were full of intricately fashioned wooden furniture, and agricultural and viticultural implements. We couldn't believe the size of the clay wine vessels. These were maybe five or six feet deep, huge amphorae, which would be buried deep in the ground and filled with wine.

'How do they make them?' asked Helen, fascinated. It was these types of vessels which were discovered at ancient archaeological digs which Georgians like to say proves that 'in Georgia was wine invented'. *(sic)*

Another visit over all too quickly. Helen and I hugged tightly at the airport.

23

Diplomatic briefing

May 2002, Tbilisi

Each week all the heads of section of the various bits of the
British Embassy met to brief the Ambassador, and each
other, on what the big issues were for the forthcoming week
and beyond. As the head of the British Council and First
Secretary Cultural I went along too to let colleagues know
about any visitors who were coming out, any new projects,
anything that might be important or newsworthy. There was
a new colleague this week, Mike, the new head of the
political section. We introduced ourselves and shook hands
over the table. He seemed pleasant. I wasn't keen on his
houndstooth jacket though.

We took it in turns round the table to let each other know
the hot news. Of late, the mood was gloomy. The Georgian
economy was not getting better, it was spiralling downwards.
The Defence Attaché briefed us on the latest on the new US
Train and Equip Program; Shevardnadze had been in
discussion with the US for some months and had invited US
troops to Georgia earlier in the year – and they had started to
arrive. The plan was that they would help the Georgians
clear the Pankisi Gorge of Muslim fighters within six
months. Having the Georgians onside for the 'War on Terror'

was undoubtedly part of the US game plan. The Russian authorities – while they wanted the Pankisi Gorge cleared of Chechen rebels – perhaps saw the presence of these US troops in their 'near neighbourhood' somewhat differently.

The new man, Mike, reported that colleagues from the British Embassy had volunteered to help monitor forthcoming local elections, along with other international organisations. Democracy was still relatively new in Georgia and electoral procedures might be weak; the country was challenged by corruption and by those who might want to maintain the status quo – it was possible that the elections could be manipulated.

Maia K fed back on media reportage, this week about kidnaps of Spanish and Georgian citizens. The possibility of kidnapping or carjacking could affect any of us and – as we knew – there was no reliable local police service to speak of. Deborah, the Ambassador, urged greater care. Another colleague reported that the guards outside his house had, far from guarding his house, stolen his car for a joyride. 'And they crashed it.' Oh dear…Who guards the guards?

It came to my turn. 'This seems frivolous against this backdrop – just to flag up that the British Council will be hosting our first major arts tour, by the Random Ballet Company.'

But my colleagues were delighted. 'You don't know how much it means for us to get access to foreign arts and culture,' said Maia, 'it means you have confidence in our country.'

'Good luck keeping the electricity on...' said someone else. 'Don't let the dancers out of your sight!'

I told them that we were moving ahead with our premises relocation project. Thanks to tireless work in particular on the part of my Office Manager, Zaza, my HQ colleagues had approved the money for renovation – at last – and we had a shortlist of possible offices. We were edging there. 'Congratulations,' said Deborah. 'I can't believe you are all still in that terrible office.'

I continued, 'We have also started an EC-funded project to do human rights training and our English language teaching activities are expanding beyond Tbilisi into Kutaisi and other cities. We'll be participating in the Tbilisi Book Fair and I'll be away at the Black Sea coast setting up a new office for the Peacekeeping English Project.' All the hard work in my office was beginning to pay off and we had more and more on which to report back.

'You have a lot going on,' said Deborah. 'That's what we like to see – it's important to keep the show on the road.'

When it came to the turn of Irakli, the Commercial Officer, he paused and cleared his throat. 'I have been contacted by a well-known British clothing and department store. Apparently they are thinking of opening a branch in Tbilisi.'

There was a silence while we considered this possibility before the Ambassador said, 'Have they actually been here?'

And we all, as one, collapsed into laughter. What were they thinking? Who had advised them that this was an 'emerging market'? Didn't they read the newspapers, or the internet? Even a quick scan would make it obvious that things were unstable. It was absurd to think, in 2002, of anyone opening a big-name shop without the risk of robbery or protection rackets. While there were indeed shops selling high-end labels such as Dior and Chanel, one could only guess how these stayed in business and who most of their clientele were – and these customers certainly weren't the kind of people who would go to this rather humdrum British high-street shop.

'I think we need to encourage them to do more market analysis and give them a frank briefing,' said Deborah.

24

New projects

June 2002, Tbilisi

My librarian colleagues, Tamuna and Nino, were preparing a stand for the Tbilisi International Book Fair. In spite of the collapsing economy and the difficulty most people in Georgia had making ends meet, reading, learning and educating their children remained a priority for Georgian parents. Adults perhaps also wanted the escapism of reading for pleasure and there was in addition a rich tradition of academic and scientific publishing stretching back through the Soviet era.

On the day of the book fair, the library team went on early to the exhibition centre to set up the British Council stand. I was dropping by for a quick check and by the time I joined them they had finished. I was impressed with what they had done. It looked lively, contemporary and eye-catching and it was a great way for us to market our library to a wide and informed audience. We were promoting UK publications and also the physical presence of our British Council office, flagging up that we would soon be moving to a modern, new office. We had to be vague about when we would, in fact, be in a new office, as we still didn't know. We had forms to fill in, lists to compile, contracts to negotiate – in a country where contracts were unusual. But the sooner we got word out that our library would be bigger, more accessible and more useful, the better.

Our neighbouring stands included the US library and information centre, the Alliance Française and the German cultural organisation, the Goethe Institut. The Director of the Goethe Institut and I chatted affably. The British Council maintained a friendly but determined competition with our cultural counterparts, apart from when we were working in partnership in which case we changed tack and worked as closely as we could.

The exhibition hall was laid out in an L shape with Georgian publishers, by far the greater number of stalls, along the main branch, while we and our foreign cousins were tucked round a corner and not so immediately obvious. There were many hundreds of visitors and the room was humming as the stall holders explained and promoted their wares to the members of the public who were strolling around examining the various exhibits. I was keen to get back to the office and was about to leave when, above the hubbub, an authoritative voice yelled out. I asked Tamuna what the man had said and she said, 'They are about to lock the doors, no-one is to leave. The President is coming!'

'Of the book fair?'

'No, Shevardnadze!' I had always wanted to meet President Shevardnadze but the British Council was simply too small a player to attract his attention.

A large party of bodyguards and security men preceded the President's arrival and all of us teetered on tiptoe like children to see where he was. The room was packed full of people. It appeared he was, quite rightly, spending quality time looking at the Georgian stalls. We could see his group was making slow progress and that they paused when they came to the end of the long row, evidently deciding whether to finish there and leave.

Shevardnadze walked over to the Goethe Institut stall. As one of the architects of German reunification perhaps he had a natural affinity with them. We were anxious he might not make it as far as our stall but as he turned away his eyes alighted on a glossy magazine on the British Council stall. He looked up at us, clearly getting ready to go and I shouted, 'Mr President! We are trying to help your country!'

He stopped in his tracks. We blurted out as much as we could about the British Council. He nodded and looked mildly interested before he and his entourage moved on.

#

When I got back to the office, Kote asked me, 'Have you heard? Peter Shaw has been kidnapped!' I didn't know Peter Shaw personally but I learnt he was a Welsh consultant who had been working on an EC-funded agricultural banking project. Apparently it was his last week in Georgia after working there for many years. He had been kidnapped while driving by men dressed as policemen – they had flagged him down and bundled him away. Nothing had been heard from his kidnappers and no-one knew where he had been taken.

#

'Well done!' said the Minister of Culture as she entered my living room for our reception to welcome the Random Ballet Company. My guests were buzzing with appreciation about the performance the previous night.

'It was superb,' said a theatre director.

'The dance was phenomenal – and the lighting and technology were out of this world. It is no mean feat to do that here,' said a journalist.

'And no power cuts!' said Johanna, my counterpart from the Goethe Institut.

I moved on to talk to some of the dancers. 'What a wonderful place Tbilisi is – such a pleasant surprise. We knew so little about this country,' said one. 'After the worst that Georgian bureaucracy and the customs agent could throw at us, Georgia has won new friends.' Indeed, getting their bulky and sophisticated equipment safely cleared through customs had been, frankly, somewhat stressful.

'Thank you for letting us show what we can do and for introducing us to these wonderful Georgian dancers,' said another of the pretty ballerinas. In addition to their performance they had also worked with young dancers, learning from each other and sharing techniques.

The Random Ballet Company was the first British dance company ever to visit Georgia, before going on Azerbaijan and then to countries in Central Asia. It was a bold and impressive production. We were relieved that it had gone so well and that, as evidenced by the cheers, encores and applause at the performance, our audience had greatly appreciated it. Andrew – our colleague in the Arts Division in London, who had chosen this group and made the UK side of the arrangements – had done us proud.

Colleagues from the British Embassy were at my reception too. Deborah and Mike, the new man from the Political Section. 'What happened at the local elections?' I asked them, as these had just happened.

'There were problems with the voters' lists, as there have not been any reliable census records taken – some people were apparently voting several times...Mikhayil Saakashvili has landed the position as Mayor of Tbilisi,' said Deborah. I vaguely remembered him.

'He is voluble and quite young – mid-30s perhaps,' said Mike. 'He had been Minister of Justice but he left Shevardnadze's party with a flourish, setting up a new opposition party, the Nationalist Movement. They have a strong anti-corruption ticket. The Mayor of Tbilisi is a significant job – doubtless he will use this position to bang a drum or two.'

'Is there any update on Peter Shaw?' I asked. It felt dreadful that we were standing around chatting and going to the ballet while the whereabouts of this kidnap victim were unknown.

'We suspect he is in the Pankisi Gorge. Work between the British Embassy, the local authorities and the British police is ongoing – trying to get to the bottom of this is pretty intense,' said Mike. Worrying times. There was a discreet cough at my shoulder and I turned to see Mr Rukhadze, of the Anglo-Georgian Friendship Society. He asked Mike to translate for him.

'It is good to bring this British dance company to Tbilisi,' he said. 'But what about the Wardrop exhibition?'

25

After sunset, sunrise

July 2002, Tbilisi

'It gives me great pleasure to introduce Dr Richard V, from the University of Sussex, and to launch today's important discussions. I am delighted that the British Council is able to support his visit and in so doing to contribute to the reform of Georgia's criminal code.'

We were at the Marriott Hotel with a working group comprised of representatives from various non-governmental organisations. Our Project Manager, Kote, had been working for a year with the British Council and he had been relentless – he had drawn on and expanded his network of like-minded organisations which were committed to positive change in Georgia. We were now working with ALPE (the Association for Legal and Public Education), the Liberty Institute, the Open Society and the Georgian Young Lawyers Association, amongst others. Some of our successful scholarship candidates were drawn from these organisations so – as a member of the various annual scholarship panels – I also knew many of these committed young people. I wasn't staying for the day of drafting and re-drafting Georgia's criminal code and I left the experts to it.

#

That evening I took Richard to a restaurant called 'Paradise Lost'.

'What an atmospheric place,' he said looking up. The restaurant was next door to the Amirani cinema and was full of silver screen memorabilia. Georgia had had a vibrant film industry in Soviet times and there were props – old bicycles, lighting equipment and suitcases – arrayed around the walls and hanging from the ceiling. It had a fabulous art deco bar, and deco lamps and contemporary sculptures were dotted about. 'And what a great name for a restaurant,' said Richard.

We chatted over dinner and I told him we were racing against time trying to keep up with all the problems in Georgia. 'This country is such an anomaly to me,' I said. 'There are massive economic and social problems, and corruption is rife. There are outbursts of violence and minimal rule of law – you know Levan and Giga from the Liberty Institute? Their office was vandalised earlier this month by an armed gang! The gang broke in, trashed their computers and beat them up...The perpetrators aren't known but the people at Liberty regularly talk out about infringements of human rights in the prisons and of minorities – they have made enemies. Then Georgia is bursting with culture, with vitality and creativity – just look at this place.' Richard agreed it seemed special.

'And there are all these almost scarily clever young people, all these young lawyers, like Kote in my office – he is a star.' I also told Richard that, relatively speaking, we had small budgets but we could do much more – we tried every way we could to stretch our pennies, such as working alongside like-minded organisations. I said we planned to put in more bids for competitively tendered European Commission-funded reform projects but it was a highly competitive market and it would take time. Richard offered to waive his fees – another star. We could now afford to buy some text books on international law for our library; we labelled the collection after him.

#

It was a lively month. A little later many of us in the office were going off to establish a new Peacekeeping English Project office in the Black Sea port of Poti. This was apparently where Jason and his Argonauts had met Medea on their quest to find the Golden Fleece.

Our own expedition was not so romantic. We needed to finalise terms with the Naval Academy, and, assuming all was satisfactory, to install the computers and check that the new office and new office manager, Gocha, were good-to-go. All the management and admin staff in the office were going. It was a five hour drive west and we set off laden with all the equipment and luggage for a night away.

It was also a trip to the seaside. Although it was a work trip, it was undeniable that we were all pleased to be getting out of the polluted city and heading for the beach. I was keen to see this mythic place.

In fact Poti was far from a seaside resort and it was hard to imagine it as ever having been anything other than a run-down port. There were pigs and chickens wandering around on the deserted main streets and the docks had seen better days. The good news was that we were able to move ahead with opening our office with no delays.

That evening Zaza said, 'We have a surprise. The Naval Academy has arranged to lend us a speedboat!' As the sun began to set over the shining blue of the Black Sea, our little team jumped on to the swanky-looking boat, ostensibly used by customs officials to chase criminals with contraband – but I wondered on this – and had an exhilarating looped tour of the harbour.

There was only one hotel in Poti, the Anchor, low on luxury but clean and with friendly staff. That night I fell asleep, exhausted after the long journey and eventful day. And was confused and surprised when my mobile phone rang at about midnight – what now? Who could it possibly be? I shook myself awake. It was Mike, the man from the British Embassy. 'I'm the Embassy Duty Officer this week and your house alarm has apparently gone off – your guards have turned off the alarm but have refused to go inside. Where are you?' I explained I was on a work trip in Poti.

'We need to investigate this, there might be a break-in. Can you get one of your British Council colleagues to go round and have a look?' I said that all the colleagues who would be able to do such a thing were with me in Poti. 'That's not great planning,' he said, sounding pissed off. I could hear chatting and laughing in the background as Mike was talking. It sounded as if he was at a party. 'I'll have to look for your house. Where do you live?'

'Radiani Street,' I told him, but it wasn't a well-known street.

'Where is it?' A good question.

'It intersects with Abashidze Street, which runs parallel with Chavchavadze Avenue.'

He relayed this to someone he was with. 'Still no clearer. I've only just arrived in Tbilisi. You'll have to be more precise.'

'Please don't worry – there is nothing worth stealing in my house anyway – it will be fine and I'll be back tomorrow!'

'No, if I have had a call-out, I need to follow it through.' The Embassy duty officer system meant that a UK member of Embassy staff would respond to emergencies for British nationals and it rotated each week. The duty officer system was essential, especially in countries that didn't have reliable police services.

'If you can get to Abashidze Street, drive away from the direction of the parliament building.' I knew he would know where that was. 'Until you get to the Coca Cola stand with the stall that sells roses on the corner with Radiani Street.' It was the only landmark I could think of and it was feeble as of course the flower stall would be shut up at 12.30 in the morning.

Mike phoned back half an hour later, apparently in a car being driven by a woman from the UN. They were accompanied by a friend of hers who had evidently been at the party they were at and the two women were chattering and giggling in the background. It was embarrassing for me to put them all to this trouble. There were few street signs in Tbilisi and it was pitch black and needless to say there was no satellite navigation in Georgia at that time. Eventually they found my house. It transpired that the wind had blown my back door open and that this had triggered the alarm. I wondered what Mike and his ladies would make of my house, nosing around in the dark.

#

The next time I met Mike at the Embassy I was grovellingly thankful to him and apologised again and again for calling him out on a Friday night. Mike told me that my ex-husband had, unknown to me, set up our security system at home to phone the Embassy duty officer mobile phone if the alarm went off. There was a spooky recorded message of Alek saying 'emergency at Radiani Street'. I wiped the message.

'Who is your deputy at the British Council for things like this?' asked Mike.

'Zaza, and he would have been round there like a shot to sort it out, had he been in Tbilisi.'

I agreed I would never again take all the management team away at the same time. 'You need SOPS,' said Mike, 'Standard operating procedures.' I had never heard of SOPs but they sounded like a good thing. Another thing to add to the list of things to do or improve. Every time I thought I had got things sorted, something else cropped up.

I did say to Mike, though, that I didn't think the duty officer should be out partying if they were 'on duty'. Mike said, 'Er, yes, you have a point, but I was totally in control and within range at all times.' He had seemed to be, to be fair.

26

New house

Autumn 2002, Tbilisi

'What wonderful books you have,' said Maia appreciatively, pulling out book after book from the cardboard boxes I had stuffed full in the days before.

'It is not time or opportunity that is to determine intimacy; it is disposition alone. Seven years would be insufficient to make some people acquainted with each other, and seven days are more than enough for others,' said Maia.

'Jane Austen. Er, er *Sense and Sensibility*?' I ventured.

'Correct,' she said, laughing at me.

Zaza had found a smaller house for me. All round it was a good move. He had negotiated cheaper rent than the previous apartment – and, as it was on the same street as our ambassador's new residence, it was safer, in the eventuality that things in the city deteriorated.

Maia came to help me unpack my collection of books and kitchen things and it was a fun diversion to laugh over books. Maia knew all the classic English (and other) authors and could quote far more lines than I could ever attempt.

I loved this new, less ostentatious house. It was built into the hillside and was perched prettily over the city below and it had a view to gaze out into. It had ethereal, daintily fragrant, pink roses in the little garden, which cascaded down below the house, and there was an uneven terrace to sit out on.

My favourite room was my bedroom. It had a generous view of the valley and had its own balcony. From the unshuttered bedroom windows I could see Tbilisi laid out before me. Churches, impressive neo-classical buildings,

blocks of flats and the mountains beyond. The bedroom was furnished with elegant antiques – a wardrobe and dressing table with inlaid woods and a curvy matching bed fit for a princess. I put a red velvet cover on

Figure 12 View of Tbilisi

the bed and red rugs on the floor and hung silver jewellery from Egypt on the walls.

I felt I might wake up happy in this room.

The living room had a large fireplace, over which an ancient Egyptian mural had been painted by my landlord. While it was an accomplished piece, I would have preferred something Georgian, or at least more neutral. 'I'm not sure about the mural,' I said to Maia. 'Is there somewhere I could buy something to cover it without damaging it?'

'I know just the place,' she said, and took me to 'La Maison Bleue'. This was a women's co-operative and many of the women there needed income to support their families. They had a workshop on an open-terraced balcony overlooking trees and a courtyard. Lots of tables were placed around the balcony and women were laying out and making their artwork. The walls of the shop were covered in silk paintings and the trestle tables were laden with painted silk cushion covers, bags and scarves. Endless, utterly exquisite artwork – some were impressionist and pastel, some bold and geometric, some of animals, some dusted with gold paint. I commissioned two large panels in reds, oranges, greens and golds of a scene of houses, balconies and trees arrayed down a Tbilisi valley.

When they were ready, Vakho – driver and handyman too – put them up. They transformed the living room.

The next day my landlord died of a heart attack. I was distraught. I said to Zaza, 'I feel so bad, I covered up his painting! I feel I must do something. Is it appropriate for me to visit his widow or show my respects in some way?' I wasn't going to refer to the painting. Zaza said he was sure his widow would appreciate it.

Before entering her house I whispered to Zaza, 'Please advise me what is appropriate to do after I express my condolences to Madame Nino.'

I have terrible hearing and as we entered the room I thought I heard Zaza say, 'Turn around near the body.' Laid out in the middle of the room, surrounded by scented flowers, was the body of my former landlord. Around the periphery of the room were many mourners, including the widow and her immediate family. I took Madame Nino's hands and kissed her and said how sorry I was. I hesitated – I wasn't sure what turning around meant. On the spot?

Flushing with relief, I followed another mourner who walked, slowly, around the coffin.

#

A few nights after moving in I lay awake looking at the few, generator-powered, lights in the dark valley below. I could see the silhouette of the distant mountains and the stars in the inky night. I still had no curtains but after the shuttered enclosure of my previous house this was blissful. The plumbing was odd, lots of clunks and shudders, probably because of all the water cuts, but I could live with that.

I woke to a spectacular red dawn and geared up for another full week. A friend from primary school days, Deema, was coming to visit. She was an anthropologist with a specialisation on post-Soviet rural communities and the author of *The Post-Soviet Peasant*. She had not been to Georgia and she planned to do some field research while I was at work. Before she arrived she had emailed me to ask about, 'The disestablishment of socialist co-operatives and whether there was any resistance?'

I had to confess this wasn't something I knew anything about – but I knew people who knew people who would (hopefully) know and I introduced her as best I could. I did have a day off though and we went to the beautiful and remote church in the Ananuri Fortress complex. When we got there, we could smell incense before we entered and, stepping into the dark, mystical cavern of the church, we were pleased to see a wedding in progress. We covered our hair and watched quietly from the periphery. Most of the church was dark but a beam of sunlight lit up the bridal couple and the priest. The groom was dark-suited and the raven-black hair of the lovely bride contrasted sharply with her dazzlingly white dress. Friends carried golden crowns above their heads and the bride had a veil draped over her elegantly coiffured hair. The bridal couple and their two witnesses carried candles and, with heads bowed, walked slowly together three times in a circular procession around the altar while the priest intoned the words of blessing. They were surrounded by family and friends and were serenaded by a choir of men whose powerful singing expanded into the church and up into the cupola above.

#

Having shown Deema a glimpse into Georgian culture, back in Tbilisi we were busy preparing to share some high-calibre British culture with our Georgian contacts – in the person of a famous British jazz musician. Our Arts Manager, Eka, was shortly leaving Georgia to follow her husband who had a scholarship in Germany. She had promised to stay until after the jazz performance and she was working flat out to make sure it all went smoothly. We had chosen the Conservatoire, usually rather traditionalist, as the venue for the single performance for an audience of 500 or so. Everything that needed to be in place apparently was but there was always a certain amount of anxiety before any high-profile event like this. Would the venue work? Would the performers arrive OK? Would they agree to stay under our wing and accept they couldn't go wandering off on their own? Would their equipment be cleared intact by the notoriously demanding and corrupt customs officials?

Eka and I went to the airport to meet our VIP visitors, keeping our fingers crossed that it would all go well. The band and support team turned out to be charm itself and said how cool it was to be in Georgia. I said to our guests, expansively, 'If there is anything you need we will do our best to help.'

One of the support team took me on one side. He asked quietly, and hopefully, 'Where are the women?'

#

The next afternoon we set up a press conference at the Metekhi Palace Hotel, where the performers were staying. We were growing in confidence with our event management and examples of British Council work had started to appear in the media – I felt we were at the point where we could be more proactive.

We arranged our room – press packs on each chair and a top table laid out in front for the lead musician, the head of the Conservatoire and me to answer questions from the journalists. Eka and I nervously said to each other, 'But what if no-one turns up?'

'I know – the British Council still isn't well enough known.' We waited.

We needn't have worried. Within minutes of the appointed time, the room was full of newspaper and radio journalists and photographers – it felt as though every TV camera crew in the city had turned up. They fiddled with their cameras and recording devices, or rustled notebooks in anticipation and chatted with some excitement amongst themselves about this famous foreign visitor. But the visitor kept us waiting. After a few minutes I made faces over the heads of the journalists at Eka at the back of the room – who, in turn, was looking nervously into the foyer of the hotel. 'Where is he?' I mouthed.

I left my chair and as we walked out of the room we bumped into the key performer himself. He was holding a video camera in front of his face. I smiled brightly into the camera, trying to look behind it to make eye contact but he held firm and continued to hold the camera. I gestured to him to follow me and I hoped he would put it down – but no! He took his seat, still holding the camera, filming the crews filming him. Why? Why? I introduced him to the press and said how pleased the British Council was to be hosting the visit of this popular and talented performer and so on. He answered all the questions put to him good-humouredly enough – from behind his camera. I imagine he had just had too much press attention and this 'turning the camera on the cameras' was making some sort of point.

He did do some masterclasses with young musicians, however, that went down a storm, and that evening at the conservatoire the musicians almost blew the roof off.

It was utterly brilliant. Almost everyone in the room including Deborah, our Ambassador, was on their feet dancing along in front of their seats. Eka shouted, 'The Conservatoire has never seen an evening like it!'

#

We barely had time to wave them goodbye before the next big event. Lord John McCluskey, the then Chairman of the Trustees of the John Smith Memorial Trust, was visiting Tbilisi that week in connection with the scholarship scheme. When I had heard of his visit some weeks earlier, I had suggested to colleagues at the British Embassy that we could aim to launch our new alumni association in my new house, if he was happy to be the VIP speaker.

'Has the Lord arrived?' asked Anka, as we hovered in my hallway getting ready to greet the guests. I had a vision of Lord McCluskey descending with a halo into my living room. And the Lord did indeed arrive, more prosaically, by Landrover with Deborah.

As well as our VIP speakers and colleagues from the Embassy we had political analysts and visiting British academics. But the most important guests were the alumni themselves from the John Smith and Chevening schemes – we had commercial lawyers, human rights lawyers, young business people, journalists, future diplomats and hopefully future politicians. People we believed would shape a better future for Georgia, committed and clever, and who would, we hoped, always retain a loyalty and affection for the UK.

We launched the Alumni Association, now a legal entity in its own right, with rousing speeches and encouraging words on the importance of learning and networking and on how important were the processes necessary for a functioning democracy and effective rule of law.

After the speeches and a series of photographs to mark the event, guests chatted. 'Did you hear that the Georgian military have successfully cleared the Chechen rebels and foreign jihadists from the Pankisi?' In response to considerable US and Russian pressure to bring order back to the Pankisi Gorge, the Georgians had mounted a successful military operation – they had been able to raise the Georgian flag there, which was promising. Apart from the broader objectives to bring crime and terrorism under control and to try to provide some form of humanitarian assistance to people in Pankisi, it was also hoped that kidnap victims, such as Peter Shaw (the consultant who had been working on an EC contract) would be rescued.

'Apparently the kidnappers asked his family for $2million.'

'They won't get it.' Maybe because he was a foreign banker it was assumed he or his family would personally have that sum of money – which was unlikely. And it is the British Government's policy (and that of the European Commission), not to pay ransoms – it could encourage even more kidnaps.

27

Crying on planes

October 2002, Manchester

I closed the door for the last time on my Manchester house of some ten years. The house had been let to tenants and was in a rough state – it was a relief that, after some inevitable blips, I had managed to sell it. Many of our pieces of furniture had been slowly eaten by woodworm and looked shabby and unloved and there wasn't much left to worry about. Alek and I could divide up our assets. I had some money in the bank now but no base, no home. Apart from in Georgia.

I flew down from Manchester to Heathrow where I was meeting some friends, Simon and Christine (both British Council colleagues), before we flew on to Tbilisi together. They were coming to stay on holiday for a week. I warned them I might not be great company. 'Don't worry, Jo, we'll cheer you up,' said Christine.

#

On the flight, Simon and Christine ate food from trays, swigged back whatever beverages were offered and watched films. I slumped in my seat next to them and wallowed in

175

my unhappiness. I was hopeless at love and had sold all my furniture. I cried. Through almost the entire flight.

#

Christine was right though, they did cheer me up. I didn't need to worry about them during the day as Simon was a fluent Russian speaker and they could go off and see the sights and keep a low profile without incident.

It was a hectic week for me at work. Amongst other things I was hosting a visit by a high-profile photographer, so to kill two birds with one stone I took him and my friends out together. It was a busy night and we all squeezed on to a bench on the creaky open air balcony at Sans Souci, an arty restaurant next to the marionette museum. The restaurant had colourful, naive art painted on the tables, walls and doors. Thoughtfully, next to the door of the WC was an identical miniature door with 'WC' painted on it for the puppets. I did my best to explain Georgian cuisine to my guests – they needed no introduction to Georgian wine. Mike from the Embassy was in the restaurant that night with my friend Maia K – he came over and introduced himself to my guests. He never seemed to be on his own, I noticed, he always had a pretty woman along too.

Eka left for Germany that week; we had a little party in the office with honey cakes and toasted her with light, sparkling wine to wish her well.

We also had some colleagues visiting from the London British Council office in connection with the premises project and a regional meeting of colleagues from Azerbaijan and Armenia to review the Peace Keeping English Project. Alongside this the country directors and office managers from the three South Caucasus countries were meeting to discuss management issues – in all we had a dozen work visitors staying in Tbilisi for two days. I asked my colleagues in the Tbilisi PEP office what we should do with them for the second evening – something different, not just a meal and pack them back to their hotels.

'I know,' said Eka. 'What about tenpin bowling?'

I was amazed. 'I can't believe there is ten-pin bowling here, what about the power cuts?'

'It never seems to have cuts,' said Lela. It was probably dodgy, maybe owned by a gangster money-launderer – but frankly, why not, for a change, let our hair down?

Along with my friends, the lawyer and premises adviser from London, my colleagues from Baku and Yerevan and all the Tbilisi PEP team, we went tenpin bowling. As I have mentioned Armenia and Azerbaijan are still technically at war. The PEP review was as much a teambuilding event as anything else, to help colleagues learn from and support each other. We split up all the groups so that the competing teams each had least one Azerbaijani, Armenian, Georgian and British person on each team. We brought bottles of Georgian wine for each team, to get the party in the mood. We had a cheerfully raucous evening.

#

Zaza and I, and our British Council premises project visitors, had also been invited to dinner by the Georgian landlady of the new office. It was one of those 'work hard, play hard' sorts of weeks. With typical Georgian hospitality when she heard I had friends staying the landlady urged me to bring them too.

Our landlady-to-be had her *supra* feast in her apartment, which she would shortly be vacating for building work to begin, as this would become the new British Council office. It was hard to imagine but the dining room – a traditional room with high ceiling and extravagant chandeliered light fittings and the usual elaborately carved dark wood furniture – would be transformed into a spankingly modern library. I had warned Christine and Simon to wear loose clothing. Sure enough it was a lavish and delicious meal with course after course after course, punctuated regularly with toast after toast and the raising of many glasses of Georgian wine.

'To our long and mutual friendship!'

'To the beautiful women!'

'To your families' health, wealth and happiness.'

'To your Queen!'

The toasts were deeply felt and lovingly shared and I had learnt, more or less, how to reply appropriately. I loved this custom and in fact had begun to find it odd when not in Georgia when people would sit down to dinner with friends and guests and just raise a glass and say 'cheers' or 'good health' or just tuck in to their meal without marking the moment with some shared compliments, good wishes, or some thoughts about the state of the world.

The lead builder, whom we were contracting to undertake much of the work, was at the dinner and he too made expansive, eloquent toasts. Leaping to his feet, with his glass raised, he finished with a flamboyant,

'To Stalin!'

Simon and Christine sat open-mouthed, flashing questioning looks at me. But I knew a good, diplomatic reply and replied,

'To a big man!'

#

Later that month I flew back to Tbilisi from a meeting in London. I was in the phase of walking and talking and working, of eating a little – but not much. Of going to sleep at night and getting up in the morning but not feeling like I was connected to anything. Or anyone.

It was a quiet overnight flight. I said hello briefly to the man in the seat next to me but neither of us wanted to talk and we flew on in silence and darkness. A few hours later I dropped my book and the man next to me jumped.

'Sorry!' He handed me the book and we ended up making small talk. I told him about my job, he about his and we expressed polite interest. He mentioned that his wife had died a few months beforehand. I burst into tears and said, 'I'm so sorry.'

He held my hand and said, 'Yes, it has been a terrible time. I have felt like I was underwater. Please don't be distressed.' I told him I had gone through a traumatic divorce and didn't know where I belonged. 'How sad!' he said, and kissed me.

Although we exchanged business cards – how prosaic – we did not see each other again. He lived in Texas.

I have got to stop sobbing on planes.

28

The man from the Embassy

November 2002, Tbilisi

Following Eka's departure I needed to rearrange the staffing structure of the office and had decided we could extend our office opening hours to six days a week. The library was as much in demand as ever and giving greater access to our books and materials was an important part of our offer. We recruited Irakli as our new Arts Manager and two new receptionists, Maka and Nutsa. As with other members of the team, they were lively, enthusiastic and full of ideas.

Rusiko also joined the team as our new English Language Adviser, taking over from Barrie. Technically he had retired but he continued to work with us on a local contract. Rusiko was pushing ahead with the English language projects, including our plan to open new English Teachers' Association of Georgia (ETAG) offices in a further five cities over the coming year. She was a highly experienced English language teaching professional, in fact one of ETAG's leading lights – another star. She had gravitas and energy and moreover was affectionate and funny.

Shortly after Rusiko arrived she and I had to go to the Ministry of Education to discuss our English language textbook project. Rusiko set up the meeting with the

Minister, Alexander Kartozia. She told me he had asked to have the meeting after dark, at 8pm that evening. There were ongoing anti-corruption demonstrations by students every day around the Ministry. 'I think he is anxious that the students will confront him, so he is going to his office very early and leaving very late.' It sounded as though the Minister felt he was trapped by his work.

That evening Vakho took us to the Ministry. On the way I asked Rusiko if she thought the Minister was a crook or a gangster, as many ministers apparently were. I just couldn't see it myself; he seemed so quiet and academic.

'I don't think he is crooked. I think he might just be ineffectual. Even if he passionately wanted to push through the essential reforms we need to improve our education system, the whole system of governance here is faulty. He can't sort things out unless many, many other things change too. Yes, he is very academic – he used to be a professor of German; he used to be Eka and Nata's teacher.'

Everyone seemed to know everyone in Tbilisi – maybe that was one of the problems in confronting the challenges. Relationships maybe mattered more than rules.

We went through a side door of the Ministry building and realised, unsurprisingly, that there were no lights. As there was no electricity. All staff bar the Minister – in a distant room along a series of pitch-black corridors, up some shrouded marble staircases somewhere – had gone home. We had no-one to ask where to go. Rusiko and I started to laugh in the darkness at the absurdity of it.

'This is ridiculous – but I have a torch!' I said.

'I have Kartozia's number,' said Rusiko and she phoned him to find out how we could find him in the unfamiliar, dark offices. She and I linked arms and made slow progress in the tomb-like Ministry building, shining the little beam of torchlight on the floor so we wouldn't fall over, then up at the doors to try to work out where we were and so on. Rusiko phoned the Minister periodically until, eventually, we found his office.

The Minister had lit candles in his office and we had an almost Dickensian meeting, discussing textbooks into the night. When we came to leave he escorted us down to the side door and, after making sure we were safely collected, he turned to go back to his office.

He seemed a lonely figure in the dark building.

#

I had a new boss, Chris, who phoned me from London to introduce himself and to check how things were in Georgia and in our office.

'It isn't boring here.' I told him we had been relieved when Peter Shaw, the kidnap victim who had been taken in June, had escaped his captors. He had had a dreadful ordeal. He had been chained in a pit for months but was now back safely in Wales. I knew my colleagues at the British Embassy had been working flat out to support him.

'Keep safe,' said Chris. 'Are things OK for me to visit, after you get into your new office?'

Assuming all the building works went ahead as planned we hoped to have moved by early February. I was relieved Chris wasn't planning to visit us sooner than that. Although I wanted him to see for himself the impact of the work we were doing, in both the longstanding projects and also the new activities we were launching, we had a tight timeline between November and February to get the new office renovated, decorated and kitted out – every week counted.

I had gone over with Zaza to see the gutted rooms that would become our new office: two floors in a building in a terrace of grand houses on the elegant, tree-lined Rustaveli Avenue, one of the most centrally located streets in the city. The bottom floor of the building was around a pretty, vine-draped courtyard occupied by, amongst others, Prospero's Bookshop, Georgia's only English language bookshop. It was a fantastic location.

Zaza was working round the clock, zipping backwards and forwards between the old and the new offices to manage this project on time and within budget, and to UK regulations and standards. It was a big ask – but if anyone could achieve it, Zaza could. We even had hard hats while we walked around the skeletal shell of an office with Levan, the architect, and Giorgi, the master builder. We discussed the floor plans, the spreadsheets, the timelines – and tried to imagine what it would look like. 'This is where the generator will go,' said Zaza. One of our biggest items of expenditure was for a proper, self-starting generator. It was all finally taking shape and we couldn't wait.

#

The building project had been going a few weeks when one morning I had a phone call from a weak-sounding Zaza. 'I'm sorry, Jo, I can't make it to the office.'

'Please don't worry, what's wrong?'

'I had an operation for a hernia yesterday. I'm in hospital!'

'Zaza!'

Vakho and I sped off to the hospital. The hospital looked trashed and the lifts to the wards weren't working. They probably hadn't been mended since before the civil war a decade earlier. Vakho and I walked up flight after flight of cracked concrete stairs. I almost skidded into a gaping hole between two steps. Far out. Vakho jumped up over the missing step, lent down and pulled me up after him. In the gaping hole of the cracked step I could see the distant stairs of the floor below.

In the ward, Zaza was lying in bed, looking pale and as thin as a pin, hardly creating a wrinkle in the bedclothes. 'Poor you – how dreadful – is there anything at all I can do?'

'I'd love a cigarette,' he said. I laughed indulgently. 'No truly,' said Zaza. 'They say I shouldn't stop, as if I cough I might rupture my stitches. I was out dancing last night and I had a hernia, so painful you cannot imagine. I will be in hospital for a week and will need to recuperate slowly.'

I told him not to worry and that we would cope. I knew it would be a struggle, though, as Zaza was such an irreplaceable member of the team and in any case the office was frenetic on a number of fronts – but these things happen and there is always a way round.

'I have already been thinking, as long as I can have a laptop and use my phone, I can direct operations on the premises project from here.'

'Are you sure? I don't want to tire you.'

'Jo, I have a busy brain – and I love my job. I love the British Council. I can't do nothing at this crucial time.' He was director of operations from his sickbed, liaising with the architect, the builders, colleagues in London, suppliers from Turkey – he kept the show on the road. What a star.

#

One Friday afternoon late in November, after a particularly fraught day, Mike, the man from the Embassy, phoned and asked if I was going to the Swiss Embassy event that night at the Karvasala Gallery. I slumped in my chair, grimacing into the phone. I truly did not want to go. It was Friday and I was drained. I wanted to be alone, as they say.

I looked at the invitation card:

The Ambassador of Switzerland invites:
(a space with my name on it)
To the inauguration of the new premises of the Caucasian Institute of Photography and New Media at the Karvasala Gallery

Dammit. If someone from the Embassy was going, it wouldn't look great if the head of the British Council – responsible as I was for all things cultural – knew about it and didn't go. I also had a new colleague, Irakli, our new Arts Manager and it would be an opportunity to introduce him to his equivalents in other foreign missions.

Home?

Or, give it a go, why not? Maybe it might be 'good for me' to get out tonight.

I gave Vakho a new brief to take me there from the office.

Mike was there in the Karvasala Gallery and under his big Georgian-looking black leather coat he was wearing that terrible houndstooth jacket he had been wearing when I had first met him in the Embassy six months earlier. He was with a friend, Andy, from the OSCE, the European security, conflict and monitoring NGO.

The Karvasala Gallery was housed in a beautiful building, a former caravanserai, where traders and camels travelling along the Silk Route in times gone past would put up for a night or two. It was freezing in the gallery – we could see our breath. As it turned out, we were part of the exhibition – wires suspended high above us had tiny cameras and the huddled group of guests were projected on to a huge screen. This was installation art, new and popular with young and young-at-heart Georgians.

The Georgian NGO which the Swiss Embassy was partnering was called *media art farm* – trendily, all lower caps – and was headed up by Wato Tsereteli. It was evidently an on trend organisation. Irakli and I agreed he should hook up with Wato as a useful new contact.

Mike's friend, Andy, asked him if he wanted to join him and his girlfriend for a meal after leaving the exhibition. Mike hesitated. He turned to me and asked if I would like to come too. He obviously didn't want to be a spare part with Andy and his ladyfriend. I hesitated.

'Yes, that would be nice,' I said, smiling at them both.

Csabas Hungarian jazz restaurant was a dark, smoky haunt, with folky ornaments artily displayed and with jazz rippling through the various rooms. We ordered red wine and spicy goulash, the speciality of the house. Andy went off to collect his girlfriend, Eka. 'Won't be long,' he said, leaving Mike and me chatting politely.

'How did you come to rock up here in Tbilisi?' asked Mike and I told him I was ashamed to admit I hadn't even known where Georgia was. I had applied to come because the job sounded enticing and challenging.

'How about you? How did you end up here?'

'I took Russian at A level back in the 70s. We studied *A Hero of Our Time,* the great 19th century novel by Lermontov, in the original text. The first line was 'I was travelling post from Tiflis...' I got caught up in the novel. It was all about adventure, amorous liaisons, danger, duels, 'passion and possibility',' said Mike, looking at me intently. 'I had to find out where Tiflis was. I joined the Foreign Office and would have loved a posting to the Soviet Union but it would have been to Moscow. It wasn't that easy to get down to the Caucasus. I was posted to Indonesia instead.'

'I had a short posting in Jakarta in the early 90s!' We compared notes on all the places we knew there. By the time Andy came back, Mike and I were deeply engrossed in conversation and started up when he and Eka sat down.

'Sorry to interrupt,' said Andy, looking at each of us with interest as the waitress delivered steaming, piquant goulash in a bowl swinging on brass chains.

When we left the restaurant later Andy and Eka said goodnight and Mike offered to give me a lift home. In the car he asked, 'Have you been to the Izida Club?'

The Izida nightclub was a small, Middle Eastern-themed club with shisha pipes, mosaic tiles and cords of fairy lights adorning the walls. We were both still wearing our decidedly non-nightclubby work clothes – in my case a brown, woollen skirt and a work top and Mike was wearing that terrible jacket. I was in my late 30s and Mike in his mid-40s and as such we were the oldest people on the dancefloor by at least a decade and we were the only foreigners there. Everyone else was 20-something, petite, chic, beautiful, almost all wearing black and smoking their heads off.

'I feel like we're in a film here in Tbilisi,' I said.

'So do I!' said Mike. 'What film? I think we're in *Casablanca*.'

'No, we're in *Dr Zhivago*!' I shouted, laughing above the music.

When Mike and I weren't dancing we were chatting and laughing and then dancing some more. The music was phenomenally good, that bass-heavy 'Buddha Bar' type stuff. One track, I later found out, was 'Ja Vida' by Christophe Goze. With its sinuous flutes and rhythmic drums it still brings back the excitement of dancing till dawn in the Izida Club in Tbilisi.

#

Later:

'What a terrible mess! It's all so complicated.'

'It's only complicated if we fall in love,' he said looking down at me.

'We won't do that,' I said quickly.

'No,' he agreed. 'I'm a bit of a bastard.'

'And I'm an ice-maiden...'

29

Roses and champagnski

'Champagnski – and it's *Brut*. I had to look all over town.'
Mike turned up smiling at my door with a bunch of red roses
and two bottles of sparkling wine. At that time only
foreigners liked dry sparkling wine – most Georgians
preferred their bubbles sweet. I was delighted with the roses,
velvety and deeply scented. 'But you do know that flower
imports are run by gangsters?' I hadn't known that. 'I'm not
really a bastard…are you an ice maiden?'

'I don't know. Maybe…'

We agreed that we would be tentative about our delicate
new relationship and, more importantly, given the intense
little society in which we worked, that we would keep things
quiet. If things didn't work out between us, it could be
embarrassing, personally and professionally.

In fact, the guards on both our houses knew all about our
comings and goings. Guards on all British – and other –
Embassy households had to record details of every visitor in
large notebooks and send the returns off somewhere.
Undoubtedly there was someone in the Ministry of the
Interior whose job it was to analyse the returns and who also
knew, therefore, that we were 'stepping out'.

#

Mike and I had to meet at the Embassy weekly meeting and I completely ignored him. My heart was beating ridiculously hard and my Embassy security pass was bouncing off my chest. After the meeting I went down the corridor to brief Maia about a work event. I also told her a few significant facts about my evening with Mike. There was keeping quiet and keeping quiet.

'Jo, be cautious, you know he's a married man. His family is coming out at Easter.' I knew he was married but thought he and his wife were estranged and I didn't know the latter. I certainly didn't want to be a home-breaker. I thanked her for telling me. I must keep up this ice maiden façade and not get more involved.

As I walked back down the corridor Mike appeared from nowhere and said, 'Jo, would you like to go to Bakuriani with me?' I knew it was in the mountains somewhere, some way from Tbilisi. 'For a weekend away in the mountains?' he said encouragingly.

Without thinking I said, 'I'd love to.' Grrr. He was so persuasive.

#

Mike and I had both been invited to a reception hosted by the Georgian Ministry of Foreign Affairs. As we were keeping things quiet, we arrived separately and each joined the throng of guests. Waiting staff circulated and served small pieces of Georgian bread topped with salty butter and caviar and other treats, and proffered trays of Georgian wine and champagne.

It was a full room, humming with diplomatic chatter. I could see Mike out of the corner of my eye on the other side of the room. Strangely, although I was giving my full attention to whoever I was conversing with, it felt that Mike was the only interesting person in the room. Stranger still, I could sense that he was moving closer and closer to where I was until we caught each other's eye with a frisson of secret recognition and briefly said hello.

We turned together to face the front as the speeches were about to start. We knew we were in for a lengthy session. There were six Ministry of Foreign Affairs speechmakers, plus an interpreter, lined up in front of the microphones at the front of the hall. The room fell silent as the first speaker was introduced. His speech was delivered and interpreted. It was an expansive and enthusiastic delivery about the significance to Georgia of warm and constructive diplomatic relations between Georgia and other countries and so on and so on. We in the audience nodded appreciatively and in due course raised our glasses or clapped when the speech finished.

The second speaker started and her words were also interpreted; it sounded similar to the first speech, if truth be told, but we all murmured respectfully when she finished. The third speaker started and – when it became clear that it was pretty much the same speech again – audience focus started to drift and the guests, particularly at the back of the room, began to talk and laugh amongst themselves. By the time the later speakers were on even the first speech givers, who were still at the line-up at the front of the room, had lit cigarettes and had turned to each other for gentle chit-chat, nodding and shrugging about some hot topic.

Mike and I felt it only fair to look dutifully interested until the last speaker had said her bit and then I turned to him and said, 'I love Georgia, don't you?'

'I do. But I love you more,' said Mike. 'Shall we go?'

And off we went.

30

Snow and dancing

Mike picked me up for our weekend away, checking before we set off that I had appropriate clothes for our mountain adventures. It was years since I had gone walking in mountains.

'I have essential supplies,' he said, pulling open a bag with two bottles of sparkling wine and a bottle of Georgian Brandy.

We set off, holding hands in the car and whooping as Mike drove down the hilly cobbled streets of Tbilisi. It was

Figure 13 House in Bakuriani

about five hours drive on misty, mountainous roads, climbing up higher and higher. And then there we were in Bakuriani, a sprawling little village of wooden chalets with broad balconies adorned with lacework carvings, surrounded by mountain tops covered in snow.

192

'*Dr Zhivago!*'

We pulled up outside the Hotel Appolon, a large log cabin of a hotel. It had been recommended to Mike by one of his colleagues at the Embassy who knew all the good places. He had referred to it as 'Otar's Place' and sure enough Otar came out to greet us and help with the bags. As we went in, Otar said something in Russian to Mike and Mike said something back. Mike whispered to me, 'Otar just said, 'your wife is beautiful' and I told him, 'I think so too'.'

'I'm sure she is,' I said. Wife or not, I was very flattered. It had transpired it was Mike's daughters who were coming out at Easter, not his amicably estranged wife.

'I don't want to be a problem in your life,' I said.

'You aren't.'

Over a welcome glass of tart *dmashni vino* – homemade wine in Russian – Otar told us Bakuriani had once been a significant ski centre in Soviet times, for lessons and training. He himself and many of his friends had been skiing champions in Soviet times. 'But times are hard. Few tourists come now.'

'We will try to help spread the word to other foreigners. It is stunning here.'

Our room was cosy and spotless, with embroidered starched linen sheets, thick duvets and wool blankets on the bed. A row of icicles half a metre long hung like sparkling daggers from the roof overhanging the balcony outside our room.

We ventured out into the fluffy deep snow, laughing and wolfing in the clear, clean air. My shoes were woefully inadequate. I was more of a café, coffee and high-heeled boots sort of person, rather than an outdoorsy type, which Mike clearly was. Mike helpfully told me how to walk uphill in the snow – he could be quite bossy – but he fell over and skidded down the hillside, to my concern and delight. I took a cautious approach and shuffled up slowly and carefully and reached the top without skidding back down – must get some proper walking boots, though.

That evening we took our place in the dining room, nodding a greeting to the only other couple at a nearby table, evidently foreigners too. The dining room was the full height of the building and was lined with pine logs. The stairs were pine and upstairs there was a pine-lined living room with a large fireplace. We tucked in to tasty, herby soup, stew thick with vegetables, homemade bread and butter, then tangy fruit with velvety homemade cream.

As we were finishing Mike turned to the other couple and made some pleasantries – in Dutch! As a ploy to impress me, this worked. Mike evidently spoke French, Dutch, Russian and Bahasa Indonesian quite well.

Later that evening we sat in front of a blazing log fire in the living room of Otar's Place, chatting to the Dutch couple about Georgian politics and about how corrupt and chaotic it all seemed to be. Mike had his arm around me as he chortled and chatted and shared our Brandy.

I'm happy. I'm so happy.

#

After the exhilaration of our weekend away I felt I should offer Mike a return date. I had been such a work-hermit though – I thought I didn't have much to offer in the way of fun things to do. I briefly thought of tenpin bowling.

'Would you like to come to Armenia with me?' I asked him.

'I'd love to!' What professional traveller turns down the opportunity to go to a new country?

#

So off we went for another trip across the Lesser Caucasus. I introduced Mike to Vakho and they chatted away in Russian in the front of the car. On the outskirts of Tbilisi we passed decrepit tower blocks, dull grey silhouettes against the snow. We saw elderly women swaddled in black coats and headscarves struggling with rickety buckets, heading towards the entrance of one of the blocks.

'They don't have water in their apartments. They have to get water from standpipes and carry it up maybe ten flights of stairs,' said Vakho. 'Sometimes people have to crack ice to get water – or they have to carry up blocks of ice and try to melt them. Some people have to chop up their furniture for firewood.'

No poverty is good. But cold, urban poverty seems especially harsh.

We crossed the border into Armenia and pulled up at the little comfort-stop that Vakho always frequented. We settled down in the dark and steamy café, along with Armenian and Iranian truck-drivers. 'Would you like coffee? Instant or ...?' asked Vakho.

'Armenian!' I said, before Mike could say Turkish.

It was a clear sunny day. Back on the road we were swept away, looking ahead into the broad expanse of shining snow laid out before us, with the volcanic peak of Mount Aragats rising majestically from the white horizon.

'Spectacular. It's colder than a witch's tit up here,' said Mike emphatically. An unusual expression. Mike had a big personality: confident, funny and openhearted. He was hardworking and organised – a planner and a strategist! He had a strong sense of duty and fairplay. And a liking for similar things to me – anything quirky, unusual or bizarre and a big taste for adventure.

And he was in love with me.

And, of course, I was falling in love with him. I had that crazy, fizzy feeling underpinned with a measure of dread that, inevitably, this heady, effervescent phase will wear off and maybe all that will be left will be the dead shell of a firework...But at the time I was too hooked, too drugged up with excitement and I had the sense that my life would be a duller, greyer, less happy place without him.

'I feel I am at home but on holiday when I am with you,' I told him.

'I'm scared to my bones,' he said.

#

Back at our claustrophobic little office in Tbilisi I turned to my colleague, Katie. 'I think I am falling in love.' She looked startled. 'With Mike. You know, that man from the British Embassy.'

Mike meanwhile asked to see Deborah, the Ambassador, on a private matter. He told her we were 'stepping out'. She was amused. 'You don't need my permission you know.'

'I know – but I didn't want you to hear via gossip.'

'Let me know if you need me to marry you both, like a captain on a ship.'

It probably was a bit like an onboard romance.

#

It was an unusually cold winter and much of Tbilisi was frozen with deep snow and ice, compacted up against the old buildings. We went out one night in the old town with some British Embassy friends and a newly arrived colleague. We took them to a restaurant which looked like an old Russian living room. Bizarrely, to get into the restaurant we had to cross a little stream under glass – with goldfish swimming in it – within the building itself.

'What a weird place Tbilisi seems to be,' said the new person. 'I love the quirkiness of it all. It's a bit of a fairytale city.'

'It's very compelling.' I had been there almost two years and felt I was an old hand.

'I keep expecting to see a snow queen or talking beavers.'

'Beavers?' asked Mike with interest.

Outside was an old-fashioned and dimly lit lamppost and, as we left, snow was falling silently around it. Our little group made slow progress as ice had frozen on top of the snowy street. I fell over with a thud. I was as helpless as a tortoise on its back. 'Don't let Mike see me,' I gasped to one of my Embassy friends as she hauled me up. How foolish I looked – ice maidens surely know how to glide over ice, not flail around on it.

Later Mike and I went back to his house which was located near the top of a steep road. Even with his powerful 4-wheel-drive car, he could not get up the ungritted, sheet-ice covered cobbled street. He had to park in a side street, halfway up. We were still wearing work shoes with shiny soles. Totally unsuitable footwear.

I need not have worried about looking foolish falling over. As we tried to walk up Mike fell flat on his face. I helped him up and fell over backwards myself. He helped me up and fell over backwards and we rolled around laughing on the snowy street. Mike's guards were about 100 metres up the hill and were watching our antics with interest – they shouted, could they help? But we ended up crawling up on hands and knees. Crazy English people.

'You are a girl version of me!'

'Never a dull moment!'

'I love you! Let's go skiing!'
Oh dear.

#

I had never been skiing before – but in all the excitement of being newly in love I was easily persuaded that I, even clumsy me, could do anything. 'But I have nothing to wear – and no skis!' I moaned.

'No problem, darling, we will find you things.' Mike borrowed some ancient-looking skis for me. He also lent me a tatty ski jacket with pink and purple triangles on it at which, I'm afraid, I inwardly cringed. I was still doubtful.

'But what about trousers?'

'Aha, I have some waterproof trousers.' He produced some pull-on 'over-trousers' in military green. I did now have my own decent pair of walking boots and endless combinations of hats, gloves and scarves. Mike, naturally enough, had his own outfit.

With our kit, off we went to Gudauri, a ski resort several hours' drive north of Tbilisi. Although much of Georgia was decaying, this resort had been reasonably well maintained and was accessible for those who could afford it. We were meeting friends of Mike's, Kevin and his Georgian girlfriend, Maka. Kevin looked tall and manly, if a little grey on top, in a grey ski suit. Maka, with cheekbones like swan's wings and as slinky as a mongoose, was dressed in scarlet and Mike, with his dark good looks, was dressed in a black ski suit. They all looked the business and they could all ski. Off they went to swerve and swoop along the icy runs, far, far above where I was, on the beginners' slope.

My skiing instructor, Laka, took a look at my attire – the old skis, the faded, elderly jacket and the green over-trousers and asked, 'How long have we got?'

'An hour.' We were both wondering what could possibly be accomplished in an hour. I swished towards him. These trousers were terrible.

Laka was extremely patient and explained about how to stand, how to go, how to stop and how not to fall over and we did the same procedures over and over again. I was hugely proud of myself that I didn't fall over but it required an enormous amount of gritty determination and concentration. I like to be on solid ground – I don't like that sensation of falling.

I was surrounded by children of about five who were skitting about with such ease and, if they did fall over, they perkily bounced back up again. It was all pretty desperate and I hated it but I was smiling away to keep the instructor happy. At least Mike wasn't around to see – he was still going up and down. One chap spotted me, though, and skied over and shouted, 'Is that Jo? Director of the British Council? Great to see you.' He was all guyed up in goggles and hat and I had no idea who he was. A minister? An important contact? I never did find out.

It was a huge relief when the hour was up and Laka and I could say, 'Farewell. Perhaps another time?' Or perhaps not.

Mike said, 'That was brilliant! Do you fancy going up to the café at the top on a chairlift?'

Après ski – that's more like it. We sat high up on the mountain top in a log cabin drinking sweet hot chocolate, surrounded by the sparkling snow and the cries and shouts of happy skiers. It was beautiful...My skiing lesson faded.

#

I wanted to introduce Mike to colleagues in the British Council but not in a dull, formal way, so in the run up to

Christmas many of us went to the Ajara night club. He didn't need much persuasion and thought they were all very pretty, the women and the men. The Ajara club was a large black room with pounding music. Mike and I were the only foreigners there, among hundreds of young Georgians dancing away their worries.

'We just want to be able to be like other young people all over the world – you know, get good jobs, go dancing, travel, all those things,' said Irakli. Things we in Britain took for granted. 'None of us can afford to go on holiday in other countries.'

'Our country seems to be going round in circles politically and we want it to go in a straight line – we want to feel we are developing. And that our politicians are held accountable,' said Kote. He had brought his girlfriend, Anna, who worked at the Liberty Institute and who was a good contact of the British Council in her own right.

Near where we had a table there were nearly naked girls dancing energetically on benches – Mike showed a keen interest. When I tried to engage him in conversation he refocused on me hazily with a, 'What, darling?' But apart from an eye for a pretty girl and, let's face it, we were surrounded by exceptionally pretty girls, including those in my office, Mike and I were very much in love. We danced the night away. Then – boom!

A power cut and we were plunged into total darkness. It was too predictable. Within minutes the bartenders dramatically set fire to the bar with vodka and in the firelight the whole nightclub carried on chatting until the power came back on. Mike chuckled, 'There's no fire escape…'

'It's not funny, you hear of terrible accidents.' It's too close to the edge, I thought.

31

Out with the nuns

January 2003, Tbilisi

I was in the British Embassy for the latest briefing meeting. The Ambassador, Deborah, kicked off. 'Just to remind us all that there will be parliamentary elections in Georgia later this year – date not yet set but likely to be late October, early November. I expect we will all be able to participate in some way, probably by election monitoring with the European security NGO, OSCE. Maia, can you keep us in the loop as things progress? We should all be extra vigilant and make sure our advice to UK citizens, and the others whom we look after, is up to date in the eventuality of unrest.' The British Embassy in Georgia was also responsible for visitors from Ireland and many Commonwealth countries.

Deputy Head of Mission, Stuart, cleared his throat and announced, 'I have been contacted by the Sword Bearer of the Lord Mayor of the City of London.' We looked at him with interest. 'He is the spokesperson of the Lord Mayor and apparently an official entourage will be visiting Ukraine in March. They'd like to add on a short side visit to Tbilisi. The purpose of these visits is generally to drum up business links between the City of London and other countries – I have pointed out that there are unlikely to be many business deals signed in Georgia at present but they are keen to come.'

'They wouldn't be funding their trip from UK tax payers' money so, security permitting, who are we to stop them?' said Deborah.

'We can put a short programme together for them,' added Stuart, 'but we need an event with some profile.' He and Deborah looked over at me. 'Could he officially open the new British Council office?'

Although Zaza had made a huge amount of progress with the premises project the reality was that there was still much work to be done before we could be fully 'live' in the new office. We didn't even have stairs in our office. We had ordered ultra-modern, blue reinforced glass stairs from Turkey and these had yet to arrive – but, come what may, we were due to move in early March. Our generator had recently spluttered to an oily death; it was so cold we were fully muffled up in the office all the time and had resorted to using a portable gas stove to boil our kettle. We just had to move. I said we'd be delighted.

'You might also get some money out of them,' said Stuart and he gave me the contact details of the Sword Bearer. Deborah meanwhile wrapped up the meeting and looked round. 'Where's Mike?' she said, looking at me. I had to confess I didn't know.

'I believe he is out with the nuns,' said Maia.

'Nuns?' said Deborah.

'I can't imagine Mike having much contact with nuns,' added Stuart with interest.

'Yes. Lt Col Chris and Mrs Siobhan Nunn. The new Defence Attaché and his wife. Mike is showing them around and giving them a briefing.' The new Defence Attaché... Maybe this offers an opportunity to pep up the PEP project with a welcome party, I wondered?

#

Chris and Siobhan beat me to it and hosted their own party shortly after they arrived. They turned out to be genial and welcoming hosts and had rustled up a lively crowd of Georgian and foreign guests who were exchanging views on the woeful state of the Georgian army, amongst other things. Mike and Chris knew each other from earlier postings in Bosnia.

'Chris,' I ventured, 'with your permission, I'd like to use your arrival to promote the new facilities at the Peace Keeping English Project office at the Naval Academy in Poti.'

'How would you like to do that?' asked Chris.

'I will arrange to host a party, you and Siobhan will be the guests of honour and we'll invite all the great and the good.'

'Uniforms?'

'Yes, please.'

'Speeches?'

'Oh yes.'

'Count me in,' said Chris.

#

I had never had much to do with the British military and had always assumed (quite incorrectly) that they would somehow order everyone around or would be more interested in promoting a military solution to some of the intractable global problems which faced us, rather than by things like training and educational activities. The more I got to know Chris and his colleagues, I realised this was wildly stereotyped and untrue. Chris was a Royal Marines officer, a Falklands veteran; he had seen much action and lost his brother to that conflict. He turned out to be one of the most open-minded and generous-hearted people I have met. He and his cheerful and empathetic wife, Siobhan, were great company to boot.

Chris was Defence Attaché for the South Caucasus and he and Siobhan (the real Defence Attachée, according to Chris) spent much of their time going between not just Georgia and Armenia – as I had done – but between Georgia and Azerbaijan as well. Siobhan, in fact, became a much valued English language teacher with all three of the Peacekeeping English Projects.

After numerous trips across the South Caucasus Chris penned the following:

Things to do on a Long Distance Car Journey in the Caucasus

1. Check underneath the Discovery for bombs and if all clear get in. Tell driver, Levan (champion motocross driver), it is better to arrive late and alive, than to die on the way.
2. Strap in tight, brace yourself for the next two, four, six or nine hours depending on where you are headed. Lock the doors because 'ere be dragons'. Do remember to take wife as bargaining chip in case of hostage situation.
3. Do not read the map. It bears no relation to the ground – especially old Soviet Army maps as they contain deliberate misinformation.
4. Do not stop at police checkpoints – they are just bandits in disguise.
5. Do pay small change to the men dressed in Day-Glo vests, carrying black and white striped truncheons, who appear wherever and whenever you park. They have families to keep and you may be the only person to stop

at their patch that month. If you don't pay, the next time you may have no car when you come back or it may be minus various essential bits.

6. Do not drink the white wine for sale in litre jars on the side of the road – it is really petrol. Do not drink the red wine for sale in litre jars on the side of the road – it is really brake fluid.

7. Do ignore all expat advice and stop for lunch at the roadside plastic table under a tree where you will be served the most succulent BBQ lamb, pork and beef with the most delicious fresh and pickled vegetables. Do try their local wine and Brandy – it is not brake fluid or petrol.

8. Do take advantage of learning German and Dutch off the back of the stolen ten-seater minibuses as they ricochet and lurch past you filled with 20-30 people with their possessions piled on top.

9. Do be prepared to talk in the past tense when you see any infrastructure that smacks of having association with enterprise, commerce, or legitimate business. 'I wonder what it was.' If you find yourself saying, 'I wonder what that is?' beware the Potemkin village.

10. Do ponder why many villages sell only one commodity. Nevertheless, do stop at the roadside stalls to buy handmade terracotta pots, baskets, hammocks, fresh bread and fruit that is completely organic as they cannot afford the stuff to adulterate it.

11. Do look out for the groups of hungover men dressed in black standing around smoking and watching the women work.

12. Above all, do remember to take lots of photographs. One day you will not be here and life will seem tame.

#

We duly launched the new Peacekeeping English Project office in Poti. Chris looking authoritative and smart in his Royal Marines dress uniform and Siobhan, blonde and chic, lined up with Ray, the PEP Team Leader, and me to greet the bigwigs at the Naval Academy in Poti. Mike came too, to fly the flag and press the flesh and generally give support. After the speeches a senior port official, one of the most powerful men in the room, approached Mike and asked him to join him and his colleagues for a private *supra*, a Georgian feast.

Chris told me he thought the launch reception had gone well. He was very supportive of all three British Council-managed Peacekeeping English teams in the South Caucasus. 'I know the Peacekeeping English Project is important and I agree with its aims, to help Georgian soldiers communicate with their allies and so on,' said Chris, 'but perhaps what matters most is not that they are better soldiers, but that they are better able to learn, to get better jobs, to help make Georgia a better place.' I loved his foresight.

Mike came back from his *supra* feast chuckling. Apparently many of the people at his meal, which included senior policemen and local businessmen, were in fact well-known gangsters. A senior customs man turned up dressed in a long black leather coat and as he sat down at the table, he put his folding stock machine pistol on the table. 'I was told he was a particularly dangerous individual. He had the dead, grey eyes of a shark.'

#

One night in February Mike was at my place and, at about two in the morning, he had a phone call from a contact. He jolted awake. 'Thanks, I'm on it.' He immediately made another call. 'I've had a tip-off that there is something hotting up near a local military barracks in the city. I'd like to check it out and it would be good to have you along.'

Mike hurried to get off to collect Chris, who had agreed straightaway to accompany him.

'Don't do anything rash – keep safe,' I said, anxiously. I could see, though, that he was eager to get out into the snowy night and find out what was going on. Apart from anything else, it was vital to keep abreast of any emergencies which could impact on the safety of British citizens in Georgia.

Could it be a coup? Even an attempted coup would signal that things were more than usually unstable in Georgia. There was much dissatisfaction within the military and they were the ones who had, in principle, the necessary hardware to take over the shaky government. Chris had only been in Georgia a few weeks and I had only been with Mike a few months. While I lay awake curious and fretting about possible dangers, Mike and Chris were driving around the unlit city, with snow falling heavily.

I saw them both later that morning at the British Embassy. It seemed the country had not been taken over nor had the government collapsed.

'Well, that was a mutiny in a teacup,' said Chris. It seemed some veteran former soldiers had over-imbibed and, acting on impulse, had threatened to take control of some tanks. It seemed their main demand was to get improved pensions and this was probably a reasonable gripe. Many of the tanks at the barracks had, in fact, fallen into disrepair but it would only take one shell from a functioning tank fired into the middle of Tbilisi to escalate things seriously – fortunately the situation was resolved after negotiation. 'I wonder what the bloody hell is really going on?'

As the newly arrived Defence Attaché, Chris said he expected he would be on-call for all kinds of exciting tip-offs and midnight sorties. Indeed, at one reception the Greek Defence Attaché sidled up to him beckoning a shared whisper and said, 'I have news for you.'

Chris leant towards him, cautious that they would not be overheard and his Greek counterpart said, 'A wonderful new restaurant has opened up.'

32

New office

It was barely believable but the great 'move' day had come. We cleared the old office. The two small rooms, the short corridor, the clunky metal door, the mouse family and the distant, frozen WC. There was no sadness saying goodbye to it.

#

'I must say this is a step up from your former office,' said Deborah, taking in the bright colours of the walls and stairs and the crisp lines of our modern furniture in the new British Council. Zaza had used all his management skills to get the office finished on time and within budget. Not least of his achievements was that the jazzy blue stairs had been cleared at the customs on the border between Turkey and Georgia. Now here they were, offering a brighter, more positive and modern way ahead – they were the centrepiece of our operation. We had public access computers and a large flat-screen TV in reception and more computers for users of an 'English Learning Zone'. Off the corridor were light and spacious offices. The library was twice the size of the old one, with more desks, books and materials and it now had an automated library system.

We had to economise wherever we could and we had not had any budget for artwork for the walls. Librarian, Nino, had painted a series of pictures which we put in the library – she was exceptionally talented. Irakli had had British Council posters from our earlier arts events framed and these adorned the corridors – it looked like an art gallery.

Our Ambassador congratulated us. Deborah, cheerful, clever and perceptive, had been unfailingly supportive, workwise, which was no bad thing in an ambassador. The relationship between the British Council and the Foreign and Commonwealth Office wasn't always a straightforward one, each having its own interpretations of British culture. As it was, Deborah and I were friendly in and out of the office and, when work didn't come first, we often went out together at weekends.

Deborah and her jovial American husband, Dick, and their pretty eleven year old twin daughters were visiting our office as an advance party – ahead of our official launch party at which the Lord Mayor of London was the guest of honour. My colleagues were busy making sure the arrangements were in place before the arrival of our VIPs.

I showed Deborah and Dick around both floors, finishing up in my own office. 'Great view from your balcony,' said Dick and it was true. From underneath the fringe of the treetops we could see up and down the majestic sweep of Rustaveli Avenue, one of the main roads through the city. Dick did not live in Tbilisi all the time, working from back in the States and in central Europe. He had a roguish sense of humour and would happily join in the dancing when Mike and I rolled back the Caucasian rugs for a party at my house. 'Can the girls and I use your public access computers?' asked

Dick. There were not many internet cafés in Tbilisi at that time and few people had their own computers. We were expecting this new facility in our reception area to be a popular resource.

'You will be the first users,' I said.

Deborah and I chatted about work. She and her colleagues had been busy arranging the visit of the Lord Mayor of London and his entourage. One great thing was that, as a goodwill gesture, they had offered to fund Mansion House scholarships. These were for short attachments to financial or legal institutions within the City of London for young Georgian high-flyers – we had been busy helping to recruit the high-flyers.

Nutsa flung into my room. 'Jo – computers! She looked nervously at Deborah. 'We can't turn them off!'

We trotted downstairs in double-quick time to where Deborah's daughters were each sitting at a computer terminal. On one screen we could see fleshy figures gyrating purposefully… 'Daddy, what's that?'

Horrified I pulled the plugs of all of the computers out of the wall. I couldn't begin to say how sorry I was but Deborah was smiling and said, 'These things happen,' while Dick said in a jocular way, 'Seen worse…Or maybe not.'

Our guards on the nightshift had evidently been enjoying the new facilities – we stepped up our password protection. 'At least your first user wasn't the Lady Mayoress,' said Deborah.

#

As it turned out our launch party went off smoothly. The Lord Mayor, his Sword Bearer, a clutch of friendly ministers and a wide swathe of significant contacts duly turned up at the appointed time. Speeches were made, all the appropriate people were thanked, the Mansion House scholarships were awarded and there was much clapping.

Members of the press duly reported how impressed they were. 'This is the best office we have ever seen in our country!' They reported that it gave hope that Georgia had a future and a chance to become a developed Western-style country. We felt we had moved from one of the worst offices, certainly in the British Council network, to one of the best offices in the country. Even other foreign organisations in Georgia at that time did not have the facilities or look of what we now offered and it went without saying that Georgian offices were not like this – but if we could do it other organisations could too.

Of course I had invited Mr Rukhadze from the Anglo-Georgian Friendship Society to the reception. 'Ah Madame Jo. Congratulations on your wonderful new office!' he said, beaming. 'Now. What about the Wardrops?' Out of the corner of my eye I saw David, a top contact from BP, and I made a bee line for him. BP was a huge investor in Georgia, having been there since 1996 working on a strategically significant pipeline from Azerbaijan to Turkey. Mindful that the country was prone to instability, they had many community development projects along the length of the pipelines. They might also be interested in public relations events in Tbilisi and beyond.

'Great office, Jo,' said David. I asked him if he fancied chipping in to hosting a *fantastic* touring exhibition celebrating historical links between the UK and Georgia?

#

We had built our platform, our institutional framework and the premises project was finished. As a team we had sorted out our contracts, our finances were robustly managed, and we had ticked all the health and safety boxes. Now we needed to maximise the impact of what we did and to do more of it. We had our first team meeting in the library of the new office.

Irakli gave us an update on arts events. With the support of our Arts Division colleagues in London he was organising a touring exhibition of video installation art and, around this event, some masterclasses for young artists. As Georgia was such a poor country, while it was important to bring examples of exciting contemporary British art, we certainly didn't want to be seen as showing off – rather, we wanted to help develop something new. With such a high level of creativity in Georgia we knew artists could learn much from each other. 'And, David Beckham!' added Irakli. We looked at him with interest. 'I have just heard back from his publicist, as I had written to ask if he would be able to visit Tbilisi at the same time as we'll be hosting a screening of the film *Bend it like Beckham*.

'What was the reply?' I asked, astonished.

'His agent said a polite no…'

'Ten out of ten for trying, Irakli – how did you think of that?' It seemed an audacious suggestion and I had no idea he had done this. It transpired that in 1996 the superstar footballer, David Beckham, had been in Tbilisi for an England football match. While watching TV in his hotel he saw Victoria Adams, Posh Spice, in a video clip of the Spice Girls and decided, 'that is the girl for me'.

'I thought he might think of Tbilisi as the romantic place where he fell in love from a distance,' said Irakli.

Kote briefed the team on the new projects we were getting underway – collaboration with the American Bar Association, the Georgian Institute of Public Affairs and other NGOs – to do more human rights training and support for the writing of textbooks on media regulation and freedom of expression. All good, solid stuff.

Rusiko fed back on the English language projects. She was forging links with the US Embassy in Tbilisi and working closely with British Council offices in other countries. 'We are also on track to open a new English Teachers' Association of Georgia office in Kutaisi, our second largest city, and also in Batumi.'

We introduced Maya D, our manager of the new language laboratory, the 'English Learning Zone'. This was a self-access facility for which learners paid a modest fee. Anuki reported that, now that we had our own suite of rooms in our office, she was better able to manage more examinations. Nata and Tamuna told colleagues that likewise they were managing a leap in library memberships and that feedback from users had been overwhelmingly positive. Tamuna told us that she was liaising with librarians from our German and French counterparts to give internships for students interested in information studies.

We had partnerships all round. We were on track.

#

My boss, Chris, made his first visit to Tbilisi and we crammed as much as we could into his programme. Irakli had arranged for the installation art reception to coincide with Chris's first night. I was pleased to see a constant stream of guests, predominantly young (our target audience for this type of event), talking to him spontaneously and enthusiastically about this innovative artwork. That evening we took Chris out for a meal, along with contacts from across our activities. The conversation drifted on and I turned to my young colleagues. We chatted about the Georgian elections due later that year.

'Wouldn't you ever want to enter public service at some point? Go into the civil service or run for office and sort it all out?' I asked.

'Absolutely no!' said Irakli vehemently and Kote and Nata shook their heads.

'No, they are all so corrupt – in order to survive, anyone working for the government has to be! They get paid virtually no salary and we can only guess what dirty deals go on.'

'But if good, 'clean' people like you never work in ministries surely Georgia will never get better? You can't expect NGOs and foreign organisations to be the ones to fill the gaps for ever and ever,' I reasoned. 'Maybe Kote (Governance Manager) should be Minister of Justice?'

We laughed at the absurdity of it. 'Then Irakli (Arts Manager) should be Minister of Culture…'

'And Nata (Education Manager) is Minister of Education!'

We decided we had a pretty good team in the British Council. Driver Vakho could be Minister of Transport and Accountant, Katie, Minister of Finance and so on. Office Manager, Zaza, would be Minister of the Interior.

#

Mike and I had been going out for four months and we were well-nigh inseparable. 'The thing is, Mike, we are just too happy. We have a few hurdles we need to get through before this might really go somewhere – what is the major issue for you?'

Mike replied, without pausing, 'If you and my daughters don't get on…That would be a deal-breaker…What about you?'

'I need to know how we feel after we have had an argument…'

#

While I had been absorbed in the new office, new projects and my new relationship, much bigger things were going on out there. All over the world millions of people had been protesting against the proposed Allied incursions into Iraq. Some of the biggest protests the globe had ever seen had taken place in mid-February and there were more into mid-March – the demonstrators were not heeded. On March 19 the Allied invasion of Iraq began. Mike and I were at home watching BBC News, hugging each other close on our sofa. We watched in horror at the bombing of Baghdad.

'This is dreadful. I'm just not convinced about the arguments for intervening…It could just lead to chaos and a free for all…' said Mike. But quite apart from the horrific scenes unfolding, we noted that the streetlights in Baghdad appeared to work. 'And look at the roads!' he said. They were smooth and well maintained. We knew we were seeing Baghdad through the lens the media was allowed, or chose, to share with us but basics like electricity and roads appeared to be working. It did seem ironic that we were living in a country which was nominally democratic but in reality where the infrastructure was collapsing and where there appeared to be little accountability by those elected to those who voted.

The heavily-guarded hillside mansions of the kleptocrats seemed to gloat above the tangled city in the valley below – where real people eked out a living.

Something had to change.

33

Springtime

April 2003, Tbilisi

It was springtime and time to meet our respective families. I was anxious that we would all get on.

Figure 14 Springtime - the River Mktvari in Tbilisi

'I hope you're eating sensibly and not drinking too much wine,' said my mother. My mum and dad had come to visit and Mike and I showed them around, starting with the market. The market stalls were heavy with fresh and dried fruits and the crisp spring air was fragrant with the scents of coriander, parsley and tomatoes.

'We don't starve here Mum – the food is wonderful.' I took them to the little provisions store near my house, with its dirty little generator chugging out acrid fumes on the pavement. I picked up some chicken, frozen in slabs, and some boxed fruit juice.

'Why is this Turkish chicken? And the fruit juice is from Turkey too? There must be Georgian chickens,' asked my dad. I didn't know. I knew there were some weird trade deals. The Georgians didn't have the plants for packaging and processing – they produced wonderful food but it was then shipped over the border, packaged and then shipped back. The final products cost four times as much.

My colleagues had heard me mention that it was my father's birthday and with true Georgian hospitality they offered to host a *supra*, a proper Georgian meal. We had the full works: the food, the wine, the toasting, the friendship, the warmth. My dad blushed, unused to being the centre of attention and being toasted to.

'Your colleagues are so young – and so beautiful,' said my mother.

I agreed. 'And not just on the outside.'

#

I had also been in touch with David Lordkipanidze of the National Museum. 'Jo, you must bring your family – I can show you the Dmanisi skulls.'

Mike and I had in fact recently been out to the archaeological dig at Dmanisi. We had visited the same day as someone from National Geographic was taking photographs. It was quite a privilege to be there, deep within the dig itself, watching as new ethno-treasures were unearthed.

David welcomed us and took us through his cavernous museum to a small, private room. 'Our museum just doesn't have enough resources to exhibit our finds properly – but some of them are absolutely unique and of global significance.' David had also invited the Dutch Ambassador, Harry, and his fiancée Loes, and he gave us each a glass of wine to warm us up in the chilly room. We all crowded round as he produced four wooden boxes lined with red satin. He opened the boxes to reveal hominid skulls of exceptional historic importance. Georgia's historical treasures are phenomenal.

#

To wind up their short holiday my parents were being true adventurers and were going overland, by the Silk Route Express train, to see Azerbaijan. I saw them off at Tbilisi train station, feeling anxious that the train would be boarded by bandits, that kind of thing.

'I hope you are wearing sensible shoes – and don't talk to any strangers,' I cautioned, but I could see my mother already making friends with a young woman in their carriage.

'Goodbye, dear Jo. We're so glad we came and we loved seeing Georgia,' said my mum, adding, 'Now I can worry about you in a more informed way.'

#

Mike's daughters, Lizzi and Katherine, also came to visit him for their Easter holiday. Nervous, I went over to Mike's house to meet them, taking little bunches of flowers. It was like having an interview but they didn't know they were the interviewers. They were very pretty teenagers, Lizzi dark and like her father, Katherine blonde and pale. While Mike and I were at work they lounged about happily, listening to music or watching any of their father's DVDs which they deemed acceptable.

We took them out and about to see Tbilisi. First to the meat market where they exclaimed at all the piglets and goats' heads laid out for sale. 'Eww Dad!' And at the heads of pigs hanging on trees on the roads out of Tbilisi. 'Dad! What's that all about?'

I discovered a different side to Mike. I had seen him at work and he was good at his job, dynamic, insightful, forceful – constantly making connections and networks. He was regarded within and outside the Embassy as a good person to have around in a crisis. With his daughters he was a caring, but firm, dad.

But how they teased him! 'Urrr, girls!' they would chant when he'd say, 'Urrr, girls! Quickly now, cross the road here!' 'Urrr, girls! Stay close!' Or other fatherly instructions.

Lizzi and Katherine seemed fascinated by Georgia. It was, I think, unlike anywhere they had ever been. 'It's all so random,' said Katherine.

'It's so extreme. The good things are really good and the bad things really bad. It looks so beautiful and so cultural but there is so much poverty,' said Lizzi. And danger – while we were watching TV one night we heard bursts of popping from the streets outside – another gun battle. They happened so frequently after dark that Mike and I didn't start up in alarm any more. When Mike took his daughters to see the churches in Mskheta, while they were looking around a huge explosion echoed from across the valley – a bomb had gone off. Mike later learnt it was an attack on a gangster by a rival.

\#

We went away for a weekend with the girls to lovely Bakuriani, up in the mountains. Driving out of Tbilisi, a policeman waved his truncheon to Mike to slow down. 'Look girls, a *pazhalsta* stick,' said Mike. 'Katherine, you are learning Russian, what does *pazhalsta* mean?'

'It means please...' said his daughter. When the policeman saw the diplomatic number plate on Mike's car, though, he gave an insouciant flick of his hand to give us permission not to bother stopping.

'The police don't get paid, or not much, and they earn their living through 'public contributions', by controlling access to things like car parks and by making up any number of driving transgressions to justify an on-the-spot fine. Then they trouser the lot – paying off other people up or down the line.'

'How sad,' said Lizzi.

When we got to Otar's place, the Hotel Appolon, the girls were delighted to find that, while Mike and I were given a welcome glass of homemade wine, they could tuck in to sticky homemade chocolate and marshmallow cake.

In the afternoon Mike arranged to go out riding with his daughters – local men brought sprightly ponies to the hotel for trekking into the mountains. I stayed behind as I had some studying to do for another Open University course. I also didn't want to crowd them out – they needed time together as a family without me in the way. I looked out the window and could see Mike, ahead on his pony saying, 'Keep up girls, keep together!' while his daughters shrieked with laughter as their little beasts did their own thing, trotting off in different directions.

That evening we played board games and cards and had more cake. Breakfast was at 8am sharp and the girls emerged, sleepy and hungry. Which was just as well, as we had mountains of food on offer – cold meats, salty farmhouse cheeses and cold spaghetti with honey. 'How random,' said Katherine but she cheered up when she saw that there was honey cake too.

#

Back in Tbilisi, we took them to the artistic old town to look around the art galleries and see craftsmen at work – jewellers, painters, potters. We had lunch on the balcony of an arty restaurant and were startled by men carrying a body in an open-topped coffin past our table. The girls were open-mouthed as the coffin and the funeral procession slowly made their way around our restaurant and into the ancient church beside it. 'Random…' whispered Katherine.

#

We had a final treat lined up, an evening out with friends watching the Georgian national dance troupe. As we anticipated, those who had not seen it before were duly impressed at this national treasure. Defence Attaché Chris leant over to Mike and whispered, 'If only the Georgian army were as well trained and self-disciplined.'

This time we were in the Soviet-style opera house, a circular building built with lots of panes of glass. As we left after the performance, Mike looked up and pointed to a spray of bullet holes in one of the windows.

Part 3 Getting Political

34

Volcano

June 2003, Tbilisi

We were to host a theatre production in Georgia, the first time we had ever done so. Often when people think of the British Council, the promotion of the best of British acting, playwriting and theatre production will be top of the list of the things they expect to see. We had specialised colleagues in London, in our Arts Division, who liaised with the various companies and who selected appropriate acts to send overseas. It can be more expensive than other activities and we usually tried to tour a production to more than one country – in this case to the three South Caucasus countries. We were delighted to learn from the London office that the play we were to show was to be *Macbeth*.

I could already imagine the reviews in Tbilisi kicking off with 'Ah Shakespeare!' During the Soviet era and beyond, Shakespeare, and Dickens and all the great international authors were widely read and quoted by appreciative Georgians. However, being the British Council, we would not be staging something stodgy and traditional. We were charged with challenging outmoded stereotypes. People outside the UK, particularly in the former Soviet countries, often did seem to think everyone goes to work wearing a bowler hat and that we can all recite the entire works of Wordsworth. If we are not like someone out of *Jeeves and Wooster*, we must surely be characters from *Pride and Prejudice*.

Therefore we had to demonstrate what was at the forefront of contemporary UK culture and to showcase the UK's modern creative industries, a substantial part of our economy. Irakli, our Arts Manager, was working at full throttle making arrangements for the arrival of the Volcano Theatre Company. This was a small outfit of three actors, two men and a woman, who had toured to positive reviews all over the world. A few days before the Volcano Company were due to arrive they told Irakli that they would be changing the production to another in their repertoire. It was called *L.O.V.E* and was an interpretation of Shakespeare's sonnets.

No problem, I thought – Georgians love Shakespeare and Georgians love 'love'. That's even better than the Scottish play, with all its gory murders and obsessive-compulsive handwashing. It transpired the Volcano Company couldn't put on *Macbeth* because their only major prop, a large metal table, had buckled in their previous performance – the other props, knives and so on, kept sliding into the middle of it – more comedic than tragic.

The sonnets are rarely acted and we were not sure how they would interpret them but I knew that there was much ambiguity about the fair youth and the dark lady and that Shakespeare may have been addressing a man in many of the sonnets. Irakli discovered that *L.O.V.E* was somewhat racy, with homosexual references – we weren't at all sure how this would go down in Tbilisi. I discussed with our UK colleagues if these racy references could be toned down, to take into account likely sensitivities in Georgia. Our colleagues far away in London said they weren't sure if this wouldn't 'jeopardise the artistic integrity' of the play but they advised us to discuss it with the actors after they arrived.

In many respects Georgia was a conservative country – in common with other Eastern and Southern European countries, homosexuality was frowned upon, especially by the older, more Soviet generation. I had been told that even carrying an umbrella apparently was a sign of not being a 'real' man – in a downpour real men would just turn up the collar of their leather jackets and get wet.

An important part of the role of the British Council is to show Britain as the open, tolerant, inclusive society it is – or purports to be – so referring to homosexuality in itself was not just OK but a good thing. However, this was the first play we had been able to host and we wanted it to go without a hitch – anything too controversial might make it difficult to do anything similar again. As it was we had challenges aplenty – the logistics of getting people and props in and out of the country and finding a theatre with a powerful enough generator to last a whole performance (and which had equipment that was compatible with the sophisticated technology the theatre group would doubtless be bringing).

We were pleased when they, and their props and technical equipment, arrived safely. Irakli and I briefed the actors on likely sensitivities in Georgia and asked if they could tone down the homosexual references – they said they would discuss it and see what they could do. I felt a little anxious.

#

We held a press conference in our library. Twenty or so journalists turned up, including one severe-looking woman dressed entirely in black – if truth be told she was a little witch-like. Rusiko provided translation. We started with some gentle questions about Shakespeare and the challenges of being a touring company. Then the severe-looking woman said, 'I have heard there are some shocking scenes in this play!' She continued, 'Are you aware that homosexuality is against the law in this country let alone being entirely immoral?'

Rusiko translated this and the actor replied, wryly, 'Of course, our aim is to convert all men in Georgia to becoming gay.' Rusiko paused and translated this back with a deadpan face. There was a shocked gasp and much scribbling from the journalists – sarcasm doesn't translate well – and Rusiko added quickly, 'He is joking!'

It was too late. It transpired that the lady in black was the Georgian Patriarch's personal journalist – I learnt that the Church not only had a newspaper, for which this woman was a key contributor, but also a radio station. That evening they broadcast a bulletin calling on everyone to boycott 'the British play'. It even has its own label! I was torn. I didn't want to offend the Georgian Church – it was not my place, as a foreigner, to be critical. I knew many people, of all ages and backgrounds, who were proud of the uniqueness and longevity of the Georgian Orthodox Church. It was at the core of Georgian identity as one of the oldest Christian countries in the world. But of course I wanted our play to go well, and for it to demonstrate the importance of diversity and tolerance in a modern society.

#

The play was due to be on for three nights. The first night, Friday June 13, was free, for invited guests. For the second two nights we had sold tickets and would be donating the proceeds to a Georgian orphanage. We held the play in the State Theatre. This was a grand old 19th century building with a long, proud history of staging dazzling and lofty works – Georgia was known as one of the cultural leaders of the Soviet Union. There were large black and white photos of great, past actors in heavy period costume and thick exotic make-up in the foyer of the theatre and along its broad, curving corridors.

With a little trepidation, that the power would stay on throughout the performance, and that the actors would indeed 'tone it down', we settled into our seats. It was a packed house and Mike and I were seated surrounded by ministers, ambassadors and other VIPs. The lights dimmed for our night at the theatre.

#

The only major prop was an enormous four poster bed with minimal, white drapery. The actors, two men and a woman, were dressed in modern clothes, which they gradually stripped off, to reveal white, modern undergarments. As they stripped, they danced and rolled and leapt. This was 'physical theatre'. They hopped and jumped on and off the bed, while reciting – beautifully – Shakespeare's sonnets. It went something like this:

All three of them leapt on to the bed and one actor said:

From fairest creatures we desire increase,
That thereby beauty's rose might never die,
But as the riper should by time decease,
His tender heir might bear his memory

And they all skipped off. The woman and one man hopped on and he said to her:

Shall I compare thee to a summer's day?
Thou art more lovely and more temperate.
Rough winds do shake the darling buds of May,
And summer's lease hath all too short a date.

And the woman and the man kissed. The man hopped off. The other man hopped on and swung from the supports of the bed, triumphantly saying:

Let me not to the marriage of true minds
Admit impediments.
Love is not love
Which alters when it alteration finds,
Or bends with the remover to remove:
O no! It is an ever-fixed mark
That looks on tempests and is never shaken

The woman and the second man kissed. Gentle titters from the audience at her faithlessness. She jumped off the bed. The other man leapt back on, saying to the man still on the bed:

Love's not Time's fool, though rosy lips and cheeks
Within his bending sickle's compass come:
Love alters not with his brief hours and weeks,
But bears it out even to the edge of doom.
If this be error and upon me proved,
I never writ, nor no man ever loved.

The two men kissed.

There was a huge intake of breath. Some catcalls from around the theatre and a clatter of seats. One man, in particular, could not get out fast enough and frantically pushed his way down his row. Sitting in the darkness, I bleated gently 'Oh nooooooo.' I cringed and dug my fingernails deeper and deeper into Mike's arm.

The actors had other props – a knife and a rose. I bet it was the same knife that did for Duncan in *Macbeth*. The climax of the play was when the girl 'castrated' at least one of the men – it may have been both, but I don't know, as by this time I was hiding my eyes.

My mistress' eyes are nothing like the sun;
Coral is far more red than her lips' red;
If snow be white, why then her breasts are dun;
If hairs be wires, black wires grow on her head.
I have seen roses damask'd, red and white,
But no such roses see I in her cheeks

With a final flourish the woman tore the petals from the rose and scattered them in the direction of the genitals of both men. The threesome stood up and bowed to feeble, uncertain applause and beat a retreat backstage – they didn't hang about.

When the lights went up my Ambassador turned to me. 'Well. That wasn't my cup of tea. It was well acted, though,' she added encouragingly. On her way out, Deborah gave a supportive, stalwart interview to a TV crew hovering outside. I was grateful to her – others in her situation might easily have distanced themselves.

The Dutch Ambassador shook my hand vigorously and said, 'Fabulous stuff.'

#

Meanwhile Irakli pushed his way along to where I was sitting. 'Jo, the director of the theatre needs to see you. Now!' Adding, 'The man who left the theatre was him.'

We ran down the corridors and stairs, first to check on the actors in the green room. 'We thought we might get bottles thrown at us!' They had done this play all over the world to rave reviews. I asked them if they had ever had a reaction like this before. 'We didn't go down too well in Northern Ireland...'

I told them not to leave until we collected them. Irakli and I – and Mike, he wasn't going to miss this – fairly sprinted to the theatre director's office, deep within the bowels of the theatre. The theatre director was shaking. I could see he was scared, visibly frightened.

'This filth!' he spat out at me. 'How can you bring this filth into this country? Into *my* theatre?' he said, waving his hands. 'How will I ever live this down?'

The room was dark but for a low ceiling light which shed a bright pool into the gloom. The theatre director was surrounded by men in black, all smoking, and at his elbow was the severe-looking woman who had been at the press conference – the Patriarch's journalist. With her notebook and pen poised for action.

I was as soothing as I could be. 'I'm sorry, this is entirely my responsibility. I am sure no-one will associate it with you or your theatre – and it is, after all, a play. Surely all good plays are meant to make you think? I am sure Shakespeare would have wanted us to think.'

'Not with disgusting stuff like this,' he spat back. His face was moist with perspiration.

'With respect, many people here tell me Georgians want to be thought of as European. In my part of Europe we believe in tolerance and we champion diversity.'

While Irakli was feverishly translating, I thought, but didn't say, that some said that Shakespeare had possibly been bisexual. I continued, 'This is an outstanding example of contemporary theatre and they have performed all over the world to outstanding reviews.'

The woman in black was scribbling. 'I don't care about other countries. I refuse to hold this production here again! Get them out of my theatre!'

Mike also tried to reason with him, pointing out the British Council had sell-outs on both nights still to come. 'What about your own costs and the money the British Council was going to donate to the orphanage? It won't look great in the press.' I didn't mind him straying into my cultural domain. He was, after all, head of the Political Section at the Embassy and things felt decidedly political.

The theatre director was intransigent. 'I don't care about the costs – we will refund all the ticket money.' He was desperate to disassociate himself and seemed to be particularly anxious about the woman in black with the pencil and the notebook.

#

We helped get the actors, and their bed, safely away through a side door.

#

Standing under a pretty old street lamp outside the theatre was a little group of about 20 women. A little huddle in sharp relief against the misty night. Some were young, some middle aged and a couple were quite old. They ran over to us and started clapping, kissing us and saying with excitement,

'Thank you, thank you, it was wonderful!'

'What a brave, fantastic thing to do…'

'I loved it!'

'How exciting to see what contemporary theatre in other countries is like.'

'We need more freedom of speech, more openness to talk about issues…'

One woman was apparently an academic who specialised in Shakespeare. 'And Shakespeare was probably bisexual anyway,' she said.

'Never a dull moment,' said Mike.

Why was the theatre director frightened? I wondered.

#

The next morning we had a death threat. A telephone call to our office. 'Do not stage this play again – or lives could be lost…And if you try, we will also cut power cables if we have to.'

We had seriously been considering trying to stage it elsewhere. The manager of a small contemporary theatre, the Basement, phoned Irakli and said she had loved the performance. She said her theatre venue was too small but she would even try to hold it in a car park just to have a chance to show it again. Other small theatre companies also offered.

The actors said they were game, but we decided it was simply too risky for them, for us and for the audience. The members of the Volcano Theatre Company did not do another production in Georgia but they did, as planned, do masterclasses with acting students and young directors, and spent their final hours in the country looking at churches – beautiful they are too but I'm not sure the actors appreciated them at the time.

Maya Z later told me that the woman castrating the men was possibly as shocking as the boy-on-boy kissing. 'A woman! Taking the upper hand? Whatever next?' She said that if the actors had been dolled up in Elizabethan costume they could probably have got away with any amount of gender-bending bed-hopping. As the actors were in modern underwear it all looked too contemporary, too possible and too threatening.

The State Theatre director probably really did fear for his life.

#

Volcano Theatre apparently took out the male kiss on their first night in Azerbaijan, the next stop on their tour, and the play went down a storm. They got braver and put the kiss back in for the subsequent performances and it still went down well. By the time they got to Armenia they were back on track and were wined and dined and fêted by the best in the land, so much had their play been appreciated.

I was pleased for them. Cynics felt this was possibly because Azerbaijanis were fed up with perceived Georgian snootiness about being so cultural and were determined to be seen to be modern and open to new things. The positive reception was all the more remarkable as, although secular, Azerbaijan is a predominantly Muslim country. Perhaps when the Armenian movers and shakers heard how well it had gone down in Baku they were determined to outdo them in their appreciation and praise. As the two countries are technically at war perhaps this was cultural one-upmanship.

#

Meanwhile, reaction to 'the British Play' did not die down in Tbilisi. Opinions on it, and the censorship of it, were lively and voluble, whether people had seen the play or not.

There was a heated exchange in the media. A late-night live TV chat show opened with a description of *L.O.V.E* and went on to debate religious and government censorship, freedom of choice and the position of women. Some of our human rights and governance contacts were on the chat-show panel. Needless to say, they were vehement supporters of the right to freedom of expression.

35

Choices

July 2003, Tbilisi

In the meeting room of the British Council our team was strategising and planning. Our broad country plan in Georgia was already set and agreed. We had four main areas, to promote:

* the learning and teaching of English through training and consultancy and through our library
* the best of UK education through management of scholarships, exams and helping people access education in Britain itself
* the best of UK arts and creativity
* more accountable and transparent governance and stronger civil society

Rusiko reported that the new English Teachers' Association offices were well underway. She and Barrie and their network of trainers were undertaking teacher training all over Georgia – the methodologies they had developed were a fusion of best practice from both the UK and Georgia and could be adapted not just for English language teaching but for any subject.

Kote told us that, politically speaking, things appeared to be hotting up in the run up to the November elections. 'Nino Burjanadze has just resigned her post as Speaker of the House and joined up with Zurab Zhvania – they are now the Burjanadze-Democrats. They will be running in opposition to Shevardnadze.' Kote added, 'Lots of organisations are running projects around the importance of free and fair elections. We need to do something too.'

I agreed but reminded him that the British Council was a neutral organisation. 'So nothing too heavy – what are the issues for young people?' I asked.

'Everyone is completely disillusioned with politics, politicians, the government – no-one wants to bother voting as they think the elections are always rigged. We need to encourage youth, in particular, to vote.' OK, this will fit with our aim to promote strong civil society in Georgia, I thought.

'Then it needs to be young, relevant and fun,' said Irakli. 'We have a jazz group coming in September – maybe they wouldn't mind if we used their performance to encourage young people to vote? We could design T-shirts about the importance of voting to distribute widely around the time of the visit.' We looked at him and at his T-shirt of the day which said 'Los Angeles County Jail'. Irakli was a big wearer of T-shirts and he had probably only worn a suit the day he had been interviewed for his job with us. We had a relaxed approach to a dress code in our office as I felt it was important for colleagues' choice of clothes to reflect the people with whom they variously worked. As Arts Manager, Irakli mixed with theatre directors and painters, dancers, musicians and the young people whom we wanted to reach – and none of them wore heavy suits. My favourite of Irakli's many T-shirts was one, which he wore out to nightclubs, which said, 'Sex Instructor: first lesson free'.

Our meeting became animated. Our ideas took shape as we chatted about how best we could contribute to having free and fair elections in Georgia. We decided we would have a slogan to encourage people to vote with the campaign strapline:

Help your country! Make your voice heard!

I updated our country plan – best laid plans and all that.

#

It was a lovely, balmy evening and Mike picked me up from the office. 'Chris asked if we fancied a 'Tbilisi Sunset'?' Off we went for a sundowner. 'I saw one of my contacts from the Dutch Embassy at lunch,' continued Mike. 'He was out with official Georgian contacts last night. They were all deeply into a *supra* feast, over-imbibing and having a whale of a time, with guns all over the table. They had lots of toasts and one man got so carried away about the *tamada*'s address he grabbed his pistol and let fire a volley of bullets into the ceiling of the restaurant – the *tamada* toastmaster, without batting an eyelid, said, 'Giorgi, Giorgi, not now...We've got guests...'.'

We joined the Nunns on their terrace overlooking the decrepit rooftops of the neighbouring houses. Acrid smoke rose from piles of rubbish burning gently on their street, while stray dogs happily rummaged. Siobhan brought a jug of 'Tbilisi Sunsets', the recipe for which was a carefully guarded secret. I asked Chris what he thought of Georgia – he and Siobhan had been in the Caucasus for about six months. 'It's like being in the '*Tailor of Panama*'.'

Chris told us about an event at which he was a guest of honour, along with his US counterpart, hosted by contacts from the Georgian Ministry of Defence. If men were men in Georgia, men in the army were men above men. When Chris was toasted for his friendship, bravery and all round military manliness, he was handed a long ram's horn containing at least half a litre of chilled white wine. The thing about a drinking horn is that, once accepted, you can't put it down without spilling it. Chris took the horn, saying, 'In the name of the friendship between our two great nations,' and drank it down to the last drop, to the cheers and admiration of his Georgian hosts.

They filled another horn and the *tamada* turned to the US Defence Attaché, giving another expansive toast and proffering the horn to him – but he held his hand up and said, 'No thank you, I don't drink.'

A gasp from the party and they looked at each other in amazement. Why did they send him here? Chris, being a true diplomat, stepped into the silence and said, 'In the name of the friendship between our three nations,' – and drank the second horn. He had to be helped to his car and I don't think he was well the next day but without question he made friends for Britain that night.

For us foreigners passing through this intriguing country, it was hard to work out how things had got as bad as they had and we worried that things were getting worse. There were power cuts every day, every night. Many foreigners, and the small number of rich Georgians who had generators, often barely noticed them but for most Georgians it was very different. Chris told us he had asked Maia K at the Embassy if she had had a nice weekend and she replied that it had been her mother's birthday. 'How nice, did you do anything special, like a candlelit dinner?' he asked her.

Maia had looked at him with a sad smile and said, 'Chris, we have had many, many dinners lit *only* by candles. My dearest wish is to be able to have dinner lit by an electric light.' Not only was the infrastructure crumbling but unemployment was rising, particularly for men in urban areas. More and more Georgians were leaving the country if they could. Corruption permeated much of public life and many private sector deals too were apparently dodgy.

'But what can we do? We are not here to intervene,' said Siobhan.

'It is hard working with this government though – I find working with the Ministry of Defence can be tough,' I said to Chris. We both worked with the Georgian MOD, he because it was his day job and me with him on the Peacekeeping English Project. It was a far from straight-forward relationship. Even if ministers signed up for collaboration, in practice often their side of the partnership was forgotten or ignored and our PEP team could find themselves starved of the resources the Georgian MOD was supposed to provide.

'It's our job to work with whoever is there, within reason – unless we break off diplomatic ties and I can't see that happening. It is better to stay through thick and thin and try to work with people for a better future,' said Mike. 'The only people who can change things, meaningfully, are the Georgians – it needs to come from them.'

'Another Tbilisi Sunset?' asked Siobhan.

#

Mike and I went back to his house. We had been together for almost a year, shuttling backwards and forwards between our two houses. I had some decisions to make. I was pondering whether Mike and I should move in together – it was a big thing for me. I didn't want to rush too fast into a new relationship, given how harrowing my break-up from my ex-husband had been. And, although Mike and I were enamoured at that time, if things deteriorated after we had moved in together, it would be much worse if we broke up. We hadn't had our first argument – I couldn't believe we wouldn't hit some rocks at some point. I decided, for the moment, to do nothing and see how things developed. Love would flourish, or fade...And time would tell.

More pressing than that decision, I had to choose when I was going to leave Georgia and move on to another job. Strictly speaking I should have been leaving in a year's time – in the summer of 2004. By then I would have done a three-and-a-half year posting, already over the standard posting of three years. Mike, meanwhile, was not due to leave until the summer of 2005. The British Council team had only recently moved to the new office and I felt that we were only just starting to make an impact and to do what we had set out to do – I worked with the best team in the world, the best office in Georgia – and the elections were coming up. Surely we could contribute to helping this dilapidated country somehow? I couldn't even think about leaving yet. I decided to stay another year.

36

More choices

'We'd like to do some 'forum theatre' in Georgia,' announced Lali.

Lali was the local head of the UK's Department for International Development. I was intrigued – this seemed different from their usual poverty-reduction projects. She had with her Caryne C.C., a British theatre director. Caryne explained, 'This is an innovative way of using theatre to empower the disempowered.'

I hadn't heard of it and I liked the sound of it. 'Almost everyone in Georgia seems to be disempowered. You might have a large audience.'

Caryne explained that forum theatre was pioneered by Augusto Boal in the 1980s in Brazil. The premise is that a short play is written, centring on a controversial, complex issue with which the whole audience will empathise or care passionately about. The play is acted – then significant bits of the play are re-run and any member of audience can say, 'Stop!' and suggest alternative choices, solutions, or scenarios. By intervening members of the audience can feel part of the play and part of the solutions.

Irakli and I were impressed. We told them about the jazz music event and the *Help your country* project we were planning. I told them that we were trying to make sure that we were doing more than just showcasing an arts event but that it should contribute in some way to what was going on around us in Georgia. I was sorry we didn't have any unallocated money to contribute to the forum theatre event, but Irakli offered to put in some time to advise on venues and production and so on. 'Your advice would be a great contribution – providing money isn't the only way to help,' said Caryne.

'What will the theme of the play be?' I asked.

'We're not sure yet, but we have some great scriptwriters lined up.'

'What about 'political corruption'? There seems to be a lot of that about.'

#

I had another important visitor.

Kote asked if a contact called Kakha Lomaia could discuss a new project with us. Kakha was the head of the Open Society Georgia – this was part of a network of NGOs founded by George Soros, the billionaire philanthropist. The Open Society had been operating in Georgia since 1994 and aimed to help democratic and transparent processes take root after the collapse of the Soviet Union. They were particularly active in the area of human rights, which was complementary to our own work.

'Jo, I have a proposal for you,' said Kakha. 'I would like to bring exit polls to Georgia for the November parliamentary elections. We have never had any form of checks and balances on voting in this country and – as you will doubtless be aware – we fear there will be a lack of transparency, to put it mildly. This will be a costly and potentially contentious strategy.'

I baulked a little and – as I had to do so often – I told him the British Council wasn't a donor organisation. 'We simply could not afford to pay for exit polls – and as for contentious, we are an apolitical and foreign organisation. It wouldn't be appropriate for my organisation to do anything politically contentious,' I told him. But even as I was saying it, I thought about the contradiction of encouraging young people to vote if the vote is worthless. Why bother trying to promote the concept of more accountable and transparent governance and stronger civil society, if we are not prepared to support the mechanisms which help to hold a government accountable? I asked if he had spoken to other organisations and he admitted that the British Council was one of the last on his list of possible partners.

'I have, in fact, tried all the major embassies and foreign organisations. No-one wants to rock the boat.' He sounded despairing.

I reiterated that the British Council's financial resources were modest and already pretty much fully committed. If we did help, there was no question of funding the entire cost.

'I am not expecting the British Council to fully fund it and I won't tell anyone how much you might put into the partnership,' said Kakha. It was a question of moral as well as financial support. In the event, I pledged what I could. A modest amount – it was what some affluent women would spend on a handbag but admittedly not any woman I knew. I emphasised about the British Council being apolitical and strictly non-partisan and that we were doing this openly and transparently to promote free and fair elections.

'If I had that amount of money to spare myself, I would give it to you,' I added.

'No Jo, this is about institutional partnership,' said Kakha. 'We need your organisation because we believe that the UK is one of those countries where free and fair elections work and your organisation has a good reputation in Georgia for your work in human rights – and I know from the Volcano play you are neutral but you can take risks.'

'I'll need to clear it with my colleagues in London.' They might not approve, I thought. We shook hands and I wished Kakha luck.

#

Kote told me he had also been in discussion with Zurab Tchiaberishvili of IFES, the International Foundation for Electoral Systems. 'They want our support to help train a network of Georgians all over the country in parallel vote tabulation, PVT.'

This technique meant that after votes were counted by the official government electoral commission, they would be counted again and recorded separately by trained, independent, Georgian counters. 'What do you think, Jo?' said Kote.

The PVT would add weight to the exit polls and would triangulate against any anomalies. 'Let's look at the budget and see what we can save – we've got to do it, haven't we?'

After consulting colleagues in London, we added to our country plan that we aimed to provide support to transparency in voting.

37

The bad old days

August 2003, Tbilisi

One warm evening I was out with Maia, sitting under the grapevines in the pergola courtyard at Reiner's Café. 'Things all seem so tense and uncertain…what's going on?' I asked her. It was always hard to make sense of Georgian politics and the pre-election period was particularly fraught.

'Who knows? But you know, it was much worse in the 90s.' She told me about the time she gave birth to her second child, Giorgi, in 1990.

'Just generally it was hard to survive – we were in and out of war. There little food, hardly any power, no water. One night my ex-husband, Torniko and I were out and we tried to help a man knocked down by a 'hit and run' driver. Torniko had picked him up from the side of the road and taken him to hospital – but he died two days later and the police turned up to arrest my husband…It was so stressful, they wouldn't leave us alone, they hounded us. I was eight months pregnant at the time. The following day I was picking up my little girl, Sophiko (who was then six years old), from school and to my horror I went into labour in the schoolyard…There was no-one left in the school but in any case there were hardly any cars, let alone taxis, on the road outside. Few people had cars; they were too expensive and there was little fuel. Any taxi drivers would only take you somewhere if they were going in that direction anyway.'

'I was lucky that eventually a man with a car did stop and took me home – I hoped I could at least drop off Sophiko with my mother but she was not at home – and where were our neighbours? It was about three in the afternoon, in November and everyone was out. I said desperately to Sophiko, please, please be good and stay here till Grandma comes home and tell her I had gone to the maternity home. We had no mobiles – in fact few people had working telephones then. My taxi driver turned out to be a kind man (it was not an easy time to be kind), and took me to the maternity home with which I had an arrangement – but no-one was there! My doctor was away and because it was likely to be a complicated birth, as I was so premature, the staff refused to see me and sent me to Maternity House number 1. In theory it was better equipped but it actually had been closed for months…The staff told me it had re-opened the day before and bundled me off across the city, all the time having the contractions and pain.'

'When I got there, the staff said, 'We are not quite open and we were not expecting to have any patients'. In fact the on-duty doctor was away drinking somewhere. The hospital was completely empty, in darkness and all the windows were open because they had repainted it. They put me on a trolley and by this time I was in agony. The only person around to help me was a young intern with a textbook who consulted it and said, 'Don't worry, it is normal to feel pain; it's a classic case.' By luck somewhere they found an experienced midwife and I gave birth to Giorgi. They left me, with the baby wrapped up in a bundle in my arms, lying on a trolley in a dark ward with open windows in November.'

'What about Sophiko and your parents?' They wouldn't have known Maia had been transferred from one maternity house to another.

'By some miracle word had got out where I was – Sophiko had been a good little girl she helped my mother, father and husband find me. It was an awful time – when I went on my scholarship to Britain I spent all my spare money on hot water bottles to send home. You see, Jo, maybe people are putting up with the current hardship because no-one can face risking it all and going back to those terrible days.'

38

Young activists

September 2003, Batumi, Ajara

The TV crews jostled and fiddled with their cameras and sound equipment in the airy hall. Invited guests were crowded in front of the panel of speakers. Our British Council banner was prominently displayed alongside the crest of the British Embassy and a banner with the logo of BP. We were back in Batumi, Ajara. I was in front of the microphone; next to me was Mr Rukhadze of the Anglo-Georgian Friendship Society and to his left was my colleague Rusiko. Behind us was the Wardrop Exhibition.

'I am delighted to welcome you to this launch of an exhibition about Oliver Wardrop, the first British diplomat to be posted to Georgia, in 1918, and Marjorie Wardrop, his sister, who translated the great Georgian epic poem, *The Knight in the Panther's Skin* into English.' Yes, I really was delighted. I thanked BP for enabling the exhibition to go ahead and added, 'While it is good to celebrate our history and our past, and the warm links between the UK and Georgia, it is also, in my view, important not just to look back but also to look to the future.' I told them that we were also launching a branch office of the English Teachers'

Association of Georgia to help give young Georgians new skills and new opportunities to do business and to travel and so on, not just there in Batumi, but in other cities too. Also that Rusiko had recently negotiated free English language learning radio broadcasts all over Georgia with the help of the BBC World Service – there was much applause – this would be a wonderful way to give more and more people the opportunity to better themselves.

I was pleased to finally get the Wardrop exhibition panels out of their years of storage and for it to be seen and appreciated – and even more pleased that BP had agreed to help fund it. Mr Rukhadze was beaming. 'But we still need to have an exhibition in Tbilisi!'

\#

Some days later, in a complete change of scene, we were dancing our socks off deep in the black-painted vaults of the Ajara nightclub to the bass-heavy jazz of our touring band. That is, Mike and I – not me and Mr Rukhadze. Surrounding us were hundreds of young Georgians, arms in the air, dancing and cavorting. Many of us were wearing the British Council T-shirts which Arts Manager, Irakli, had designed. Printed on the T-shirts was a silhouetted figure, one arm raised making a V for Victory sign against a splodged X. In English it said 'Make your Voice Heard' alongside Georgian script which said 'Help Your Country'.

In between tracks the lead musician yelled, 'Hey, Tbilisi! Hey, guys, don't forget to vote – stand up for your rights!'

Before the performance Irakli and I met the band and I asked if they would mind if we used their performance to get out some messages about voting in the run up to the

November elections. The bandleader looked sceptical. 'I don't want to do anything political.'

'Yes, yes, I know, neither would we,' I said. 'This is entirely apolitical – this is just because so many young people are cynical about voting at all.'

'Aren't young people meant to be cynical?'

'Yes, but this is their chance to change things – just talking about all the problems isn't enough. I know you are only in Georgia for a few days – this country is, to be frank, going down the drain...And it could be such a great place. Ordinary

Georgians deserve better and elections are their opportunity to act and to hold their government accountable!'

He nodded thoughtfully and he looked at the T-shirt Irakli was holding. 'Would you wear this?' asked Irakli.

'Good T-shirt,' said the musician.

Figure 15 Irakli and Nata at the Ajara Club

It was just as well he said yes. All over Tbilisi there were also striking red posters, designed by Kote, our Governance Manager, emblazoned with the words 'Jazz in Support of Fair Elections'.

We distributed dozens of the T-shirts to journalists at our jazz event press conference. Kote had arranged another course of human rights training with GIPA (the Georgian Institute of Public Affairs) and had visiting consultants from Leicester University and Queen's University Belfast – he made presentations of the T-shirts to the human rights students. We handed out the T-shirts to as many people as we could at the Ajara nightclub.

Figure 16 Kote and Jo at the Ajara Club

I had herded together our visitors who were in town and they were dancing along with us too. This week we had Embassy colleagues down from Moscow and Dr Richard V from the University of Sussex, with whom we were still working on reform of the Georgian criminal code. I don't suppose it would have been the sort of event Dr V would normally have gone to but he came along and joined in, even donning a British Council T-shirt. There were also friends from the alumni, our human rights contacts and arts contacts. We danced the night away together. I shouted to Richard over the loud, clubby music, 'Are you enjoying yourself?'

He yelled back, 'Make Your Voice Heard!'

#

The following evening Richard and I chatted over dinner in one of Tbilisi's folky restaurants. We were entertained by dancers in traditional costumes with scarlet coats and flamboyant hats, and drummers and flautists in black coats slung with bandoliers of silver gun cartridges. Our guests included significant human rights contacts – from the Liberty Institute, the Georgian Young Lawyers Association, the Association of Legal and Political Education (ALPE), partners from the American Bar Association and other friends of the family. Needless to say there were many toasts, to Richard, to teamwork and partnership, to the possibility of a brighter future for Georgia.

Kote leaned forward and told Richard and me, 'Many people here with us tonight have also been involved in the preparation of a documentary film in which leading intellectuals and civil society leaders gave frank views on the current state of the country – we need to speak up and tell it how it is.'

'I keep hearing about a movement called *Kmara* - what's it all about?' I asked.

'*Kmara* means enough in Georgian. Students are mobilising to try to break through the political apathy that is stagnating our country,' said Anna from the Eurasia Institute. 'They have painted the word 'Enough' all over the city and they have been protesting outside the State University demanding the resignation of the government.'

Kote told us that many NGOs – such as Liberty, ALPE, the Young Lawyers – were actively supporting the *Kmara* movement. 'It's not just NGOs, also theatre and film directors, people all across civil society are working together to try to encourage free and fair elections.'

Mark from the US NGO, the National Democratic Institute, told us that James Baker, the former US Secretary of State, had visited Shevardnadze in July and had given him advice on how to run elections. USAID were trying to help computerise the election rolls. 'But I'm worried the voter lists will still be incomplete – there's a long way to go,' said Mark.

Richard looked round the table and said in an aside to me. 'Isn't everyone so young?' I agreed that it was noticeable that most of the activists and campaigners were under 35.

'They have a different outlook, perhaps, as they grew up after the collapse of the Soviet Union.'

#

It wasn't just about making sure people used their right to vote – it was also about making sure that votes cast were real. Kote and I met Zurab Tchaberishvili of the Fair Election Society, IFES, to launch the training on parallel vote tabulation. We were co-funders of the PVT project, which was entirely new in Georgia. The trainees – maybe 50 people at this session out of 80 in all – were from all over the country and they were being trained in vote counting, independently of the government officials tasked with doing this. These trainees in turn would be training others to share the methodology as cost-effectively as possible.

Zurab, Kote and I together each said a few words to open the training session, to underline our support for free and fair elections as one of the cornerstones of a functioning democracy. I told them that the British Embassy would also be funding official T-shirts for the election monitors to wear on Election Day – being visible was part of encouraging transparency. Zurab emphasised the dedication and commitment of the PVT volunteers. If things got nasty at the polling stations, the parallel vote counters would be doing something very brave. They would be at the heart of helping their country.

#

Meanwhile, Kakha Lomaia from the Open Society NGO had been successful and had brought on board a partnership to fund the exit polls. The informal partnership line-up was his own organisation – the Open Society Georgia Foundation – plus the Eurasia Foundation, the independent TV company Rustavi 2 and the British Council. The Eurasia Foundation was a grant-making NGO which aimed to increase social justice and economic prosperity; at the time it was predominantly funded by USAID.

Hosting an exit poll would be a big thing. Like PVT, exit polls had never been held in Georgia. It would be a new thing for voters to be asked, after they had voted, for whom they had voted – and for those statistics to be gathered in a non-partisan, accountable and transparent way.

Accordingly, our exit poll partnership held numerous press conferences to let the public know that, this time, their votes should count. That was the plan, anyway.

39

Observers

September 2003, Tbilisi

Mike and I were on our way to a dinner party hosted by a
Georgian friend of Mike's, Goga. As we drove I noted, not
for the first time, that there was a lot of welding underway
throughout the city.

Goga was a Georgian businessman who had worked in
Moscow on various enterprises and who had a finger in many
pies. We had the sense that some of his activities in African
countries some years earlier were fairly dark. Mike knew him
through his friend Kevin, as they were all keen motorbikers.
'How can you ever get up to speed on your bikes?' I asked.
'The roads are so pitted with pot-holes.'

'That adds to the thrill,' said Goga. 'Actually it would be
good to get these roads sorted out, then we could really let rip.'
Goga was urbane, intelligent and a little mischievous. He loved
skiing, biking and nice cars. He had invited a great mix of
friends to the dinner party. A British man from the European
Bank of Reconstruction and his Georgian artist girlfriend.
Other cosmopolitan Georgian friends: a businessman who also
headed up a wildlife charity; a famous film director who
additionally lectured on business processes at the university; a
famous dancer who was also a photographer. I said I was

impressed at how multi-talented many Georgians seemed to be. 'Perhaps, but remember our jobs pay very little. No-one could live off only one salary and many people have to have two or three jobs to make ends meet. The economy here is collapsing.'

'That's absolutely right,' said one of his friends. 'Here in Tbilisi if you are lucky to have a good education and friends in the right places, you can get new opportunities. Friends helping friends is the only way you can survive. It's people in rural areas, where there are literally no paid jobs, that have real problems – that is painful to see.' All those men in black hanging around at roadsides in the villages, waiting for something to happen. Often while their women get on and do all the family things like cooking and cleaning, raising children and in many cases being the breadwinner.

'I notice that there always seems to be welding going on – literally all the time, day or night. Is that 'mending and making do' or are there building projects going on?' I asked.

Everyone laughed at my naivety. 'Perhaps a little – but more likely they are stealing the metal for scrap. Pylons have been known to collapse because there's nothing left to support them.'

'It must be interesting to work in Russia,' I said to Goga. Relations between Russia and her tiny neighbour Georgia were often fraught. He nodded and said it was indeed interesting.

'We like the Russians,' said one woman. 'We're just not keen on Putin.'

Goga raised his glass – as host he was *tamada*, the toast master. 'To Mother Georgia, to my mother, and to the mother of my children. To women!'

One of his friends toasted back, 'To friendship!'

Goga raised his glass again, 'Yes, to friendship. I am happy to have you, dear friends, around me. With you there is no *obligatsia*, and for this I thank you.' I could only begin to imagine the complex murkiness of a world underpinned by *obligatsia* rather than the supposed transparency and accountability of a world based on the rule of law. 'I would love to live in a clean Georgia,' said Goga. 'I would pay more tax, if there was somewhere decent to pay it to. I'd like to move from the black economy to white. I consider myself grey, at present.'

#

'Fancy joining us for a night at the Likani Palace?' asked Siobhan, the real Defence Attachée. She and Chris – the official one – were taking a break during one of their many official trips across the South Caucasus. The Likani Palace was near the spa resort of Borjomi. It had been built in 1892 by a Romanov Grand Duke who was Viceroy of the Caucasus in the imperial years. In the Soviet era Stalin often used to use it as a country retreat in his country of birth. We didn't need persuading to visit it.

It was pouring with rain when we arrived. At first glance it appeared to be a pretty little palace, with curvy balconies and turrets but like many other buildings in the country, closer to it was shabby. It was surrounded by a neglected and sprawling garden complete with classical statues and an ornate but empty fountain. 'It's like the *Fall of the House of Usher*, said Chris as thunder shook the sky and lightning flashed around us.

The lower floor of the palace was a dark labyrinth of corridors and servants' rooms. Upstairs were splendid but faded bedrooms with ornate, high ceilings, heavy decorations and enormous lumpy beds. Siobhan and Chris had the dubious honour of sleeping in the bedroom – and possibly the bed – almost definitely slept in by Stalin and before him by the Grand Duke Nicholas Mikhailovich. Each corridor had a rickety chair on which sat a stern *baboushka*. These elderly women guarded the corridors fiercely and looked suspiciously at us when we passed. They looked as if they had known Stalin himself.

There was an odd bathroom arrangement at the palace. One had to go down the long dark corridor from the bedrooms to reach a single, cavernous bathroom with an imposing porcelain bath in one corner, a washbasin in another and, in its own corner, a toilet. It appeared to be completely unmodernised. It was not a cosy room. I couldn't help wondering who had been there before me doing their ablutions in this very room.

In the afternoon, after the storm abated, we went for a long walk around the valley surrounding the palace. The orange and red leaves of the autumnal trees dripped and shivered. Routing back we were slowly approached by an elderly man carrying apples. Chris cleared his throat to say, 'No, thank you, we don't want to buy any apples.'

The little old man looked up at him. 'I am not selling them to you. I am giving them to you.' Chastened, we felt we had to give him some money to thank him for giving us the apples.

Nearing the end of our walk we passed a number of little chalets around the palace. 'These look lovely – let's see what they look like inside,' suggested Siobhan and she and I peered inside one – and popped out just as quickly when an English-sounding voice said, 'May I help you, ladies?'

While we appeared to be the only guests in the palace, minibuses with 'Organisation for Security and Co-operation' (OSCE) across their sides were unloading a number of new, foreign-looking guests who were to stay in the chalets. As it transpired, the English-sounding voice belonged to a retired British army officer. He and the other minibus passengers were apparently an advance party of Election Observers and Monitors, who had arrived in Georgia for training ahead of the November 2 elections. After a little more social chit-chat it further transpired that the army officer was a friend of Siobhan's brother. What a small world.

To celebrate the world being small we felt we deserved a sundowner. We noticed some rather incongruous cocktail glasses in the window of a modest little bar near the palace. Chris asked the waitress, 'Do you do martinis? '

The girl said yes, she certainly did. Stirred, not shaken, as it turned out.

40

Hotting Up

September 2003, Tbilisi

If the Volcano Theatre play we had hosted a few months earlier had been an eruption, the 'Theatre for Change' was like an inferno.

The Basement Theatre was hosting this innovative play. The manager of the Basement was one of those who had offered to help us when our Volcano Theatre production of *L.O.V.E* had faltered back in June. Now they were working with the UK's Department for International Development and the British theatre director, Caryne C.C.

The Basement was actually in a basement off Rustaveli Avenue and one hot evening Maia K and I and about a hundred of us were crammed into it on long, low benches for a performance of the play, *The Choice*. As far as I could see there were only two other foreigners in the audience – I recognised a woman from USAID and another from Save the Children.

The actors were all students and were breathtakingly good. In spite of my non-existent Georgian and with the help of Maia whispering pertinent translation I could easily follow the issues. Caryne had worked with talented Georgian playwrights and they had developed a short but hard-hitting play with themes that every Georgian could identify with in some way – political corruption, bribery and the challenges that face people who try to lead an honest, ordinary life in the face of grinding poverty and lack of employment opportunities. The play had tragedy, comedy, some professional dramatic effects and clever political satire. This was unusual in Georgia and even I could guess which minister they were parodying. They made great use of what looked like Monopoly money – it changed hands several times.

The plan was that the play would last about an hour. This first version of the play involved a central character of an idealistic young man who wants to make a difference and who decides to run for political office. He starts out promising to make things better for those he knows and for those who voted for him. Through a series of choices and decisions, however, all too inevitably he is drawn into the turbid, grubby world of corruption and deception. It was like a Georgian *No Longer at Ease*, that powerful novel by Chinua Achebe about idealism and corruption in Nigeria.

After the first play certain key sections were to be run again – bits of the play where the characters had made decisions that had further implicated them in corrupt practices. Any member of the audience was invited to join in and become part of the play and suggest other ways, other choices that might just have a better result. It was the first time participative theatre had been presented in Georgia. However, after about 45 minutes into the initial play – power cut.

We were plunged into the blackest, hottest darkness. The temperature was in a humid upper 30s. We sat wondering if there was a generator or if the lights would miraculously come back on. When it was clear the power would not be resumed we all fumbled about and found we had two torches in the audience. I had a feeble one and the woman from USAID had a huge one. We surrendered these, candles were lit and lighters were flicked on and off. The actors continued stoically. It was hell-like in the basement.

The actors then re-ran bits of the play and the audience was invited to interrupt and shout out alternatives or different choices. It was utterly compelling and there was a lot of participation. The audience was *living* in the play – even those, like me, who lived on the periphery of most of the issues. One woman got up and threw the toy money back in the face of the actor playing the Corrupt Politician screaming, 'SO MUCH FOR YOUR ELECTION PROMISES – TURN ON OUR ELECTRICITY!' To hysterical cheers from the rest of the audience…The play toured the country and everywhere it was presented audiences were engaged, enraged, ignited.

#

October 2003

'Jo, some young artists would like us to support them to do a painting marathon,' said my colleague Irakli.

'Tell me more,' I urged.

'The National Library is allowing about 30 artists to set up easels and to paint all day on the theme of 'Make your voice heard', before the elections. The artists are all broke.' Young artists always are…'Can we spend about £200 to buy painting materials?'

Yes, we could. On a chilly October day, they set up their easels in the National Library and painted for free and fair elections. It was a big hit with the independent media which covered the event virtually all day.

#

Meanwhile, on the streets in Tbilisi and cities beyond, the *Kmara* student activists, the Georgian Young Lawyers and all their cousins from the Liberty Institute and others were out in force. Demonstrating – waving flags – writing graffiti. If Tbilisi was a woman she may have been fragile and bruised but she wasn't submitting – she wasn't beaten yet. More foreign election observers were arriving in planeloads for the presidential elections on November 2.

Things were hotting up.

41

Elections

We could feel change in the air.

It was snaking and rippling through the country and people were talking, murmuring, shouting to each other. Some were angry, some were fearful. There was a fear that change might make things worse – it might destroy what fragile security there was and the old horrors of civil war and anarchy might creep into the vacuum. Some people though thought, 'enough was enough' and that change might bring more opportunity, prosperity and fairness. It was worrying and uncertain – but there was hope.

#

Before the elections my office had to make sure we and our customers, visitors and offices were safe. If there were scuffles or violence around the polling stations, things could get out of hand. We rehearsed evacuation procedures for non-Georgian nationals – we stored copies of essential documents for an emergency office safely offsite – we reviewed our business continuity plan to make sure it was shipshape and up-to-date. British Council offices everywhere have to manage risks and we had a list of suggestions to consider and for which we needed to have a contingency plan. I looked down at my checklist. 'Just to refresh our memories, our risks might include violence on the streets, civil insurrection, terrorism, war, bombs, earthquake, floods, collapse of banks, collapse of infrastructure – electricity, water, gas...'

'We have already had more than half of those,' pointed out Tamuna.

'We are resilient and prepared,' said Zaza. He was working at full pelt.

'OK, right now we are focusing on the risk of civil insurrection,' I said. A key thing was to keep the TV and radio on all the time. Zaza, Vakho and I additionally had two-way radios which linked to the British Embassy, which we could use in the eventuality that mobile phone networks went down. We three formed the core of an incident control team, supported by Gogi (our IT and techie guy) – we would advise other colleagues on what to do.

We discussed who would do what if there was fighting on the streets or if streets were closed. The default was to close the office and for everyone to stay in their homes. Vakho would be an essential part of the communications strategy, as he had a motorbike and would be available to zip around the city to keep everyone up to date if necessary. He nodded, looking pleased with this arrangement. Tamuna would liaise with Zaza to make sure we closed the library swiftly and with due consideration to our visitors and Anuki had a drill for what to do to cancel the UK exams she managed. Many of the exams we invigilated took place on the same day throughout the world so this would need careful management.

'What visitors from outside Georgia are we due to have this month?' I asked.

'We have the regional team meeting of the Peace Keeping English Project at the end of November – we'll have colleagues from Armenia, Azerbaijan and visitors from Central Europe,' said Ray, the PEP Project Manager. Irakli mentioned that we had another arts exhibition of video installation – the artist would be coming out for five nights at the end of the month.

'Right,' I said, 'let's tentatively agree that these should go ahead, on the premise that we reserve the right to cancel these events at short notice if need be – the Embassy will advise us.'

'We also have an audit due this month, with two colleagues coming from London,' said Accountant Katie. Although we had worked hard to make sure everything was in place and all the financial procedures and contracts were as robust as they could be, an audit is never anyone's favourite thing – it's like going to the dentist.

'Perhaps we can advise them that there is rather a lot going on in Georgia at the moment?'

#

Sunday November 2

The elections were underway. Mike had gone with some of the Embassy staff to provide informal monitoring of the voting while I stayed at home. I had just received the latest pack of Open University materials for my next MSc course. This one was on 'Institutional Development'. I opened it all up and then thought, 'Forget this...' I phoned Mike to ask him what was going on.

'It seems totally disorganised,' he told me. 'As we'd feared, the electoral voters' lists are all over the place. Some of the polling stations just couldn't cope and have started to register people by adding their names on the spot – and some people don't seem to be able to vote at all. It's far from transparent. The bully boys are having their way...'

#

Monday November 3

The following day my colleagues came to the office, crowding into the management team's room and reporting back to each other.

'I voted! – So have I – Me too!'

'What were the polling stations like?' I asked.

'Long, long queues.'

'So disorganised.'

'I saw fighting outside the polling station.'

'I saw fighting inside!'

'Did you see anyone doing exit polls or parallel vote tabulation?' I asked. Most had but some hadn't.

'I saw the international election monitors, you know, OSCE.'

We kept the new flat-screen TV on in reception. This showed cable TV such as BBC World, Euronews and CNN. It wasn't as informative, however, as what was on the stubby little black and white TV that Zaza had perched on a chair in the management team's office upstairs, as this showed Georgian channels. The independent Rustavi 2 TV station, in particular, seemed to be reporting broadly and incisively. One elderly, frail woman shouted at a TV interviewer, 'I have nothing – I have nothing left to take away! But I have a vote!'

As Mike had seen, apparently many names were missing from voter registration lists, so many people didn't even have that. 'I can't vote if my name isn't here,' shouted one man angrily. Actually more than one. As had been feared, the voter lists were in a woeful state.

Tchiaberishvili, the head of the International Society for Fair Elections, which had arranged the parallel vote tabulation, called on Nana Davdariani, head of the Central Electoral Commission to ensure the counting would indeed be free and fair. It was hard to see how the voting could be fair if the lists weren't accurate – but it was worse even than that.

Stories emerged of astonishing, eye-popping examples of ballot stuffing. Men arrogantly walking into polling stations, laden with guns and boxes containing hundreds of alternative, faked votes. A man lifting up his jumper and tipping out a tumble of vote papers on to a counting table. Men holding up a polling station at gunpoint, stealing voting boxes and stuffing them in vans, chucking them in the river.

While we watched the TV, transfixed, my colleagues were receiving and sending text messages and phone calls. The room was alive with talk and speculation. Rustavi 2 reporters continued to report. 'And now we have the preliminary results of the exit polls.'

'Hush, hush, exit polls!' Our room went quiet. This could be important.

The reporter continued, '…was conducted in 500 precincts and among 23,000 voters around Georgia, by the US polling firm, Global Strategy Group. This organisation was contracted by the Rustavi 2 broadcasting company with the financial support of the Eurasia Foundation, the Open Society Georgia Foundation and the British Council.'

I breathed in tightly.

'The National Movement opposition party leads the November 2 parliamentary elections.'

We gasped.

'The exit poll results are:

1. Saakashvili's National Movement 21%
2. Shevardnadze's party, For New Georgia 14%
3. Natelashvili's Labour party 14%
4. Burjanadze-Zhvania Democrats 8%
5. Aslan Abashidze's Revival Union 7%
6. New Rights 6%
7. Other parties 30%'

Irregularities notwithstanding, put simply, this would mean the opposition party headed up by the young, pro-West politician, Saakashvili, was winning and Shevardnadze's government party had lost.

'Remember this doesn't count,' said Kote. 'It's what the government's Central Election Commission say that matters – and what will be really interesting is what the parallel vote tabulation results say.'

#

I hurried back to my own office to look on the internet for other angles, other ways to verify or check on what was going on. I found the freshly released report from OSCE/ODIHR, the Organisation for Security and Co-operation in Europe/Office for Democratic Institutions and Human Rights.

While trained Georgians were doing the exit polling and parallel vote tabulation – for which the results, as with the official count, would come in later – external checking of the probity of voting and counting was undertaken by an International Election Observation Mission from a number of European organisations.

The international mission had been in Georgia since early September with 34 long-term experts deployed in Tbilisi and six regional centres, supported by 450 short-term observers. They had observed elections in 1200 polling stations – almost half. In theory voting should have been undertaken along internationally recognised lines and the international monitors had checklists of things they expected to see – and of things they should not see – on which to report back.

OSCE's report said the November 2 elections in Georgia: *'Fell short of a number of international standards for democratic elections. Inaccuracies in the voter list seriously challenged the fundamental guarantee of universal suffrage and lessened voters' confidence in the state administration.'*

They conceded that attempts had been made to update the election code and noted that the media had been allowed to report on a proliferation of parties, so political pluralism was evident. The election monitors noted, however, that there were serious violations of ballot stuffing; ballot destruction; use of pre-marked ballots; multiple voting and in some cases 'implausible turnout' of voters at some polling stations – in other words, substantially more people voted in a village than were known to exist. The report also noted that government civil servants had been participating as campaign managers for 'For New Georgia', Shevardnadze's ruling party – this was illegal. The international monitors had seen many examples of voters, and Georgian election observer groups, being intimidated, either by physical obstruction or, on some occasions, by violence.

OSCE were particularly concerned with voting in Ajara – here there was *much* evidence of implausible turnout and some serious acts of violence. They noted that the *'political environment in Ajara dissuaded political parties from campaigning.'* I wasn't surprised at that. Ajara was where Aslan Abashidze ruled his sinister state-within-a-state.

There might have been some 'freedom' in the election process, but 'fairness' was being tested.

#

Tuesday November 4

Back in the office we were crowded round the little TV again. It was important stuff – this was the release of the preliminary official results being announced by the head of the Central Election Commission, Nana Davdariani. She looked harassed. 'Any irregularities are down to 'human error'. There is no evidence of wrongdoing.'

My colleagues angrily chorused, 'What? How can she say that?'

'What did we see with our own eyes?'

Davdariani continued, 'These are the preliminary results – please note that these are not the final results. In particular, the results from Abashidze's Ajara Revival party are not yet officially declared.'

'The results so far are:

1. Shevardnadze's For New Georgia party 21%
2. Saakashvili's National Movement 18%

3.   Natelashvili's Labour 12%
4.   Burjanadze-Zhvania Democrats 9%
5.   New Rights 7%
6.   Other parties 33%'

In contradiction to the exit poll results, the official results indicated that Shevardnadze's party had got more than Saakashvili's National Movement.

'It's all crazy,' said Kote. 'The numbers don't make sense!'

'Who are the Labour Party?' I asked.

'They are led by Shalva Natelashvili. They are sort of left wing, older. Natelashvili doesn't like Shevardnadze much but he likes Saakashvili and the others less. Zhvania and Burjanadze, meanwhile, are both Western-leaning reformers and neither much like Saakashvili, but they like the Labour and Revival parties even less.'

It was confusing.

'We are now revealing the result of the parallel vote tabulation (PVT) organised by the International Society for Fair Elections (IFES),' said the Rustavi 2 presenter. The presenter was, in fact, one of our alumni from the John Smith Fellowship Scheme.

IFES had deployed 2500 observers on the day to conduct PVT in 550 precincts, about 85% of all polling stations. Some observers had faced obstruction and even violence. The reporter took a breath and we waited.

'The PVT results are:

1.   Saakashvili's National Movement have 26% of the vote.
2.   Shevardnadze's For New Georgia party 19%
3.   Natelashvili's Labour 17%
4.   Burjanadze-Zhvania Democrats 10%

5.   New Rights 8%
6.   Abashidze's Ajara Revival party 8%
7.   Other parties 12%'

The results of both the exit polls and the parallel vote tabulation, and the International Election Monitoring mission observations, appeared to show unmistakable evidence of massive electoral fraud on the part of the government.

I tried to make sense of it all. 'So the process of consulting the electorate was, evidently, deeply flawed but even those flawed results are being ignored.'

The TV showed images of Mikhayil Saakishvili – Misha – the young leader of the National Movement, out on the streets surrounded by men in black – hundreds of them. The street looked familiar. 'I'm going to see from the front of the building!'

Zaza and I ran through my office and on to the balcony and we looked down. Sure enough there were people massing around near the Central Election Commission which was up Rustaveli Avenue to our left, on the other side of the road. Down below we could also see people walking purposefully towards the parliament building which was a few hundred metres to our right. Zaza and I looked at each other and hurried back to get a different view from the TV in his room. Thousands of people were taking to the streets, demanding that the 'real' votes were recognised – or else that Shevardnadze admitted that there had been electoral fraud and allowed a fresh election. The city had been cordoned off to prevent people coming in from other cities and it was swarming with military personnel and vehicles. Rustavi 2 TV station broadcasts showed, however, that more and more people appeared to be mobilising.

We watched and waited.

42

Demonstrations

As usual Mike drove us to work, coming down from his house high up at the top of the valley, driving down through the cobbled back streets and into the main avenues of the city.

Tbilisi, however, was anything but usual. All over the city at every major road intersection there seemed to be a road block with tanks and armoured vehicles and hundreds of troops, predominantly young. We had heard they hadn't been paid for months, their uniforms and boots were shabby and they were hungry. Some of them were holding riot shields, some wearing balaclavas and ski masks. Many were holding guns. There were also demonstrators everywhere. Without doubt many of the demonstrating men were also carrying handguns.

'It's unreal. Look at all these people!'

We passed large groups in almost every open space, mostly men but some women too. Some were carrying flags, holding them up

Figure 17 'Change is coming!'
(Darren Woodcock)

276

high and waving them. There were the *Kmara* 'Enough' flags – a white background with a silhouette of a clenched fist. Some people were carrying the Georgian flag, a black, white and maroon flag and also one I didn't recognise, a white flag with five red crosses. We saw a young man standing on a rubbish bin hanging on to a tree with one arm and in his other hand a loudspeaker. He was perhaps shouting comradely encouragement to the mass of people below him but absolutely no-one appeared to be looking at him. All the men in leather jackets below him were standing around chatting to each other, smoking and hugging their arms against the cold.

As well as demonstrators and security forces, the city was heaving with media. Camera and radio crews and journalists were everywhere, clasping their equipment and notepads, chasing the burgeoning stories.

Mike dropped me at my office. He had to drive on to the Embassy out at the Metekhi Palace Hotel; it was some way from the city centre and from there he wouldn't be able to immediately see for himself how things were developing on the ground – I knew that he would spend most of his time driving all over Tbilisi seeing different officials and trying to keep a finger on the pulse.

The central location of the British Council office gave me a brilliant vantage point from which to see the demonstrators. 'Keep me posted if you see anything and stay in, stay safe. I love you – not boring here, is it?' said Mike, as he kissed me goodbye.

I rushed upstairs to turn on the two TVs. If you weren't on it, you were watching it. Colleagues arrived in dribs and drabs. Not Governance Manager Kote, though, nor Irakli, the Arts Manager.

'Things must be serious, the international press are here,' I remarked. BBC, CNN and Euronews journalists were reporting from Tbilisi. We flicked backwards and forwards on the flat-screen TV downstairs in reception, to see what the foreign correspondents were making of it – the stories were mostly the same.

'Georgia...Corruption...Politically, economically unstable...Energy and material shortages...Life hard for many people...Challenged elections...Demonstrators in increasing numbers...Opposition leaders calling for fresh elections...' said Damian Grammaticus, the BBC reporter.

Saakashvili, always surrounded by throngs of people, got a lot of airtime and he was voluble, a firebrand in many languages. How the European and US media must have loved him. 'We are here for peaceful demonstrations,' said Saakashvili. 'Shevardnadze has refused to admit or believe there were falsehoods, refused to allow a recount or fresh votes!'

Other opposition party leaders, Burjanadze and Zhvania, were out on the streets too. Giorgi Baramidze (one of Zhvania's men), was in the crowds near the Chancellery building and called on the young troops to be 'clever and careful' – don't fire on the demonstrators...

The demonstrators were evidently not necessarily supporters of the same political party. These were groups of people who were fragmented and lacking in focus – but there was a general and growing feeling that 'enough was enough'.

Irakli turned up at the office wearing a badge that said 'Press'. 'What's that all about?' I asked.

'I wouldn't have been able to get here if I didn't have this on,' he said, 'the streets are cordoned off all over the place.'

We hurried back upstairs to watch the little old black and white TV. The crowds were gathering outside parliament and beyond that in Freedom Square. Outside parliament was a huge screen, maybe four by six metres, on to which the

unfolding events in the city were broadcast. Rustavi 2, the independent TV station, had somehow managed to set up the screen. It was an impressive sight. This was before social networking so television broadcasting, this screen and mobile phones were powerful media. The screen, beaming out the Rustavi 2 TV broadcast, showed the crowd how big they were as a group and where else people were.

Figure 18 The screen in front of Parliament (Darren Woodcock)

More and more people joined them – not just young men but women carrying babies and holding children's hands, and elderly people. People like this had been demonstrating in Tbilisi against Soviet rule on April 9 1989 – and had been gunned down by Soviet troops.

Vakho came bounding in to the management team office and said, 'Quick, watch Euronews!' We thundered down our blue glass stairs to watch the TV in reception. There was Vakho being interviewed.

'Vakho!' we chorused.

'No-one believes these results,' said Vakho to the Euronews interviewer. 'The government party has committed electoral fraud. All we want is for our votes to count and for things to change for the better in our country.'

'I hope you didn't say you were from the British Council – we are apolitical!' I said, anxiously.

'No problems, Jo, I didn't tell them where I worked. I was a 'man in the street'.' And there were plenty of those around.

I went back to my office to phone Ray at the Peacekeeping English Project in the Ministry of Defence to check how things were with his team. 'We aren't doing much – all our students are away working on more important things. We're catching up with our admin.'

'Keep a low profile Ray.'

'It all seems peaceful out our way,' he reassured me. The Georgian MOD offices were some way away from the city centre.

'Let's hope it stays that way...'

#

Figure 19 Demonstrators, media and soldiers (Darren Woodcock)

Although I went to my office over the next few days, it was impossible to get any work done. I mostly watched TV, trawled the internet and leant over my balcony to try to see what on earth was happening on the busy street below. Zaza, the Office Manager, and Irine, our Accounts Assistant, kept me company from time to time during their cigarette breaks. We strained to see up and down Rustaveli Avenue and tried to count the swelling numbers of demonstrators who made a daily pilgrimage towards parliament and increasingly to Freedom Square.

I phoned Mike periodically to give him our rough estimates of how many people appeared to be marching.

There were more people carrying the *Kmara* flag and the white flag with the red crosses – we noticed there were increasing numbers of women, girls and families.

'Some of the women are carrying roses…' said Irine.

#

Sunday November 9, Tbilisi

I didn't want to go to London. I had to go back for work meetings, not least to brief another new boss, Bob. I didn't want to leave when things were so tense and so exciting and I didn't want to leave my colleagues at a difficult time. Zaza and I had rehearsed the contingency plans a hundred times – we did another test run in the office and checked that our alternative offsite office could function.

Mike said, 'Look at it this way, Jo, with you out of the way, Zaza and the British Embassy have one fewer British national to worry about. If things get bad, you would have to leave anyway.' Which was true. Barrie and Ray were still in town but it would be hard to meet more laid back, sensible and experienced men.

'I'll miss you,' said Mike. 'We'll be together soon.' We were only going to be apart for a few days as he also had to return to London on business. I would miss him too – we were a team.

Off I flew, fretting.

#

Monday November 10, London

Email from Zaza, Tbilisi to Jo, London

Dear Jo,

Hope you are doing well. The situation here is still difficult. The President met some of the opposition leaders but unfortunately the negotiations resulted in nothing as the President declared he was not aware of any violations of election procedures and had no authority to make any decision affecting the results. There are more and more people coming from different regions and the temporary daily manifestations have turned into a permanent one in front of the parliament building – the road there is blocked to traffic all the time. But we are open as there is little likelihood of violent outcomes in the nearest future, the office is accessible and (thank God) all the facilities are functioning. Though general tension is rising in the population.

One more thing, regarding the Wardrop Exhibition in Tbilisi State University. Mr Rukhadze informed me that they would like to organise the exhibition to open on November 24.

What do you think?

Warm wishes from us all, Zaza

#

You can imagine what I thought.

#

Tuesday November 11, London

Phone call London to Tbilisi

'Zaza, I hope you are all OK!'

'We are fine, Jo – we're watching events from over your balcony. We've had library users coming in to learn English and use the computers and then they go down the road to join the demonstrations. We closed the office now, though, just in case. Yes, the main opposition leaders, Saakashvili, Zhvania and Burjanadze, met with Shevardnadze on November 9 and Shevardnadze said he wouldn't resign over a few young people waving flags – he said something about, 'it would be different if it was a million people signing a petition', so now there is a massive petition. They say a million names are already on it!'

'I wonder where this is all going? Keep me posted, Zaza. Take care!'

Dear oh dear, oh dear, oh dear.

#

Thursday November 13, London

Email from Mike, Tbilisi to Jo, London

Darling,

The latest official figures on the vote counts are all over the place…All the EU ambassadors met Shevy a couple of days ago and urged dialogue and not forcible methods to solve the stasis. Deborah is working round the clock. And the US Ambassador has been accused of being behind the demonstrations – crazy, but you know what the rumour mill can be like. In reality, of course, he will be keeping a watchful eye and urging peaceful dialogue.

Can't stop, things to do, people to see.
I love you, together soon,
Mike

#

Friday November 14, London

Phone call London to Tbilisi

'Hi Kote, what is the latest? I'm finding it hard to keep up…' I knew he would be deep in the heart of it, he knew so many key people.

'Jo, you would not believe it, it is all such a fantasy. They just released their latest 'official' figures. 110 per cent of people in Ajara voted for Abashidze's party, Revival! Abashidze will now go into a coalition with the Shevardnadze party which, according to these 'official figures' would give them almost 40% per cent of the total vote in Georgia.'

Aslan Abashidze's Revival Party in Ajara had somehow achieved 19 per cent of the total vote in Georgia. No mean feat considering only 10 per cent of the population lived there.

'That's incredible – it's is beyond belief...'

'Yes, these figures are completely fabricated – Abashidze just made up the numbers.'

'Do they think no-one will notice?' I said, astonished.

'Well, we know that Shevardnadze travelled to Ajara a few days ago and talked to Abashidze.'

'I thought they hated each other?' I asked.

'Yes, but maybe not as much as they both hate Saakashvili. Aslan Abashidze apparently wants a greater role in Georgian politics or he threatens to secede.'

The Georgian state had already potentially lost South Ossetia and Abkhazia. Shevardnadze couldn't afford to lose Ajara as well. The biggest fief in the fiefdom was apparently holding him to ransom.

'All that, for this? Kote, I'm speechless, I'm so sorry. What about the opposition leaders?'

'Saakashvili is calling on people not to demonstrate over the weekend, but to have a 'day of action' on Monday. He wants Shevardnadze to resign and won't talk to him.'

'What about Burjanadze and Zhvania?'

'They want dialogue – for Shevardnadze to cancel the elections and call fresh ones. This new threat of Abashidze possibly joining forces with Shevy is worrying everyone. Zhvania, Burjanadze and Saakashvili are talking together far more now – but it's all very uncertain.'

'Stay safe, Kote and keep me posted!'

#

Wednesday November 19, London

After work in the London office I went back to my new flat

and sat watching what had been going on in Tbilisi on any TV channel I could find, and I trawled the internet for news. I learnt that the newly 'elected' parliament was due to convene on November 22. I found a TV clip of Shevardnadze meeting the press and appealing to the young people behind the demonstrations. 'I warn you and urge everyone – you could be my grandchildren – you cannot do this. Since I am alive, since I am elected President, I will not allow society to tear itself apart. If people confront each other war may follow – the threat is real.' He didn't say this in a threatening way. He looked genuinely baffled – as if there was only a problem with a few silly young people out on the streets. Yellow leaves were falling into the chilly autumnal streets in Tbilisi.

Tedo Japaridze, the head of the National Security Council and one of Georgia's most senior officials, supported the President. While he accepted that electoral violations had possibly occurred, he pointed out that Shevardnadze was in a difficult and isolated situation. He said the President was, in effect, being blackmailed into stepping down by people making radical speeches and massing in the streets but he felt most people did not want the threat of violence. 'Under these circumstances I support the announcement by the ruling party concerning the opening of the new parliament.'

Abashidze sent busloads of his Ajaran supporters to Tbilisi. Rumour had it that they had been bribed – but it was so difficult to know what rumours were true, or partly true, or how much was false propaganda. The TV coverage made it look fevered. Pro-government supporters were now rallying in front of parliament, carrying sticks...anti-government supporters were everywhere else.

I saw one of the opposition leaders, Nino Burjanadze, being interviewed. She said Shevardnadze had squandered his earlier achievements. 'I was proud to have a president who was friends with some of the most important people of the 20th century. I'm truly sorry things have come to this point. The president had the chance to have his name written in gold letters in the history of Georgia.'

There was agitator, Misha Saakashvili, saying to the masses, 'We want peace! The only way to have peace is to replace this irresponsible, dangerous President and we, the whole Georgian nation, we together can do it!' All around him there was rousing singing and dancing in the crowds. Oh Georgia – always an opportunity to dance together. Then footage of a stream of cars hooting up and down Rustaveli Avenue – cars and buses crammed with young families, old men and women. Chanting, 'Misha! Misha! Misha!' If Abashidze could bus in supporters, so too could the opposition.

Soldiers in lines were holding their riot shields, looking nervously out from their balaclavas, eyes darting from side to side. More and more people were carrying red roses to the demonstration.

#

Thursday November 20, London

'Shevy won't easily step down,' said Mike. Mike had come back to Britain for a few days on business.

The Georgian Central Election Commission had released the final 'official' set of results that day and we sat poring over them alongside the 'real' results from the Parallel Vote Tabulation.

Official and PVT results:

Party	Official results %	Place	PVT %	Place
For New Georgia (Shevardnadze government party)	21	*1*	19	*2*
Democratic Revival (Abashidze, Ajara)	19	*2*	8	*5*
National Movement (Saakashvili)	18	*3*	26	*1*
Labour	12	*4*	17	*3*
Burjanadze-Democrats	9	*5*	10	*4*
New Rights	7	*6*	8	*6*
Other parties	14	–	12	–

'How can the government keep sticking to these fabricated figures?' I asked, exasperated. 'How did your presentation go?' Mike had just made an official presentation to his Whitehall colleagues.

'I told them that I don't feel the Georgians have any appetite for violence with the horrors of the 1993 civil war still fresh in their minds,' said Mike. 'And that it is highly unlikely these demonstrations will make a difference unless the opposition can develop sufficient critical mass against the bully boys and those with vested self-interest who control the ballot boxes – if they are under threat, would they fight for survival? It is all still so unclear. The opposition is clearly popular but they are too fragmented and will they be allowed to keep on the pressure? No-one really knows if there is sufficient opposition.'

I was annoyed. 'These demonstrations have to make a difference! What is the point of us saying 'democracy' and free and fair elections are worth standing up for, if they don't make a difference? They aren't just concepts!'

' Maybe it just isn't the right time in Georgia – my feeling is that Shevardnadze might call for fresh elections and then these opposition groups can get their act together – perhaps the civil society institutions in Georgia are not yet firmly enough in place?'

'The institutions will never be firmly in place if things carry on as they are!' I said.

'You can't want sudden regime change!' said Mike.

'I'm not saying we intervene for regime change – we know that doesn't work! I'm only saying we can hope for something better for Georgians and we can encourage those who can make a difference. We are not imposing our values – the Georgians are asking for our help. It is my job to try to know what young Georgians want – and they want their government to be accountable, to work!' I was yelling. 'And just because it is potentially inconvenient for us and our country doesn't mean we shouldn't encourage it. I have lots of Georgian friends who want change. It isn't a whim – it's for jobs, heat, light, opportunity. Why should they stay forever in this hell? I think this is the Georgian people's chance, now, to stand firm!'

'People could be killed – you know how trigger-happy people can be – you can't want that!' Mike was frustrated by the unpredictable situation.

'Of course not!' I shouted at him. 'I just think this is the closest they have ever, ever been to self-determination. You said yourself it is virtually a failing state – you can't want that either?'

We both knew it was fragile – few government institutions functioned. There were fewer and fewer jobs, raging corruption, shaky rule of law. The next step from failing state was a failed state...Anarchy...Civil war. Georgia had already had those within living memory and she didn't need them again.

'You aren't really an ice maiden, are you? Will you marry me?'

43

Revolution

Saturday November 22 2003, Tbilisi

We arrived back at Tbilisi airport in the early hours of Saturday morning. Vakho was there, waiting to drive us back into the city. My new fiancé agreed with Vakho that we should not go through the centre of the city but skirt around the dark back streets. We could see barricades near the State Chancellery building and beyond, manned by soldiers standing near military vehicles. Dispersed about the cold city were groups of hard-core opposition demonstrators huddling around beaten up, charcoal-smouldering braziers.

'They say there are about 100,000 people during the day,' said Vakho. 'The big crowds will be back in Freedom Square at daybreak.'

'What's been going on?' I asked. We had missed valuable hours of developments during our flight back.

'Nobody really knows – but thousands of extra people have come in from the regions. So many cars and buses full of people. And Tedo Japaridze, the Chair of the National Security Council, was on TV yesterday evening – he called on Shevardnadze to admit the elections were a fraud.' Japaridze was one of Shevy's top officials and he had made a crucial about-turn.

'This changes everything,' said Mike.

#

Mike spent the morning phoning his contacts. Periodically the lines would jam.

Irakli phoned me. 'Jo, I think the revolution is starting... What should we do about the art exhibition?'

I hadn't forgotten about it. We were hosting an installation art exhibition at the Karvasala Gallery, the Silk Route watering hole where Mike and I had had our impromptu date exactly a year earlier. Our British Council launch reception was due to start in the early evening.

'The art work and the artist are here. She came in a few days earlier to set it all up and she has done a few activities already. The invitations to the reception have gone out and details of the exhibition have been in the press.'

'Where are you?'

'I'm here at the gallery.'

The gallery was some 100 metres down from Freedom Square, the focus of the demonstrations. I told Irakli to stay where he was and that Mike and I would come down – we could decide what to do there. The exhibition wasn't the only event the British Council was hosting that weekend. I phoned Ray, the team leader of the Peacekeeping English Project. He and his colleagues had been hosting a regional review meeting and there were participants from all the South Caucasus countries and some from Central Europe. The visiting participants were staying in a centrally located hotel, which was where their workshop meetings were also being held. It was so centrally located it was just down the road from the parliament building – near, in fact, where the other big crowd of demonstrators were congregating.

'We're all fine,' said Ray, 'but it has been hard to keep our participants' minds on English teaching methodology. We have all been peering out the window at all these crowds.'

'Don't leave the hotel Ray.' We agreed to keep in touch.

I phoned Zaza to find out where he was. 'I'm in the British Council – the demonstrators are still coming past our office on their way to the Parliament building. I wanted to make sure everything was all right here – we have closed the office though, to be on the safe side.' Zaza said he would join us at the art exhibition.

'The newly 'elected' government is due to be opened in the Parliament building this afternoon,' said Mike, coming off a phone call, 'but apparently Saakashvili, Burjanadze and Zhvania are boycotting the session. Let's get down to the city centre so we can assess what on earth is going on.'

#

The city was massing with people, walking purposefully towards the city centre. There were more barricades, with young, conscripted soldiers in riot gear looking out through their visors. As we drove, I tried to see their eyes. They did not look aggressive but anxious.

There were empty buses everywhere, parked untidily around the periphery of the city centre. The cold air was heavy with cheap petrol. The pro-reform demonstrators were evidently not just from Tbilisi. Their numbers were swelled by busloads of people from other cities, Rustavi, Telasi, Gori, Zugdidi.

Figure 20 Rustaveli Avenue (Darren Woodcock)

I phoned a colleague in the

British Embassy to discuss the situation. 'Things might be teetering into a revolution!' I bleated.

And our colleague said, 'Can you give me half an hour? The Rugby World Cup Final is on and England is playing Australia...'

#

While the England rugby team were apparently engaged in an historic win against Australia we were in the Karvasala art gallery.

The roads in the quaint old town seemed quiet.

'Let's go ahead with the reception, Irakli.' I couldn't imagine anyone actually turning up. Wato, the man from our trendy partner organisation *media art farm* (all lower caps), and our contemporary media artist were at the gallery.

The video art exhibition was all set up playing on several large screens around the chilly gallery. Wine, snacks and flyers were laid out. Ambient music was playing softly. 'It's all so 'British Council',' said hard-nosed political officer Mike. Many of my British Council team had come to help with the reception, but not Kote – he had more important things on his mind.

Young men and girls drifted into the gallery. They were mostly dressed in black and some were holding Georgian flags. Some had *Kmara* flags and some of the girls were carrying dark red roses. They had evidently broken away from the demonstrations to come down the road to see the British Council exhibition – we were hosting revolutionaries!

A TV crew came in to cover our event – I was astonished. They asked me to give an interview and, with the camera rolling asked, 'Please tell us what this exhibition is all about.' The standard request about any event. I was struggling to think of a reply that would in some way connect our event to the real world. I couldn't imagine how this interview would go out on TV – who would possibly watch it?

'Contemporary media art is important because it is a way of helping people to think independently and to explore new ideas and to challenge accepted norms,' I said. 'Just because something has always happened in a particular way doesn't mean it is the only way. What is exciting today is what is going on out there, on the streets around Freedom Square –'

Someone shouted, 'Come in here! Parliament is being stormed! Come in here!'

The TV crew and I immediately abandoned my interview. We all ran together, following the direction of the voice. We crammed into the gallery guards' room. This was a cramped, untidy, behind-the-scenes room which had a large old black and white TV, broadcasting grainy footage. Mike and I, the guards, British Council staff, visitors with revolutionary flags, the video artist, even the TV crew crushed in together – we saw a mass of men heaving their way through the seemingly solid doors of the cavernous parliament building.

Shevardnadze had just been addressing the new parliament, as if nothing was going on outside. 'The President will only resign according to the constitution,' he said. 'I am dependent on the will of parliament and the people and it will happen according to the constitutional framework. I believe I have support from each political party...'

The demonstrators had hammered on the door of the parliament building and the security personnel had stood aside. The crowd poured in – shocked, we watched their progress unfold. A man holding a rose high up above his head, was leading the way, followed by others, many others.

'That's Saakashvili!'

Saakashvili was booming, 'Resign! Resign! Resign!' His words echoed across the crowded, chaotic hall of the parliament.

Shevardnadze continued, 'I want to thank the opposition, the constitutional opposition...'

The pushing and shoving further down the room gained a momentum that the MPs in the middle of the room could no longer contain. In frozen fascination we watched the demonstrators, like a homogenous organism, swarm forward. They climbed over the tops of the chairs, over the tables, towards the front of the room. Shevardnadze appeared to ignore the ruckus unfolding, until his bodyguards seized him and bundled him to a side-door. The Silver Fox was jostled out, one of his men holding a Kalashnikov above his head.

Saakashvili's crowd surged forward. Those at the head of the pack reached the front of the room, scattering papers, jumping on tables, hammering a ceremonial hammer and triumphantly drinking tea from Shevy's cup. The crowd yelled, 'Misha! Misha! Misha!'

Now Saakashvili was at the front of the room holding a rose, surrounded by men waving large red and white flags and the *Kmara* flags of the student protesters. Georgian music started to fill the room.

Our TV crew had vanished and had rushed to where the action was unfolding.

'Oh – my – God! Oh my God! Oh my God!' we chorused.

'This is some film...Are you sure it isn't scripted?' asked the video artist.

'My daughter! My daughter! My children!' said my colleagues, suddenly worried about family at home.

'The British Council!' said Zaza, seriously concerned that the parliament stormers were so close – maybe 300 metres – to our office. They could easily become looters.

Was this a power vacuum? Had a failing state failed altogether? We jolted back to the reality of worrying about what we should do next – was it safe to get home? I discussed with Mike and Zaza and barked, 'Yes, go home! Things might get worse...Avoid the central streets, don't be tempted to get involved!' I phoned Ray – we agreed that his visitors should on no account leave their hotel.

Vakho took our visiting artist back to her hotel. I told her not to leave till we came to get her the following day. 'No fear of that,' she said, 'I'm not going anywhere.' She didn't look as if she was greatly enjoying her weekend in Tbilisi.

#

Sunday November 23

The next morning Mike was constantly on the phone and I watched TV endlessly. 'It's all very confused. Shevy has declared a state of emergency and says the criminals responsible will be punished,' said Mike. 'Damn – the mobile phone lines keep going down – the networks are overloaded,' he said, picking up his satellite phone. On TV we saw pictures of the chair from Shevardnadze's office. It had been destroyed – hacked to pieces and burnt.

Saakashvili was on TV pretty much non-stop, surrounded by supporters.

Burjanadze had declared herself Acting President under the constitution and she called on Shevy to hold fresh elections as the opposition parties had declared the November 2 ones null and void.

What would Shevardnadze do next? He hadn't gone yet. We saw Shevy hosting a press conference. 'We can discuss

Figure 21 Mikhayil Saakashvili and supporters (Darren Woodcock)

anything. If they want to speed up presidential elections or have a re-run of parliamentary elections but only after the violence has come to an end.'

'But the demonstrators weren't being violent, were they?' I asked Mike. 'Well, they stormed parliament and burnt his chair,' he pointed out. 'We heard that some of the army might be siding with Burjanadze as Acting President,' he added – but nothing was definite. It was all so fluid.

We also saw that Igor Ivanov, the Russian Foreign Minister, had arrived from Moscow to try to act as a mediator. He spent all day going backwards and forwards between the presidential palace and the Parliament building, which was now held by opposition party supporters. Ivanov said that there might have been electoral mistakes but that these should be sorted out 'in the realm of the law' to avoid chaos. The last thing the Russians wanted was total chaos on their doorstep. The US too urged dialogue and compromise, for the avoidance of confrontation and for calm to be restored.

#

That evening Mike went off to the British Embassy on the other side of town. Meanwhile I met Irakli, the video artist, our art partner Wato and Ingrid, his Belgian girlfriend. We had dinner in the *fin de siècle* restaurant, Paradise Lost. The one with bicycles hanging from the ceiling and waiters dressed in black with long white aprons.

We feverishly discussed developments, aided by watching a black and white TV attached to the side of the elaborate *art nouveau* bar. Most of the time there was little to see apart from the crowds outside parliament or in Freedom Square. The big screen was still in front of the parliament building so the demonstrators could see the same images we could – either themselves or Ivanov's plane sitting at Tbilisi airport. We could see tanks and soldiers hanging around wearing balaclavas, surrounded by demonstrators. The soldiers were probably the same age as many in the crowd. Neighbours, cousins, schoolmates.

There was much debate on TV about whether Shevy would flee to Russia – or would he ask the army to fire on their own people? If shots were fired what would the Russian government do? What would the US, or any other government, do? If one bullet was fired, it could be a spark to ignite a war – it wouldn't take much for excitable young men, or indeed desperate older men, to put their firearms into use.

We speculated in a blue fug of cigarette smoke.

'The revolution this...'

'The revolution that...'

'Is it really a revolution?'

'Fuck the revolution!' said our visiting artist.

Sacrilege, we thought. She was only in Georgia for a few days and had come at an intense time. 'Can I go back to my hotel and you can tell me when it's all over?' Easier said than done, given how tense it was and how potentially dangerous it might be outside. The hotel was only across the road so Irakli escorted her there and hurried back to join us.

Behind the scenes, we could imagine there must be discussions and debates, arguments and agreements, shouting, yelling, appeasing, alliances formed and broken. The most likely outcome was that Shevardnaze would call for fresh elections and that these would have to be free and fair. It was assumed he would stay on as President while a new government would be elected in.

At one point on the TV they reported that Shevardnadze had gone, flown off to Moscow. We knew better, as I was in mobile contact with colleague Nutsa, who told us she was in mobile contact with Shevy's granddaughter. Nutsa's friend reliably reported that she and others in his family were with him at home and that he was sitting in his armchair – in his living room in front of a roaring log fire. It was odd to think that this ageing man, once so powerful and influential in the Soviet Union and so instrumental in *perestroika* and *glasnost* and the deconstruction of the Soviet Union – and with that gaining the independence of his own country – was now pondering what best to do. Surrounded by his family, young and old, sitting in front of a roaring log fire.

More talking behind the scenes, more people in power deciding what to do with the power they had.

What to do?

What to do?

Then, on the television, we saw someone put a rose down the barrel of a gun. Other girls did the same. We could see that military units had apparently started to switch sides. Soldiers were now holding roses, looking sheepishly at the pretty girls in the crowds. Men jumped up on to the tanks, pushing more roses down the gun barrels. Saakashvili embraced soldiers. 'My brothers!'

Zhvania and Saakashvili went to the presidential palace with the Russian Foreign Minister, Ivanov.

Shevardnadze, Saakashvili, Zhvania and Ivanov emerged from the last of endless meetings – they looked in shock.

Then it came. The TV reporter announced, with a tremor in his voice, that Shevardnadze was stepping down.

That Shevardnadze conceded that there had been some electoral fraud. The President said, 'If I use the rights I have, it would lead to bloodshed – but I have never betrayed my people.'

#

From all over the city, perhaps deep in the remote countryside too, came a roar. We all roared. Everyone at our table, everyone in the restaurant, the waiters in their white aprons, everyone was roaring and leaping up and down.

We ran out to Chavchavadzhe Avenue, Tbilisi's main thoroughfare, and everyone was roaring there too. The city had gone beserk with delight. Cars driving around honking and hooting, streets overflowing with people waving flags, waving at each other. Soldiers making a V for victory sign and laughing, running down the roads. Fireworks exploded over the city, along with a crackling of celebratory gunfire, turning the night air smoky and aromatic, silhouetting the cars and buses.

I phoned my parents – worried and remote – to shriek, 'THEY DID IT!'

It seemed impossible now that the government guns would be turned on their own people.

Mike had spent the evening in touch with his network of contacts in Tbilisi and his colleagues in London. It was about midnight. He phoned me and yelled, 'What's your location?' and I thundered, 'PARADISE LOST!'

Mike drove through a city wild with delirious crowds. People were pouring out of their homes and restaurants and wherever they were to join the demonstrators and celebrators. When he arrived we hugged and hugged. 'Never a dull moment darling!' yelled Mike above the din of the celebrations.

The waiters had disappeared into the street party, flinging off their white aprons.

'Come – come with us,' said Wato and Ingrid, and we went back to their flat just around the corner. 'It was our screen,' said Wato, of the big screen outside parliament, on which Rustavi 2 had shown their broadcasts of the demonstrations and of the opposition party leaders going amongst the crowds. The *media art farm* screen had played its own part in showing the demonstrators what was going on and how big the crowds were. It was the same screen Mike and I and Irakli had been shown on exactly a year earlier at the Karvasala Gallery when we were part of the Swiss Embassy/*media art farm* installation art exhibition.

We toasted and talked into the small hours, loafing on low benches strewn with prickly tapestry cushions, about what the new Georgian freedom would bring. We figured that Shevardnadze must have realised his hungry, under-resourced army, would not support him.

'They are saying it is the 'War of the Roses' – the red roses against the Silver Fox.'

'Or the 'Rose Revolution'.'

'How could Shevardnadze not have known how desperate people are here?'

'People get removed from reality if they have been in power too long and they are surrounded by people who want the status quo to remain.'

Shevardnadze didn't seem to be personally corrupt, I said.

'But some of his cronies are – they have creamed off tons of money...'

#

To be there in Tbilisi, that night!

We were high on hope and expectation. Here, surely, was a chance that things could get better in Georgia.

#

'We are assembled', he said, 'to discuss and counsel together.
The sun of my days is set, a moonless night is before me.
The full-blown rose must scatter the face of the earth with its petals.
But the bud on the branch unfolds, filling the garden with fragrance.'
Knight in the Panther's Skin verse 35
Shota Rustaveli

44

Shevardnadze's chair

I woke after a couple of hours' sleep with a wolfish hangover. Mike had to get over to the Embassy and to try to assess what the consequences of the weekend's events would be and I had the Peacekeeping English review meeting to close. We were still going ahead with our project workshop – the show must go on.

Walking into the conference room at the PEP hotel I bumped into Chris, the Defence Attaché, who looked a little rosy-cheeked and yes, even more wolfish than me. 'What a night!'

Chris addressed our PEP colleagues. 'The aim of the Peacekeeping English project is all about helping people across the world communicate with each other and by this to try to understand each other. I am sure we have all been endlessly watching television and you will have noticed how many of the younger generation in Georgia speak English or want to be able to. I truly believe that mastering the English language is important for peace, and for prosperity, in this volatile world.'

I added that I was glad everyone was safe and that they had evidently heeded the warning not to leave the hotel during last night's dramatic events. Two of my colleagues shifted in their chairs and looked at each other. The participants introduced themselves – needless to say there was high excitement. Eva, the woman from the Czech Republic said, 'I lived through the Velvet Revolution in Prague. I didn't think I would live through another!'

After the pleasantries Chris and I got ready to let them get on with the workshop. I wished them all the best and reminded them that things were still edgy and to be careful out there. As Chris and I were leaving Matt and Sergey from the Armenia PEP office intercepted us.

'Jo, we need to come clean. We stormed the parliament yesterday!'

'You aren't even Georgian – it could have been a bloodbath!'

'Can we make it up to you? We have a present for you,' said Matt. Armenian Brandy? Matt handed me a stick about 20 cm long of splintered, battered wood. I looked at it. It had small metal studs along it. I asked him what it was.

'A bit of Shevardnadze's chair'

'We've both got even bigger bits.'

They were not only present in the great mass of men (and a few spirited women), ramming into the parliament building, Matt and Sergey were right in the thick of it. I blanked from my mind the possible alternative outcome of what today would have been like if the soldiers had fired.

Later that day I had my piece of history sawn into three pieces. I gave one to Zaza, for keeping the office safe from potential looters – he had slept in the office while our guards kept guard on the street. Another piece I gave to Kote – he had been in the thick of it. The third bit I kept. I have it still.

It later transpired that Shevardnadze's chair was the only bit of collateral damage. No cars were set on fire nor shops and offices torched or looted. More remarkable still, there was no bloodshed, no fighting and political tribalism was suspended.

Part 4 Impact

45

New broom politics

We were swept along Rustaveli Avenue amongst a delirious crowd. It was a sharp, sunny, optimistic day. Mike and I, of course, had not joined in the protest demonstrations against electoral fraud in the Georgian elections in November. It was not our place to do so. But we sure as hell joined in the celebrations.

It was the day of the inauguration of the new President, Mikhayil Saakashvili. We had decided not to drive but to walk down from our hillside house along with thousands of other people who were converging outside the parliament building for the inauguration ceremony.

'The city looks so spic and span.' It really did. The wide boulevards and cobbled side streets had been swept of dead leaves and litter. Street lampposts and doors had been painted. Shop fronts and government windows been washed. If Tbilisi was a woman…she looked sparkling and fresh. Excited and full of hope. Her beauty emerging again.

Enterprising street vendors were selling little flags. 'They have brought back the ancient flag – the white one with the five red crosses. They're undergoing a rebranding exercise,' said Mike. We bought some and I waved mine as energetically as

*Figure 22 Inauguration Day
January 2004*

anyone there. Almost everyone was carrying one of these flags and elegant larger versions of these hung off lampposts and high off the tops of the major buildings. Not only this flag, we noted, but the European Union flag was hung high outside the parliament building.

It was a family day, with groups of men and women and their children, older people, teenagers and young people, thronging, chatting and happy.

#

After the collapse of his government Shevardnadze in effect retired from public life. Unlike other deposed leaders he did not flee his country – it was clearly important to allow him to stay in his own country without fear of prosecution. He was quoted as saying, 'A liberal state requires those structures that can guarantee the sustainability of a fledgling nation. Regrettably many of my colleagues did not take the right path – I did not receive accurate and adequate information from them…Ultimately it was my fault.'

We also heard he had said, 'But I did everything the Americans asked of me.' Perhaps Shevardnadze felt the structures needed for reform were already in place – and he still apparently maintained that the November 2003 elections weren't totally rigged. Perhaps those around him shielded him and he just didn't see the everyday misery in Georgia?

When Shevardnadze had stepped down, under the constitution Nino Burjanadze, as Speaker of the House, stayed as Acting President until presidential elections were arranged for January 4 2004. Zurab Zhvania became Prime Minister and Tedo Japaridze became the Minister of Foreign Affairs.

Figure 23 British Ambassador Deborah Barnes Jones monitoring the January 2004 election

For these new presidential elections Mike and I had gone along with our Ambassador, Deborah, as she was an election monitor. The British Council provided a consultant to monitor and evaluate the exit poll process – these elections appeared orderly and far better organised.

Apparently 96 per cent of the electorate voted for Saakashvili and this result was deemed to be free and fair. This was an extraordinary vote of confidence. Expectations that he and the other reformers would deliver were, needless to say, very high.

#

In the cheerful crowd for the inauguration there was dancing and good-humoured jostling as we waited for the speeches.

'Look, there's one of my guards.' Sure enough one of the young men who had had to sit in the little hut outside my house was standing to attention in a smart new uniform. He smiled in recognition as I waved at him. We bumped into other people we knew. The Minister of Defence, David Tevzadze, tipped his peaked cap at me. 'He seems so perky.'

'He hasn't lost his job yet,' said Mike.

'Jo, have you heard my news?' It was Rusiko from my office in the excited throng of people. 'Colin Powell, you know, the US Secretary of State, is here for the inauguration. The US Embassy has invited me to the reception for them as one of the hundred most important people in Georgia.'

'Rusiko – you certainly are!' The US had a massive presence in Georgia, and this was an honour and was recognition of her, and her colleagues', work in helping to spread the teaching and learning of English. I had been astonished to read though in the (foreign) press that some thought the Rose Revolution was US-sponsored or a CIA coup – or that it was somehow planned and orchestrated by George Soros as the man behind the Open Society. Extraordinary. You couldn't manage a coup like a project – managing projects was hard enough.

Quite the reverse – there was a widely held feeling, including with Burjanadze and Zhvania, that if Shevardnadze had conceded electoral fraud in November and had allowed fresh elections, he himself could have stayed as President until the presidential elections in mid-2004.

The OSCE had summarised that it was a 'lack of political will to manage a genuine democratic election process which provoked a political crisis'. Undoubtedly the huge swell of public dissatisfaction had been encouraged, informed and nurtured by Georgian non-governmental organisations, many of whom had received support from organisations from other countries.

We had had quite a few warm emails at the office from our NGO contacts. 'This could not be possible without the assistance we Georgians received from your organisation and the whole international community. We always feel your support and especially so during that week. I hope we will manage, again with your assistance, to build a new Georgia.'

To us the Rose Revolution was a spontaneous, unexpected and organic result born out of the desperation of millions of ordinary Georgians. A critical mass of opposition to the status quo had been achieved. Undoubtedly many foreign organisations contributed – we could also see the poverty and malfeasance – but the calls for change were co-ordinated and led by Georgians.

There was a lot of post-revolution discussion too on the role played by the Rustavi 2 TV channel. Did it go over the line of objective reporting? Their continuous broadcasting of the results evidently encouraged the disparate opposition parties and led to the swelling in numbers of demonstrators. The presence of foreign media too undoubtedly contributed to the growth in confidence of the demonstrators. I don't know if they went too far. I have often wondered whether the news makes the media or the other way round.

#

On inauguration day, although there was widespread delirium, not everyone was pleased. We bumped into one of our cleaners, and sensible friend, Maka. 'Bah – this was not a revolution. It will be the same and we will have younger, more stupid, politicians – but let's see what they come up with.'

People climbed up trees along the avenues near the parliament building to get a better view. Saakashvili's voice boomed out to a cheering crowd.

'Two weeks ago an election was held which was assessed by the entire world as the most competitive in Georgia's history. You have chosen a united Georgia, a Georgia without poverty. We have confirmed that Georgia's democracy is developing...I want to thank the opposition; because there is no freedom without dissenting opinion...We share a common love of Georgia and a devotion to democracy.' He thanked others too, the journalists, human rights activists and NGOs.

'Strengthening democratic institutions will be my priority. A strong judiciary and army and civil society. We will continue to move, with even firmer steps, towards NATO. This aspiration is not against any of our neighbours' interests, nor is it aimed at alienating any of our neighbours. We should stretch the hand of co-operation to Russia. We should be friends, we should be closer.'

A military parade followed. Soldiers, smart and newly kitted out with US guns – Special Forces personnel dressed head to toe in black – rocket launchers, armoured vehicles and so on and so on. Planes flew overhead – then helicopters, dropping red rose petals on the crowds below.

Petals fluttered down on to our upturned faces.

#

February 2004

Some weeks into February, one lazy Saturday morning at home, Mike and I decided to lay our cards on the table – and it was *our* home. I had moved in with Mike, to the delight of my colleagues. By doing so we would save money on my rent and security and the money could be ploughed straight back into British Council projects – more needed than ever.

'So, what cards have you got?' asked Mike. I looked down at my pile of business cards as we were literally looking through these to try to work out what was going on.

'Kakha Lomaia.'

'Where has he come from and gone to?'

'He was head of the Open Society – he was the man with whom we worked on the exit polls. He's the new Minister of Education!' I put Kakha's new and old business cards in two separate piles.

'And Zurab Adeishvili, who worked with us on human rights training and textbooks is the new Minister of the Interior. One of our John Smith scholars, Gigi Ugulava from one of the legal reform NGOs is the new Deputy Minister of Security.' Ugulava had been working with the British Council on another human rights training project and had been a big player behind the *Kmara* movement. Zurab Tchiabershvili, whom we worked with on parallel vote tabulation, was the new head of the Electoral Commission.

'There is a new Minister of Defence, now Gela Bezhuashvili; he used to be a deputy so there is some continuity there,' added Mike. We went through our pile of cards. Name after name had shifted from jobs in civil society directly into ministerial or senior government positions. I had liked the former ministers of education and of culture – but they couldn't stay. The aspirational generation of reformers had arrived.

'Out with the old, in with the new. The new ministers are so young – most of them are barely 30 years old,' I said. 'And have you noticed – they are almost all foreign educated?' In fact most of the new government had been on scholarships in the west. In the US, in Germany, in France, and, indeed, a substantial number in the UK – our alumni.

'Don't these new ministers have to be elected Members of Parliament first?' I wondered.

'Apparently not – but perhaps they see a foreign Master's degree as a qualification of sorts. I hope they don't overdo it. They have some capable elder statesmen they shouldn't overlook – too many of these young firebrands could be dangerous,' said Mike.

Under Shevardnadze Tedo Japaridze had been a deputy foreign minister, Georgian Ambassador to the US and Chair of the National Security Council. Under Saakashvili he was briefly Minister of Foreign Affairs but was now off to the Turkey Black Sea Co-operation Organisation. It appeared he had been sidelined. 'That's a shame,' said Mike. 'We always assessed him as one of the sensible and experienced players. He was one of the few people who seemed to be able to understand the dynamics of Georgia's relationship with the West, and balancing that with Russia. The new government has a *massive* job ahead of them – they need to think about stability and security.'

Within weeks the new administration worked fast to address some of the most pressing issues – they had released their manifesto to crack down on corruption, to sort out pay and pensions, improve the economy and foreign relations. The new politicians in Georgia aspired to NATO and EU membership. Many observers, however, including Mike, assessed that Russia would see this shift to the influence of western institutions as a threat. 'Saakashvili is dangerously keen on 'territorial reintegration' into Georgia of Abkahzia and South Ossetia. He would do better, in my view, to sort out Georgia's economy and provide a carrot of economic opportunity to people there,' said Mike.

There were virtually no jobs or possibilities for progress for ordinary people in those regions. In fact, little had changed since the separatist civil war of the 90s. If Georgia was able to develop itself as an example of economic progress, this might encourage those living in the separatist regions to develop constructive economic ties.

It was a real challenge for Saakashvili though. There were still over 200,000 internally displaced people, many of them in Tbilisi, from those two places. A high proportion of a population of four and a half million in Georgia. Not only did many of the deeply impoverished ethnically Georgian IDPs want to go home, others – particularly in Tbilisi – wanted to reduce the strain their presence put on the wider Georgian economy. Saakashvili's supporters included a number of hawks who felt that the US-trained and equipped Georgian military would be able to mount a campaign in South Ossetia, in particular. At the outset of his presidential political campaign Saakashvili himself had publicly declared his support for a policy of territorial reintegration and many in Georgia expected him to press for this – it was part of establishing national pride.

Russia, however, would see this as a provocation – they claimed those remaining in South Ossetia and Abkhazia wanted to be independent and wanted Russia's protection. Russian military forces there described themselves as 'peacekeepers'. The Russian state perhaps saw maintaining these frozen conflicts as a way of creating a degree of instability in Georgia, a country they wanted to keep within their sphere of influence. The new President Saakashvili could apparently be mercurial and impulsive – it might be all too easy for the Russians to provoke him and the Georgians into some poorly thought through plan.

'To give Misha credit, they have moved fast to clear out the police and get cracking on tackling wider corruption,' added Mike. Within weeks there were newly recruited police with new uniforms, cars and kit – the police had a new code of practice and had undergone human rights training. They were getting substantial assistance from USAID. No more police waving *pazhalsta* sticks at random motorists for fines – sorting out the police force would be a huge step forward.

In the revolutionary zeal to press ahead, however, there were a number of questionable practices. While Shevardnadze appeared exempt from the new anti-corruption drive, the new government started to arrest men and women believed to be significantly corrupt. Some of these dramatic arrests were filmed. Old men fleeing, one literally being pulled off a stationary plane on the tarmac at Tbilisi airport – another arrested at home at dead of night and led out from his home in his pyjamas. Sentences of those deemed guilty could be commuted if they gave pots of money to try to fill the empty treasury coffers. Many of those arrested were almost definitely guilty – but there were questions from members of Georgian civil society, and from us foreigners. In the rush to get things done, legal corners were being cut – where was the rule of law?

The new, young government had enormous challenges ahead.

46

Musical chairs

The trainer at the front of the room said, 'It is important to include your commitments for purchase in this spreadsheet which links to the master spreadsheet which in turn links to the financial plan template. Don't forget your accrued lump sums...' After all the political excitement, we still had day jobs to do. The senior members of our office, Zaza, Katie, Kote and I, were on a mandatory management course and we would then be training other colleagues in the office. It was a warm day and the sunlight was shining brightly into the stuffy room – it was quite hard to concentrate on the finer detail.

Kote's mobile phone buzzed and I frowned at him. He looked discreetly at it, raised his eyebrows and quietly left the room. The trainers handed out pieces of flipchart paper to the various tables for us to do an exercise. Kote returned some minutes later, shaking his head and smiling. In a low voice, he said, 'Jo, that was the Minister of Justice. He offered me the job of Deputy Minister.' I dropped my marker pen.

It was the biggest honour to be offered a position like this and for Kote it was an opportunity to be able to shape policy in one of the most vital areas in Georgia. It was also brilliant for the British Council – he would be a significant player in what had become one of our most important ministries. It was not a foregone conclusion that he would go, however. It was still so uncertain and fluid. The new Georgian government had huge obstacles to overcome, not the least of which was that there was no money in the Treasury, even to pay ministers' salaries. Salaries with the British Council were not high but rather mid-range compared to other foreign organisations – but we were reliable and had wider benefits in our terms and conditions than the new Georgian government might be able to offer.

For me, in purely practical terms, the timing was not great for Kote to leave. We had just signed a contract with the European Commission to deliver a major training project, the Procuracy Reform Project. This project was designed to improve governance in a key power ministry – all judges and key staff were to be trained in human rights and management of judicial staff. This was a major success for us and was an important area in Georgia's institutional development, but it would be a challenge to deliver it. Kote had been a pivotal part of winning the bid; he was due to be the contract manager and he had a detailed knowledge of the Georgian and UK reform issues and of British Council systems – he would be hard to replace.

When we broke for lunch I said, 'Kote, whatever you need to do, you have my full-hearted support.' Georgia needed people like Kote at the helm. If all the good people stayed with foreign organisations, then we were part of the brain drain. If, on the other hand, we could be a conduit for helping good people learn new skills and use their talents within Georgian structures, it was quite the opposite. He accepted the Minister's proposition.

Shortly after Kote was headhunted, so too was Nata, our Exchanges Manager. She was leaving us to join the Mayor of Tbilisi's Office; another central and influential position. The new President had been the previous Mayor of Tbilisi. Another overhaul of the staffing structure in my office was called for – an opportunity not a problem. More interviews, some promotions and some new appointments later and we had a dynamic, new team.

#

I visited Kote some weeks after he started work. The Ministry of Justice was just down the road from my office so I walked, which in itself was a brilliant feeling. It was springtime and the air was as fresh and crisp as a green apple. I thought of earlier times when foreigners were told they would be risking their safety or possessions just by walking down Rustaveli Avenue – it genuinely felt that things were changing.

Kote's secretary ushered me into his room. It was an impressive room with a window on to Rustaveli Avenue below and Kote had one of those imposing desks that important people have. Kote asked his secretary to bring us coffee. When she closed the door we burst out laughing at the strangeness of his new situation. He was now one of a small group of young Georgian reformers and they had to deliver big, positive changes. With all the excitement, expectations in Georgia were high. 'Kote, how does it feel? How are you coping?' I asked him.

'Jo, I have to say it is weird. I can't tell you how much there is to do and it's hard to know where to start – but we are a good, strong team.' He gave me his new business card. 'We still don't have government email addresses – I'm using a hotmail account!'

'It's great that you are here, though Kote – you are in the right place to help address at least some of the challenges. What an office you have – remember when you joined the British Council when you and the others were crammed in behind the library shelves?'

'How are things at the British Council? I miss you all.' I told him we were as full-on as ever. His successor, Sopho, was fantastic and we had managed to get the new Procuracy Reform Project mobilised. We had a new project manager for it and would also shortly have a new British Ambassador. I asked him about the game of 'musical chairs' going on with his government colleagues.

'Saakashvili is certainly keeping busy. He calls us his kindergarten as we are all so young.' Saakashvili was only in his mid-30s himself and most members of the new government were in their early 30s. The Minister of the Interior looked like Harry Potter. The new Minister of Foreign Affairs, Salome Zurabishvili, had actually been the French Ambassador and she had been rapidly 'naturalised' – I had heard some at the French Embassy were embarrassed by this defection but I imagine some were also rather pleased.

'Nino Burjanadze is staying as Speaker of Parliament; she is sticking by the President for the time being.' They had been rivals before the Rose Revolution.

'How is the Prime Minister getting on?' I asked.

'Zhvania is going flat out sorting out the new tax code. It needed a thorough overhaul. Social taxes will come down by a third, income tax will be halved and they are planning to make things easier for business.' It had been so complex that few people or organisations had paid tax properly – by simplifying it and enforcing the new tax laws, the Treasury could start to pay for public services. It was a vital part of cracking down on corruption.

'Kote, good luck with it all.'

'Keep me on the list when the office goes out socialising.'

I told him we'd have him out dancing again.

\#

I couldn't stay long chatting to Kote as I had to go to the State Prosecutor's Office to help with interviews for new staff for our new project. The British Council, with our Spanish and Danish consultancy partners, was managing the European Commission-funded Procuracy Reform Project. The EC had been a significant development agency in Georgia for some years. Since the inauguration of the new, reformist government they had committed many million more Euros towards major reform projects to help overhaul significant ministries.

The British Council had signed the new contract in February and had one month to put the new team together. Our new team leader, Pam, was an American-Irish former judge and she had hotfooted it to Tbilisi as soon as she could. Pam was determined and feisty and had an eye for the absurd, which was no bad thing. Pam, Sopho and I ran a series of interviews to find her an Office Manager. We explained to each applicant who we were and what the structure of the PRP office would be – that Pam would be the boss, I was her boss and Sopho would oversee contract management.

One particular candidate was a beefy man, slouching in his leather jacket. His experience on paper looked great. He answered most questions well. Pam then asked, 'How do you think you will get on working with a team comprised mostly of women?'

'That's no problem – I wouldn't let them boss me about, oh no. I'm my own man. I don't like women being bossy.'

Pam ended up with a team of focussed and forceful women to support her. They needed to be. The State Prosecutor's Office was one of the power ministries, hard-edged, riddled with crime and corruption and with some of the biggest challenges to overcome. Our project focused on human rights training for judges and other staff and it couldn't confront all the issues – but it would be a start.

#

As well as Pam's arrival, we had a new British Ambassador, Donald McLaren, McLaren of the McLaren. A Scottish laird, no less.

I also had an aunt, Annie, visiting Europe from Canada and who was in Tbilisi for a few days. We decided to take them all sightseeing to the 'dry bridge market', the antiques market down near the river. Mike, Annie and I called outside the Ambassador's residence to collect Donald and his wife, Maida. Although it was April and technically spring should have been in the air, it was freezing that morning. We were all in our winter gear, muffled up against the cold. I rang the doorbell and waited – and waited some more. Eventually the door was opened by Maida, looking elegant and blonde in a long dark coat with a fur collar.

'We're running a little behind schedule,' she said and disappeared. I went back to our car and we sat there waiting. Five minutes later we were still waiting.

'You go this time,' I urged Mike. He rang on the door. And waited. Maida emerged again and said, 'Give us a few more minutes…' Eventually they were evidently ready to join us. Out stepped Donald, in a kilt.

'I wonder how the Ambassador's outfit will go down at the market?'

The dry bridge market was under and around a bridge that had quite a long bank before it crossed the River Mtkvari. One bit of the market had sprawling blankets laid out in all directions selling every conceivable widget and gadget. Another bit had rickety little stalls under canvas to protect the antiques from the elements. The stall holders were literally selling the family silver. It was sad to think of all the people who had to give up their treasures – it was like chopping up the piano for firewood. There were Georgian daggers, guns, jewellery, bits of chandeliers, copper pots, agricultural equipment, silver cutlery, paintings, carved boxes and on and on.

There was also a place where men looking for work would congregate, standing around or holding signs that said 'experienced builder' or 'carpenter' or 'any job considered'. It was perhaps like many places in the Great Depression in the 1930s. As we had anticipated, Donald in his kilt on this icily cold day raised more than a few curious eyebrows amongst the *babouschka*-like ladies and the hard men in black leather jackets. Donald and Maida chatted away affably in Russian to the stall holders. 'They were asking if he had cold knees,' said Mike.

\#

We had taken Annie to a few parties and to see a few sights but for her last day she was on her own. 'I have never been there myself but would a day trip to Gori to see the Museum of Stalinism be of interest?' I asked. Stalin, or Josef Jugashvili, was born in Gori (a shortish drive from Tbilisi), in 1878. He had spent his early years there before moving to Tbilisi where, instead of becoming an Orthodox priest, as his mother had wanted, he became a Marxist revolutionary.

Annie came back from Gori full of her impressions. 'I was taken round the Stalin Museum by a lady called Nino; she was so elegantly dressed, so neatly turned out. Nino showed me room after room, pointing out all the items of interest: 'This is his school desk', 'This is his desk from the Kremlin', 'This is a death mask' – gruesome. And on and on, and all so respectful of Stalin as such a great son of Georgia.'

When the tour was over, Annie admired some beautiful roses growing in the garden. The tour-guide dropped her guard and said, 'People keep stealing them. We plant them, we tend them but our roses get stolen. People take them to Tbilisi to sell them in the market.'

Annie asked Nino whether her family had known Stalin, and she said, 'Yes, we hate him. My family lost everything, all our land, because of him.'

47

MPs and Union Jack bikinis

May 2004, Tbilisi

After giving it some thought, I crouched down in the aisle of the aeroplane and whispered, 'Excuse me please, Madame Burjanadze.'

Nino Burjanadze, Speaker of the House, looked up from her reading. 'Could we talk about the proposed English for Parliamentarians Project?' I asked her. She must have hated being approached by people all the time in her down time but she nodded her assent. I hadn't wanted to tower over her so I knelt down in the aisle. We had briefly met before but in a job like hers I was sure she would not remember me. I said I understood from our new Ambassador – whom she could not forget – that she was keen to have English training for MPs and other staff in the parliament.

'Yes, that's right,' she nodded, 'it is so important for our decision-makers to be able to communicate with people from other countries and to be able to access information and ideas.' Many MPs would be fluent Russian speakers and that was vital too but also having English skills would open new doors and create new opportunities. Not least because massive new projects and loans for reform of ministries and infrastructure were under discussion with the

World Bank, the European Commission and so on – much needed institutions were, at last, being built.

'We are keen to help,' I said. 'We'll bend over backwards to pull a project together as soon as we possibly can. It would be good to have a reception to launch it and get the press in to publicise it.' She offered the parliament building as a venue. I was delighted.

#

At the end of April I had been back in Britain catching up with friends and family. While I was there I had an email from my friend, Maia K, at the British Embassy. She told me, 'Ajara is about to fall after awful things Abashidze has been doing. He has blown up buildings and bridges!' When I got back to Tbilisi in early May the papers were full of headlines like: 'Aslan has fled! Ajara is free!' It was like Narnia Through the Looking Glass. The despot, Aslan Abashidze, had been overthrown in a popular revolt and he had fled to Moscow. Prime Minister Zurab Zhvania said Ajara would retain its autonomous status and that there would shortly be truly free and fair elections there. Businesses and properties held by the Abashidze clan were confiscated: houses, pharmacies, cars, bank accounts.

#

As we got to know Donald, the new Ambassador, we realised he was quite a character. He was as a proficient bagpipe player and delighted Georgian guests with his piping at British Embassy receptions – but he was often late to meetings. I got used to bringing work with me to the Embassy in anticipation that our weekly round-table meeting would be running late. On several occasions I was more than a little aggrieved to have dragged all the way across town to a meeting which it then transpired, at the last minute, had been cancelled. His secretary, Marina, would apologise, 'I'm sorry, Jo, apparently the Ambassador had a late dinner party last night.' Disgruntled I thought, hang on, I was at that dinner party and I am here at work.

I wanted to talk to him about the forthcoming reception at the parliament to launch the English for Parliamentarians Project, which we had pulled together against the clock. When I eventually did see Donald he was charm itself and said, 'Do whatever you need to. Yes, yes, the Embassy will pay for the project if the British Council does all the work. Yes, we'll pay for the reception if you arrange it.' Which was fine by me.

#

Back in my office I sat down with my colleagues, Maka and Nutsa, to work out all the arrangements for the English for Parliamentarians reception. Anuki, who managed our UK exams work, saw us hard at work, plotting and planning. 'I never have an opportunity to do much in the way of public relations in connection with my exams work,' she said.

I asked her to join us. 'Exams can seem like all work and no play. How can we make them eye-catching and 'sexy'?'

'Bikinis are sexy,' said Nutsa. So, putting our heads together, we decided to buy Union Jack bikinis as prizes for top achievers and to use the English for Georgian Parliamentarians reception also for an award ceremony.

'Do you think they will be popular? What if men are the top scorers?' I asked.

'We already know that all the top achievers for this session are young women and Georgian girls love fashion.'

This was certainly true and it was also the case that the Union Jack was quite iconic in Georgia.

We finished our plan and duly arranged to send out invitation cards, on thick white Embassy-crested cards, with elegant curly script saying:

Her Majesty's Ambassador, Donald, the McLaren of the McLaren invites:
(a whole host of important contacts, MPs, ministers, press)
To: The launch of the English for Parliamentarians Project
At: The Parliament of Georgia
(and the time and date)

#

We were in the parliament building with our trusted caterers, Reiners, setting it all up well in time before the arrival of all the VIP guests. A solid staircase led down into a cavernous marble-floored room. At the bottom of the stairs was a platform and on this we had arranged for microphones on stands for the speakers. These would be Donald, as host of the party; the Deputy Leader of the House, Mikheil Machavariani; my English Language Adviser, Rusiko; and me.

Shortly before 7pm, the time the party was due to start, it was all set up and media representatives, TV cameramen and press journalists had arranged themselves at strategic locations. I stood at the bottom of the stairs getting ready to greet guests – and wondering where the host was. 'Where's the Ambassador?' I asked my colleagues – but nobody knew.

Guests started to arrive: VIPs, MPs – some of whom would be learners in the project – members of the English Teachers' Association of Georgia. I was busy greeting them and moving them on to my colleagues who ushered them into the reception area. Still no sign of Donald as guests started to mill around chatting and snacking.

The three winners of our exams competition, not yet out of their teens, were standing giggling in a row to the left of the microphones. Anuki was with them, holding the Union Jack bikinis for the prize-giving later. The PR woman from the Parliament building said, 'We need to start, the Deputy Leader of the House is a busy man – he can only stay for the speeches and then he needs to go.' Out of the corner of my eye, I could see my colleague Maka, waving at me discreetly and pointing.

'Yes, yes, but we can't seem to get hold of the Ambassador,' I said, adding, 'perhaps he is dealing with a crisis…'

I scooted over to Maka. 'What is it? Where is he?'

'He's...' She hesitated, pointing again. 'He's in a cupboard under the stairs!'

What?

I opened a door under the large white marble staircase. Like so many under-stairs cupboards it was evidently a cleaners' cupboard. Sure enough, surrounded by mops and buckets and cleaning rags, there was our Ambassador, along with my friend Maia K, his head of Press and Public Affairs.

He was waving a scruffy piece of paper and she was frantically writing. 'Ah Jo, yes, we've almost finished.' With a flap of papers Donald joined me for the speeches.

The Ambassador started his speech and as soon as he said his first sentence there was cheering. He gave the speech to launch the project on the learning of English, in

Georgian. I was impressed, as were the guests. Georgian can be a devilishly difficult language for foreigners. What Donald had asked Maia to do was write down a phonetic translation of his speech, in which he gave the commitment of his country to the development of democratic processes in Georgia. He paid tribute to the British Council for arranging for the teaching and for the materials on political processes we had provided. He wished the learners good luck with their studies. No wonder they were cheering.

The Deputy Speaker then said, in English, 'There is a Georgian saying that for every language a person knows, they are valued as that many people. So 'be as many people as you can be'.' This was picked up as a strapline in the press.

I thanked them both and said how honoured we were to be involved in the project and how important it was for the British Council to help provide new skills and so on. Also that – on another of our activities which we wanted to celebrate – a new, young generation of learners were excelling. Maybe one day they, too, would be members of parliament or leaders in their fields. We handed out the Union Jack bikinis to the winners of the exams competition to more cheers from the guests.

48

Guns and mountains

June 2004, Svaneti

Mike and I had long wanted to visit the remote mountainous region of Svaneti. It was outstandingly beautiful and had its own unique language – but it was unruly, with feuding mountain tribes and criminal gangs. It bordered the breakaway region of Abkhazia and, although the so-called borders were patrolled by Russian peacekeepers, in reality the area was a conduit for smuggling and banditry.

Apart from wanting to see this beautiful part of Georgia for ourselves, I wanted to meet Eteri, a young English teacher who worked in the Svan capital, Mestia. She needed more resources and help. She had sent me an email when she heard about the British Council's expanding work and, now we were more established in Tbilisi and other major cities, I felt we could start to reach out to more remote parts of Georgia.

At the time few outsiders, including Georgians from Tbilisi, visited Svaneti and the region was seen as a little remote from Georgia proper. Maya Z in my office had a thousand 'Svan jokes' along the lines of 'have you heard the one about the Svan, the Russian and the Armenian etc?'

'There is no rule of law at all there and snipers, bandits and kidnappers hide in the forests – you will need bodyguards,' said Gigi Ugulava, Deputy Minister of Interior, when Mike had discussed our intended visit with him. We concurred.

I knew it was an exceptionally poor part of Georgia and this trip wasn't for tourism but to take English language teaching materials. Before we set off I also loaded up boxes of my old books, videos and clothes and when my colleagues heard they brought toys and clothes. We knew it wasn't much but sometimes a little goes a long way.

Vakho drove us to the city of Zugdidi where we met Eteri. She was with her driver in an old Lada. We got our bags out to transfer them to the Lada and asked Vakho if he wanted to change his mind and come with us. He shook his head and said, 'No, Svaneti is too crazy for me.' And this from the man who had worked in Chechnya.

We had arranged a rendezvous with our Georgian army bodyguards, who would take us on the first leg of our journey to Svaneti's capital, Mestia. The four men had heavy machine guns, bandanas, shiny sunglasses and military fatigues with vests stuffed full of kit – they looked like alley cats that had seen a fair bit of action. Their car was a beaten up Russian jeep. It had a row of bullet holes in a spray across the top of the windscreen. '*Seriouzny*?' asked Mike, pointing at the bullet holes.

'*Da, seriouzny*,' agreed the chief bodyguard. They had been engaged in fighting with bandits only a few days before.

We set off through the deep forests, climbing higher and higher up again. Our guards looked from side to side for glimpses from within the dense trees of reflected metal or glass shining in the keen sunlight which might locate a possible attacker.

We made a comfort stop for a picnic and the guards came over to chat. They showed us their guns. Mike slung a gun strap over his shoulder and the men then offered a gun to me to hold. I spent four years at a Quaker school and we used to debate ethics such as 'would you ever touch a gun?' and I remember that I had reluctantly concurred that I would only do so to save my family's life or a similar catastrophe. Here I was being handed an AK47 for fun.

We eventually got to Mestia which had an expansive, utterly deserted square, surrounded by a number of imposing buildings, one of which was burnt out – it was entirely gutted. 'What happened there?'

'That is the police station. It was burnt down last week. This often happens.'

Our lodging was in a modest farmhouse and our room (maybe someone's bedroom cleared out to make room for us), was simply furnished. Mike gave a whoop of delight as he pulled out an old shotgun which was nestling behind the dressing table.

The following morning we journeyed higher up into the mountains. First we picked up Peter Nasmyth, author, photographer, traveller. Peter looked amused at our entourage. He travelled everywhere without any tra-la-la, with a modest rucksack on his shoulder, a camera and notebook. Peter was a long-time Georgiaphile, hopping backwards and forwards between London and Georgia and writing books such as *In the Mountains of Poetry*. He had been visiting Mestia researching a new book and today he wanted to go higher up still to meet some friends in their mountain hamlets.

We were accompanied by yet more men, this time local police bodyguards. One portly, moustachioed chap, who was in an army uniform that no longer fitted, was evidently the boss. Another younger man was wearing a jacket and pinstriped trousers, dress shoes, a flat cap and had an old

Figure 24 Svaneti towers

rifle on a strap over his shoulder – he looked like a Free French fighter from World War II.

We transferred from Eteri's car to the local guards' jeep. Dotted about were the famous Svaneti towers. These were tall, simple angular buildings with narrow slitted windows, apparently built for feuding and sieging. When things got tough a family could retreat inside, bed down and take pot-shots at neighbours through the slits. Beautiful little children wearing faded clothes and pretty kerchiefs on their heads looked curiously at our unusual party.

We parked up and walked on foot up the steep meadows towards little houses high above us. Peter N led the way, scooting nimbly up the precipitous hillside, followed closely by Mike and one of the young, fit-looking guards. Then another guard and Eteri, then me, huffing and puffing. The Free-French guard (a heavy smoker perhaps) and the chubby guard followed us some way back. We reached the summit of the hill which was perhaps about 1500 metres in altitude. The air was so clear, the sky dazzlingly blue, the meadows vivid green and sprinkled with flowers. Whiter than the whitest thing I have ever seen was snow on the mountain peaks.

We met Madame Marta and her husband, possibly the oldest people I have ever met. Their modest wooden house was surrounded by a fenced enclosure in which sat a plump pig and a cow, with chickens free-ranging all around. Madame Marta was tiny, maybe four and a half feet tall and she was wearing a long dress with an apron and a headscarf. I

calculated that if she was 90-something, she would have been a child when the Russian Revolution happened and during the First World War; a teenager when Georgia was absorbed into the Soviet Union and in her 20s when the Second World War broke out – she might have been like the rosy-cheeked apple pickers in the Soviet posters.

Figure 25 Madame Marta's summer house

I wondered if she had lived in that house all that time. 'This is just our summer house. In the winter we go down the mountain to stay with family in Mestia. Would you like some special tea?' Mike said her Russian accent was impeccably pure. She made us tangy herbal tea in an ancient samovar. We had taken chocolate and biscuits and we had a jovial tea party. The wooden walls of her little house were plastered with colourful advertisements from ancient magazines and a curling old map.

After tea we went out into the pastures and Madame Marta showed me the herbs from which she had made the tea. The guards were hanging about smoking on the hillside. Marta barked at the rather fit one – he was about 6'4" and broad-shouldered – 'You there! Pick flowers for the lady!' Startled, he bent down to pick me a posy. Marta was half his height and possibly almost four times his age. The guard had doubtless seen service on the border with Chechnya, and in the lawless and dangerous Pankisi Gorge, so picking flowers wasn't in the normal course of his working day.

When we said our thank yous and farewells we walked back down to our vehicle and crammed in. We had eight passengers in the jeep – four visitors and four guards. It reeked of petrol and needless to say we had no seat belts – there were at least four machine guns. The driver (the chubby guard), grimly surveyed the route ahead of us and set off, taking a deep breath and holding on tight to the steering wheel. It was barely a road and it was steep. As we gained momentum, we bounced and lurched over the ruts and potholes, hanging on to anything we could reach. Fifteen minutes of being rattled like dried peas in an old tin can and we were back down the mountain side in Mestia. 'I think we should have walked', said Peter faintly.

'I don't think some of their guns had safety catches fully on. They could have gone off at any jolt,' added Mike.

The real business of the trip was to talk to Eteri about how we could help with training more English language teachers in Svaneti. Internet was unreliable, even picking up phone signals could be a challenge, but there was always a way. I gave her all the materials plus the donated clothes and toys and I knew they would be well used. Eteri would later be trained as an English language trainer by Rusiko and Barrie and would then be equipped to share her new techniques and materials. From her remote mountain top, she was our newest recruit to the English Teachers' Association of Georgia.

#

We were trying to cram in as much activity as we could into our trip out of Tbilisi. We opened a new branch of ETAG in the north-west Georgian city of Zugdidi, for which Rusiko came up from Tbilisi.

More significantly I wanted to visit a women's centre in nearby Abkhazia. We had already provided them with some English teaching materials with the help of a British NGO called Conciliation Resources but I wanted to see for myself what the issues were for them and to give them more materials.

Abkhazia, bordering Russia and with a Black Sea coastline, was one of the breakaway regions. Following a brutal civil war in 1993-95 it was now in a state of 'frozen conflict'. Few Georgians were allowed to visit Abkhazia, including the many internally displaced people now resident in around Tbilisi. The territory was heavily guarded by Russian peacekeepers. Likewise, few Abkhaz went into the body of Georgia. As Abkhazia was only recognised by a tiny number of countries as an independent country (Russia, Syria, Venezuela), those who wanted to travel abroad did so on Russian passports.

It felt very distant.

I had liaised with the UN and for this visit Mike, Rusiko and I transferred to a UNHCR vehicle to go over a long, lonely bridge into Gali, just over the border into Abkhazia. We could see that, in its day, Gali would have had a Riveria-type appearance – but now there were crumbling villas and war-damaged buildings rotting away in the semi-tropical vegetation. In many ways it reminded Mike of the aftermath of the war in Bosnia in the 1990s. More than ten years after the conflict in Abkhazia, there was no sign of reconstruction.

We were met by Tsira, a pretty young woman in a stylish minidress with her blonde hair up in a *chignon*. The exterior walls of the teaching centre were pockmarked with bullet holes and the windows were protected by bars as in a prison. In this it was no different to most of the other buildings we had seen there. Inside, Tsira introduced us to 20 or so other teachers. All women, they were all dressed up as if for a party. As indeed it turned out to be.

'We have baked you a cake as our guest of honour,' said Tsira. It was a large cake topped with a layer of chopped jelly, coloured red, clear and green, arranged in the shape of the union jack flag. 'I'm sorry it has green bits rather than blue, but we couldn't get blue jelly.' I said I had never seen such a wonderful cake. I cut the cake and we had speeches and modest toasts to friendship and learning and peace. 'We don't care about politics. We just want our country to be normal – for our children to have the chance of jobs.'

We gave each other tight hugs when we said goodbye.

49

Out of the frying pan and into the fire

Autumn 2004, Tbilisi

Figure 26 Tbilisi balcony

Mike and I were strolling around the beautiful old quarter in Tbilisi. It looked clean and refurbished. Calmer than it had done for many years. New businesses, restaurants and shops were opening up, house fronts were freshly painted, the roads had been mended. It might only be a façade, but it was something and it was a start. It had always been a quirky, arty part of Tbilisi and now it was even more striking.

We discussed what our next steps should be. We had been together for almost two years and we were now both due to leave Georgia the following summer. We had to decide, soon, what to do – whenever there is uncertainty, try to plan.

'OK,' said Mike, 'we have three options, no four, no, OK there are loads of options.' He carried on, 'I give up my job and follow you – but I am only five years off retirement so it makes sense for me to keep going. Or, you give up your job and follow me – but your career is on the up and after Georgia you want another challenging, exciting job.'

He paused and I said, 'We could try to get jobs in the same country – or we try to get jobs in neighbouring countries.'

Mike added, 'Or we both leave our jobs and find work with other organisations so that we can be together. Or both go back to London. Or we split up.' We looked at each other. 'I'm not keen on going back to London, how dull,' said Mike. I agreed. I loved being in the field – I loved networking, meeting new people, leading a team, the whole 'intercultural' thing. And the London office always seemed way too political for me...

'OK, let's look at a map and see where possible posts might come up,' I suggested. As most posts followed a three-year rotation it was broadly possible to predict. We knew our respective organisations well enough and how our own skills sets would map against likely needs in the various countries. My preference was to work in a developing or transitional country. Mike was most likely to work in edgy, challenging places. When we got home, we looked at an atlas. The countries that jumped out were Sierra Leone? Afghanistan? Iraq? Pakistan? A Balkan country? Ukraine? We both set about investigating and applying for new posts.

#

Things were evolving again in my office and it was good that they were. Irakli was headhunted by the Ministry of Finance to be an adviser. I was impressed. 'Not the Ministry of Culture, Irakli?'

'If you remember, Jo, I did arts things in my spare time before I joined the British Council – my day job was in insurance, but things were such a mess then in that sector, it was in its infancy.' I did remember. I had thought Irakli's entrepreneurial and managerial skills were spot on. He was going to be an important member of an important ministry. Since the revolution the government had evidently been working flat out to streamline archaic bureaucracy in the banking and insurance sectors. Western trained business people, a number of them British-trained alumni, were at the heart of reforming the business sector. Things appeared to be making progress.

Sopho had been headhunted too, to do a three-month secondment with the Institute of Migration, helping monitor Iraq's first democratic elections. So we interviewed for new staff and Iki, Lela and Paata joined the team. Katie had worked hard to get her ACCA accountancy qualification, Nutsa was doing evening classes for an MBA. In fact everyone was learning new skills somehow.

#

New Year's Eve 2004

At the end of another eventful year, Mike and I had been back to Britain for Christmas. We flew back to Tbilisi on New Year's Eve and arrived, panting, at the flat of one of our friends just before midnight.

'Quick,' said Roy, 'each grab a glass!' He lived in a modern apartment block about ten floors up. Roy had five other guests and we squeezed out on to his balcony together. He filled our glasses with champagne for us to toast in 2005 with a, 'Happy New Year! Happy New Year! May 2005 be a happy one!' We chorused, and clinked our glasses and kissed, and looked out at the nearby explosions. People were setting off fireworks all over the valley of the city – spectacularly so from the balconies of neighbouring apartment blocks, filling the midnight air with the sharp smell of gunpowder.

'How pretty! Fantastic! Superb! Hang on – isn't that? Machine-gun tracer fire?!'

Yes, people were firing rounds of ammunition from the balconies of nearby blocks of flats, high into the night sky.

'Oh my God! – Duck! – *Fuck*!'

'Mind the glasses,' said Roy faintly, as we beat a retreat indoors.

What goes up must come down!

#

While we were back in Britain Mike was told his next post would be in Afghanistan. Oh my. I still didn't know the outcome of my own application – I had applied for the job of British Council director there too. We wanted to be together. We would have to wait and see.

50

Holding firm in spite of everything

February 2005, Tbilisi

One morning early in February Mike's phone rang. I could hear from his responses that something serious had happened. 'When? God, that's terrible...Where? God, I hope this won't destabilise things. Yes, I heard he was trying to broker a peace deal over South Ossetia.' Who were they talking about? I was all ears, and looked for more clues in Mike's expression. What was going on? He hung up his phone.

'Zhvania has been found dead.' The Prime Minister! This was shocking news. 'In the flat of a friend. Apparently he was poisoned by a leaking gas heater.' It seemed barely credible but it was possible. We had had some terrible heaters in our old office – how many homes and offices must still have those dodgy old gas-buckets? I did wonder how a Prime Minister would be allowed to be exposed to one like them, however. Zurab Zhvania was one of the three key leaders of the Rose Revolution and he had died in mysterious circumstances.

Undoubtedly he was a great loss to the country. Many had admired his level-headed objectivity. A political commentator on the South Caucasus, Thomas de Waal, described him as the 'head' to the ever emotional Saakashivili's 'heart'.

Mike spent all day on the phone. 'There's already wild speculation around the circumstances of his death.' Conspiracy theories mushroomed. Was it indeed an accident? Was it something purely personal, not political? Or was he murdered because he had been trying to broker a deal with South Ossetia, by those who wouldn't benefit from a change in the status quo, certain 'outside forces'? Or by someone in Georgia itself? In one of the opposition parties, or closer in?

The wider region was volatile. Ukraine, a country with close ties to Georgia, and some similarities in its relationship with Russia, had just gone through a revolution of her own. This was the Orange Revolution and the inauguration of the pro-West President, Victor Yuschenko had taken place in late January, only some weeks before. Most Georgians and many others welcomed this but not everyone in the region was pleased with the developments in Ukraine.

Zhvania's death posed a potential threat to the stability of the young government. Georgians didn't need political fragmentation to threaten the delicate progress they had made in reforming their country. And they *had* made progress. In spite of challenges they held firm to their reform agenda. It was just over a year since the Rose Revolution and the new government had become more experienced and more confident. They had introduced swathes of anti-corruption measures to clean up the public sector. One visible manifestation was that the establishment of a new police service created a fresh feel to the city. The officers were smarter in every sense of the word and they drove sleek, new VW patrol cars. What a change from the old policemen; standing around smoking in their Soviet-style uniforms, harassing ordinary people. Tbilisi felt less threatening.

Young reformers were also working flat out to reform tax systems and the banking sector. It had become increasingly essential to use contracts and modern management and business methodology. There appeared to be greater transparency – perhaps fewer deals were now done late at night by men in black over good food and a lot of wine.

The reformers were working hard to develop accountable institutions, improve systems and sharpen their governance. By so doing they hoped to qualify for a major Poverty Reduction Support Credit under the World Bank. This was a huge programme designed to support public sector management, to improve electricity and gas sector services, to make it easier for private sector development and to improve social protection. As a result of the revolution, huge sums of new donor aid and assistance had been agreed with the Georgian government. World Bank, US and Scandinavian money went into improving essential infrastructure: roads, water supply, street lighting. The EC was training civil servants on European structures. The UK's Department for International Development was helping support tourism.

Many of the young people working so hard to transform their country were educated in other countries – they had been on scholarships in the USA, in Germany, in France, at the Central European University in Budapest. Many of them had been to the UK – our alumni from the FCO's Chevening programme, the John Smith Fellowship scheme and the Mansion House scholarships given by the Lord Mayor of the City of London. They had become influential in government and had risen to the top in major law firms, banks and across the media. Crucially some chose to stay outside government, to continue in advocacy and human rights NGOs – it was vital to have those who would speak out to keep the government in check when they got overconfident, or had cut corners in their race to reform – and this was happening. The reform process wasn't perfect. But it was a start.

The UK-Georgian Professional Network – the formal alumni association – had developed into an active NGO in its own right. It became a true think-tank of people who understood the best of what Britain could offer and who understood the reality of the challenges facing their country, thanks to its committed members. Bright, articulate and forward-looking, they were helping to transform Georgia. Education is the key.

51

Impact

March 2005, Tbilisi

A major advance for many of us was that we no longer endured the same frequency of power cuts. Life could begin to approach normality. In spite of this, one dark and snowy night *clumsy me* slipped backwards and fell with a thud on to an icy kerb…I broke four ribs.

EXCRUCIATING

It was my own fault. I was wearing totally unsuitable shoes.

While I was recuperating, Zaza stepped up from Office Manager and covered my job too. He and Tamuna, our head librarian, visited me at home to brief me on work. We had just extended our office to provide a bigger library with innovative facilities unique in Georgia.

'Word is out about our new 'Kids' Corner' in the library,' Tamuna told me. 'The President's little boy came – his bodyguard didn't want to leave his gun with our guards!'

'What did you do?' We couldn't turn away such a top contact and equally we couldn't relax our 'no guns' policy.

'The guard finally agreed to leave his gun in his car but he sat in the children's corner. Mari gave him comics to

349

read.' I pictured the security guard. Doubtless tall and dressed in a black suit and with an earpiece – reading children's books while perched on one of our lime-green, diminutive children's chairs.

Zaza briefed me about other work. The Procuracy Reform Project team had trained every judge in the country on human rights and management – no mean feat. We were hosting wave after wave of visits to and from UK. Artists and academics, musicians and management consultants, trainers and TV journalists. More friends for Georgia, more friends for Britain.

Zaza told me that David Lordkipanidze, the director of the National Museum, was going from strength to strength. David had mobilised enough partners, including the French and German cultural organisations, to host an exhibition of spectacular gold items. These had been found recently at the Vani archaeological site in West Georgia and were dated from the fourth century BC. 'We think we can afford to contribute to the partnership,' said Zaza. At last.

#

One afternoon I had a phone call from a senior colleague in London. 'Jo, I'm phoning regarding your job application…I'm afraid we have not been able to offer you Director Afghanistan.' Oh no! That was where Mike was being posted and I had wanted to work there too. 'However, we are still offering you a promotion – we would like you to be our Deputy Director in Pakistan.'

Oh my.

52

Saying goodbye

I had hosted many parties to welcome and say goodbye to lots of people and now, after almost five years, it was my time to go – the farewell party circuit cranked into gear. Many people knew Mike and me through work so at some of the receptions we appeared as a double act. We had a number of big events to which good friends, Georgian and foreigners, came. It was quite overwhelming. The ambassador also graciously said, 'Both of you let my secretary, Marina, know six top drawer guests and let's have a dinner to wave you off at the Residence.'

It was a small group at our VIP farewell. Donald and Maida, Mike and me. My former colleague Kote (Deputy Minister of Justice); Giga Bokeria (MP and alumnus of the University of Leicester), Kakha Lomaia, Minister of Education, Irakli Alasania, Chairman of the Abkazh Government in Exile, a deputy from the Ministry of Interior and another from Foreign Affairs. This was a high-powered group. We had both worked hard during our time in Georgia and these men were now close contacts. These sorts of events always brought out the speeches and as we know most Georgians love making speeches anyway. It was an opportunity for someone to say a few words of appreciation about what difference the departing person, or in this case two persons, had made. Donald said a few appreciative words about each of us and each of our guests did too with much raising of the wine glasses. It was all too easy to blush.

Donald praised Mike for his contribution to building Anglo-Georgian relations during an action-packed time and for his work to help build capacity and skills in the Georgian ministries with which he worked. Giga Bokeria mentioned the Chevening scholarships, informing the other guests that I had been on his interview board back in 2001. It seemed a lifetime ago.

Kote raised a glass to me and said, 'To the nicest boss I have ever had.' Blush!

Giga Bokeria exclaimed, 'What, nicer than me?' and we all laughed – he was known for being a firebrand and was pretty hardnosed. Giga and Kote had worked together in their NGO days.

Kakha Lomaia, Minister of Education, then said, 'I would like to share with you that without Jo, the Rose Revolution may not have happened.'

Laughter and then silence, as Donald asked, 'How can this be?'

The minister continued, 'In the summer of 2003, as you will remember, I was heading up the NGO, the Open Society Georgia. You might also remember how much I wanted to put in place the system of exit polls to help counterbalance the likelihood of massive electoral fraud. My organisation couldn't possibly do this alone. I asked everyone, all the foreign missions, all the big aid and donor agencies, for their support but none of them were prepared to contribute. I went to see Jo and I outlined my vision – and Jo thought about it and said she could help. With her pledge of support I went back to other organisations and enough came on board. We got the trainers out, instituted exit polls for the first time in this country's history. And, as we know, the exit polls, and the parallel vote tabulation, provided evidence of electoral fraud – from that came the peaceful demonstrations. The rest is history. *Didi madloba* Jo. Thank you very much.' He raised his glass in a toast.

Oh my…

I thanked him and said I was honoured if he felt I had contributed to helping Georgia in some way. Of course, I knew it was their vision and persistence, along with the hundreds of thousands, the millions, of Georgians who had stood together to try to see positive change, that resulted in the Rose Revolution. I knew, and no-one knew more than they did, that the real challenges were still ahead – that they still had to meet the huge expectations from those who took part in those momentous days. I wished them luck. I raised my own glass in a toast to a prosperous, stable, vibrant Georgia.

'To Georgia!'

#

Mike was leaving Georgia for good, a week ahead of me. We had already done a three-way pack: some stuff back to Britain, some with me to Pakistan. A small trunk and two suitcases were going with Mike for his two-year stint in Afghanistan. Holding up his beloved (awful) houndstooth jacket that he had worn when we first met, Mike had said, regretfully, 'I don't think I will have much use for this in Kabul.'

I gently took it from him and put it out of harm's way with the stuff going back to UK. Tucking it deep down.

I held up handfuls of my sleeveless party tops. 'I don't think I will have much use for these in Islamabad.' That was OK, there would be new outfits to wear there, new friends to make, new places to see, new projects to manage.

Finally, the logistics were in place for our move. All we had to do was say goodbye.

#

Vakho drove Mike, me and my colleague, Nutsa, to the airport. Nutsa was there too as on the same flight as Mike's was the winner of the TV programme *The Clever Kid Competition*. This was a spinoff from *Who Wants to Be a Millionaire?* It had become the most watched TV programme in the country and the 11 year-old was flying off to Britain to take up his prize for being the cleverest kid in Georgia – his prize being one month's free tuition at an English language school, paid for by the British Council. Nutsa had managed the British Council arrangements.

At the airport Nutsa went off to help the cleverest-kid-in-Georgia and his parents at the check-in and make sure everything was OK. The clever kid was quite a VIP for us.

This was late August and Mike and I didn't know when we would see each other again. We hoped to be together before Christmas. We both felt that, for the moment, our jobs needed to come first and until we got to our respective new jobs, we had no idea what priorities would confront us – or how reliable the only flight between Islamabad and Kabul, a UN charter flight, would be. I didn't know how we would cope with the distance between us – with the challenges in both, very challenging, countries. I wasn't averse to taking risks but worrying about Mike going to Afghanistan put things on a new plane.

It was, I imagine, like saying goodbye to a lover going to war.

'Jo,' said Mike, pausing as he put his hand on my cheek, 'we don't swim in the shallows do we? You know how much I love you. We'll be together again soon. Let's make it so.'

I whispered, 'Never a dull moment...'

Nutsa appeared breathlessly at my other elbow. 'Jo – the Clever Kid – there is a TV crew here and they want to interview you!' *What?*

I turned to her. 'Nutsa, I'm so sorry I can't...I really can't.' As – of course – I was crying. 'Can you do it?' Nutsa was quite a junior member of our team and ordinarily I would have fielded any interview at a moment's notice. But, for lots of reasons, I felt Nutsa should do it – it was her big project and frankly there was no comparison between her glowingly pretty face and my blotchy one on camera.

'I'd love to!' She ran back across the forecourt of the airport to be interviewed.

Mike went up the stairs towards immigration and I stood at the bottom waving forlornly.

The house felt hollow when I got home.

#

After Mike left I missed him with a passion and we phoned each other every day. I didn't have much time to be bored or lonely though. I was getting everything ready for my successor, Lena, who was arriving the following week. I colour-coded and cross-referenced a wad of hand-over notes; I wanted to leave her some reference points to try to explain where we came from and what we had done – so I tried to encapsulate almost five years of 'making friends for

Britain', to hand on the baton to my successor, frantically trying to make it all make sense.

Revolution, earthquake, a new office in Armenia, a royal visit and a premises project. I had had three bosses in almost five years. Worked with three British Ambassadors in Georgia and one in Armenia. And with two, very different, governments in Georgia. Made many, many trips to Armenia and clocked up a lot of travel to Azerbaijan and beyond.

I had arrived married to one man and was leaving engaged to be married to another.

In many respects, though, what mattered almost as much as any of that was the honour of working with my colleagues in the British Council in Georgia and in Armenia and all the friends I had made within and beyond the office. I laughed often, had occasion to cry too and it could be exhausting – but we felt we were in some way contributing to something greater than ourselves.

#

The British Council team went out for a final feast and we sat chatting and reminiscing. One last time for walnut dips, pomegranates sprinkled like jewels on dish after dish, tangy sauces and succulent meats. One last time to savour aromatic *Saperavi* wine. One last time to toast and toast. We toasted Mike *in absentia*, and I said I would never forget the happy, happy times I had lived in Georgia – not least because this was where I had met him.

'What a shame you couldn't have got married here.'

'We could have project-managed your wedding like a British Council event.'

'Impact assessment, minute-by-minute planning!'

'I could waive the thing about not talking to each other during the party,' I said.

How great that would have been. Tbilisi weddings set off in a long convoy of cars, driving at speed along the major streets such as Rustaveli Avenue and around Freedom Square, with all the drivers continuously honking their horns – and my colleagues knew how to throw a good party. However, Mike's divorce had not yet come through. While my own divorce was short, sharp and painful, Mike's was amicable, practical and, by comparison, quite a slow process. His final papers were expected any day.

Lively and rhythmic music had filled the room while we dined. Men on neighbouring tables spotted the beautiful girls on ours and asked Anuki and Nutsa to dance. There they were, parading and gesturing and gliding flamboyantly in the middle of the restaurant while the rest of us clapped and laughed.

Amongst other kind and thoughtful gifts, my colleagues gave me a photo album which I treasure. It has photos of all of us as babies and as adults. This was long before digital photography or when photos could be easily scanned. The baby photos in particular were touching as they each gave something irreplaceable. It was decorated throughout by sticky notes with flowers drawn by hand in fluorescent highlighter pens. The album was introduced by a little poem: *From time to time, the usual moment seems terribly beautiful.*

#

On my last day, we had a mournful drive to the airport and everyone in the office came. We stood in a huddle in the departure hall.

Goodbye – goodbye – goodbye – good luck! Thank you for everything – I'll miss you – we'll miss you – goodbye…

357

Inevitably, tears welled up. I walked to the top of the stairs at the airport and looked back and waved one last time at these dear friends. I turned away and walked to immigration to go through the usual procedure. The immigration official took my passport and opened it in the bored way of people who have to do the same thing over and over again – then looked up to check my face against the photograph. He saw my red, tearful eyes. He was surprised. 'Are you OK?' he asked, solicitously.

'I'm sad to be leaving Georgia.'

'I could refuse to give you an exit stamp?' he offered helpfully. I laughed.

'No. It's time to go.' Not least because I am sure my successor, Lena, couldn't wait for me to get out of her hair and to be able to take the colour-coded, cross-referenced baton I had handed over to her and run with it. Lena and her new team had things to do, projects to improve, new people to meet and relationships to build.

On the plane I was pleased, at least, to find I had three seats in a row to myself. As soon as I could, I pushed the arm rests up and lay down across all three seats. The stewardess asked if I would like anything and I asked for a cup of tea and a pillow. She left me to the serious business of crying into the pillow. She must have wondered what was wrong. Perhaps she thought someone I knew had died or I was going through some romantic trauma.

I really must stop crying on planes.

53

Arriving again

September 2005, Islamabad airport

Some weeks later I had arrived in my new country, Pakistan.

It was early in the morning and already quite hot. Islamabad International Airport was buzzing and bustling with plane loads of new arrivals. There was a long queue at immigration. After my 'illegal immigrant' experience in Armenia, I had a slight anxiety that my papers wouldn't be in order – I dreaded the possible inconvenience and embarrassment of being hauled off somewhere for questioning.

I made it through immigration without incident and collected my weighty luggage – my suitcases were packed full to bursting. I hauled the bags on to a trolley, tired and overwhelmed by all the noise, and I am sure I had that confused 'just-arrived' look. To a chorus of yells of 'taxi', 'Madame, taxi!' and a general hubbub, I struggled to push my luggage-laden trolley out into the arrivals hall. I emerged to where all the drivers and relatives and friends of arriving passengers were pushing and thronging. I scanned the crowds. There were hundreds of people rammed up against the long barrier, calling and beckoning. Many men wearing long white *jalabiya* and women and girls dressed in colourful *shalwar kameez*.

I looked for someone with my name on a piece of card, as I was expecting a British Council driver to collect me – and was so relieved and pleased to see him, holding up the sign with my name on it. I waved and smiled broadly at him, pointing at the sign and at myself, nodding, and he smiled back in greeting.

Then I noticed, standing next to the driver – with a smile on his movie star face – was Mike.

Epilogue

Georgia beyond

June 2013, Tbilisi

'Jo, have you noticed something?' I had to look out at the valley below us to work out what Mike meant. 'The lights are on – it's night time in Tbilisi and the lights are on – and there is no rumble of generators.'

Mike and I were back in Tbilisi, having a cocktail at the Betsy Hotel, taking in all the changes since we had lived there during those heady days surrounding the Rose Revolution. We did indeed get married. Not in the exciting surroundings of Kabul or Islamabad – which we attempted to organise – but when we were back in Britain on leave, in the rather prosaic venue of a registry office in Dorset. A few days after we got married, we flew back to our respective countries. When the time came again for us to move on, I decided that, although I loved the British Council, I loved Mike more and I resigned. I became an 'accompanying spouse' for his last posting in Kingston, Jamaica – the British Council had an unusually small operation there and there was no possibility of a job with them for me. We decided that Kingston was like Tbilisi with palm trees, a big compliment indeed. I did eventually go back to work for the British Council as a friend of the family – a consultant – and a series of assignments for them often took me to Asia and kept me busy in Britain.

As soon as we could, Mike and I went back to Georgia on holiday, as tourists.

#

In spite of continuing challenges, Georgia had come a long way since the Rose Revolution in 2003. There were some major achievements of remarkably rapid institution-building. The low level corruption and institutional decay to which Georgia was prone before the revolution was tackled head on. In 2003 the independent watchdog, Transparency International, had ranked Georgia 133 out of 175 countries for perceptions of corrupt practices in public and business life. By 2018 Georgia ranked 41. The United Nations Development Programme has redefined Georgia as a High Human Development country – not as high as the resource-rich Russian Federation but overall levels of poverty are lower than in neighbouring Azerbaijan and Armenia.

The reformers behind the Rose Revolution did indeed update laws, implemented a transparent taxation system and modernised banking. The civil service was streamlined and became more functional. These and other reforms helped to dramatically reduce public sector corruption. Police were held accountable to enforce the laws and there was a notable decrease in violent crime.

There had been hundreds of thousands of internally displaced persons housed in appalling conditions in collapsing hotels. Many of them had been moved to live in specially constructed satellite camps – while far from an ideal situation, their situation was preferable to what they endured beforehand.

We noted that Tbilisi was busy with shops – including IKEA – Carrefour – Next. Not everyone likes them but, after all the earlier deprivations, it was good for ordinary people to have extra choice. The city had even more quirky and elegant bars, clubs and restaurants – modern offices and banks. Many of the beautiful old buildings lining the hilly streets had been restored; balconies repaired and façades painted in glorious pastels. Ancient streets had been uncovered and pedestrianised and there were yet more artisans displaying their wares in enticing little shops. Roads had been renamed and signposted. The main road toward the airport was renamed George Bush Street – the airport itself was a shiny, chrome and glass, modern gateway.

There were tourists everywhere. Planeloads and busloads of them from all over the world. Taking pictures of the grapevines curling around the pretty balconies or wandering through the old quarter. Making their way along smooth new motorways to sample Georgia's many wines in the vineyards far out in the countryside. Or strolling through the art galleries and world-class museums to wonder at the ancient gold and enamel artefacts alongside stunning contemporary art.

Batumi had become a flamboyant palmtree-fringed centre for casinos and other seaside entertainments. Kutaisi, the third city, has become the legislative capital.

#

'How are things for you now?' I asked friends, anticipating a 'happy every after' response. From what we could see things had not reverted to the pre-revolution chaos we had lived through when we had first arrived in the country.

'Oh, our politicians are terrible, such corruption!'

'Is it still so corrupt? I thought things have improved here. Tbilisi seems so vibrant and prosperous – and I heard you pay taxes and that the civil service is functioning now,' I said.

'Oh yes, the economy is doing much better and we don't have to bribe everyone to get simple things done – and yes, the education system has improved so much. Oh and yes, healthcare is better too…but the guys at the top, who can trust them?' A common problem in many countries.

'You seem to have water, gas and electricity, all at the same time?' I asked.

'Of course – yes, of course we do. It is hard to remember those days. Some things have changed so much we have become used to them now. But Jo, the worst times were in 2008. The Russians invaded us!'

While they were busy tackling the economy and corruption, Saakashvili and his government also, naively, attempted to take on the Russian Federation. Increasing military tensions between Georgia and Russia over the self-proclaimed republic of Abkhazia – including Russian troop reinforcements there – led mercurial Saakashvili to send a pre-emptive force of Georgian troops into South Ossetia. Maybe at the back of his mind was that this would be a diversionary action away from Abkhazia and perhaps it was an attempt to reintegrate South Ossetia into Georgia. Territorial reintegration of both these breakaway republics had been a strongly emotive part of Saakashvili's election campaign in 2003.

He seriously misplayed his hand. Evidently Saakashvili's pro-Western Georgian government anticipated that NATO, and the US in particular, would support them. However, there was a brutal Russian retaliation. There was no rescue from the West, no cavalry support.

'We were terrified, Jo!' Anka told me. 'I was in Tbilisi with my husband but our three little children were at my brother's ski school up in the mountains in Bakuriani. Misha Saakashvili appeared on TV, his face was ashen, shocked. He told us Russian tanks were going to invade Tbilisi and that we should prepare for the worst!'

Understandably, many people in Tbilisi panicked – there was a run on food and fuel and phone lines collapsed. Anka and her husband leapt in their car to make the three hour journey to Bakuriani to get their children. They drove fast until they reached the city of Gori. 'But the highway was blocked there – I was weeping to my throat, it was the worst feeling. We couldn't get to my children. The police stopped us, they told us Gori had been bombed!'

Russian tanks had entered Georgia and got as far as Gori, about an hour's drive from Tbilisi. Taking any route they could, it took Anka and her husband eight hours to reach Bakuriani, driving over perilous and unfamiliar mountain roads in the dark.

'We had to keep stopping to ask directions – and no-one knew what was happening with the invasion but we heard hundreds of people had been killed! And I felt so bad, Jo! The world was falling apart for us – if our country cannot protect us and we cannot protect our children? What can you trust?'

They stayed the night in Bakuriani, anxiously debating what to do, where to go. They decided to travel back to the capital in convoy with another four cars. 'We made it safely back to Tbilisi. We had to go so slowly and we saw the woods burning near Borjomi. Our soldiers and road blocks were everywhere. It was terrifying...'

The Russo-Georgian war was short but vicious. According to an EU report, in the five-day conflict, 412 Georgians (of whom over two hundred were civilians), 67 Russians and 365 South Ossetians were killed and over two thousand people on all sides were wounded. The conflict was ended with foreign diplomatic intervention and the Russian troops withdrew. In effect the conflict strengthened Russian hold over the self-proclaimed republics of South Ossetia and Abkhazia.

#

Georgian confidence was deeply shaken by the Russian invasion in 2008. Saakashvili's misjudgement will have contributed to his eventual downfall in 2012.

Nine years after the Rose Revolution, the Saakashvili-led United National party government was voted out in Georgia's first smooth democratic change of government. In spite of that government's many achievements, the Georgian people by now expected to be able to hold their rulers accountable in a way that previous regimes had not been. Some of the positive developments were overshadowed by ever increasing demands for reform, transparency and accountability.

Saakashvili himself stepped down from presidential office in 2013, as was constitutionally required, having served two terms. After his party's electoral defeat there was considerable political retribution. Saakashvili and some of his top ministers were accused of varying degrees of criminal or corrupt behaviour – some charges may have been politically motivated. Saakashvili infamously went on to become involved in Ukrainian politics. Giorgi Margvelashvili, whom I had known when he was the head of the Georgian Institute of Public Affairs, was elected as President. In 2018 he, in turn, was replaced by Salome Zurabishvili (who had been Minister of Foreign Affairs under Saakashvili and before that, the French Ambassador to Georgia).

Before and after the Saakashvili government, while standards of living have evidently improved for many people and low level corruption has been massively reduced, there is still evidence of high level cronyism. The press is not perhaps as free as it should be and shady deals are perhaps still concluded by powerful men in dark rooms consuming good food and fine wine into the wee, small hours.

As in many other countries, political life in Georgia seems to have polarised between older traditionalists and younger modernisers. The Russian 'offer' might be compelling for a number of Georgians. However, for most Georgians, the last thing they want is a return to being under the influence or control of their powerful northern neighbour.

Georgians are rightly proud of their independence.

#

Many of my former colleagues from the British Council and the Peacekeeping English Project went on to set up their own businesses, some as management consultants and advisers. Others have become senior public servants in Georgia. Some are now working in senior international positions in London, Strasbourg and New York. Maia K left the British Embassy and worked at senior level in the Georgian Ministry of Foreign Affairs, before being posted as Georgian Ambassador to Norway.

As for the British Council in Georgia, it is still going – stronger than ever – from the office on Rustaveli Avenue. Zaza is not only the Director of the Georgia team but of all the South Caucasus countries, working with the stars, Maya D, Tamuna, Eka, Gogi, Luiza, Vakho and Katie.

It was not just Mike and I who found Georgia an exceptionally exciting and romantic place. Some of our British and other foreign friends met each other there and subsequently married. Other friends met and married dashing and beautiful Georgians.

People still fall in love under the grapevines in Tbilisi.

June 2019

Bibliography

I have tried to be factually accurate and have consulted widely. Any mistakes or inaccuracies are unintentional and are mine alone.

Abramia, Natia, *Culture Smart! Georgia – Customs & Culture*, Kuperard, London, 2012

Burford, Tim, *Georgia: The Bradt Travel Guide,* Bradt Publications, 1999

De Waal, Thomas, *The Caucasus: An Introduction,* Oxford University Press, 2010

Edisherashvili, S and Iremashvili, G, *The Rose Revolution*, Advertising and Publishing Company, Tbilisi 2004

Gahrton, Per, *Georgia: Pawn in the New Great Game*, Pluto Press, London 2010

Gorgiladze, R, *Joy of Sharing – Georgian Feasting Culture*, Cezanne Publishing, 2012

Jones, Stephen F, *War and Revolution in the Caucasus: Georgia Ablaze*, Routledge, UK, 2010

Karumidze, Z and Wertsch, J V, *Enough! The Rose Revolution in the Republic of Georgia 2003*, Nova, New York, 2005

Medzmariashvili, E Ed, *100 Museums of Georgia*, KLIO Publishing House, Tbilisi, 2012

Mitchell, Lincoln A, *Uncertain Democracy: US Foreign Policy and Georgia's Rose Revolution*, University of Pennsylvania Press, 2009

Nasmyth, Peter, *Georgia: In the Mountains of Poetry*, Abingdon, UK: Routledge, 2006

Plunkett, R and Masters, T, *Georgia, Armenia and Azerbaijan*, Lonely Planet, 2004

Russell, Mary, *Please don't call it Soviet Georgia*, Serpent's Tail, London, 1991

Steavenson, Wendell, *Stories I Stole*, Atlantic Books, UK 2002

#

The Messenger

Georgian Times

Georgia Today

#

International Election Observation Mission – Parliamentary Elections, Georgia – 2 November 2003

London Information Network on Conflicts and State-building – Crisis and Renewal in Georgian Politics: the 2003 Parliamentary Elections and 2004 Presidential Elections, Broers, Lawrence and Broxup, Julian

OSCE/ODIHR Election Observation Mission Post-Election Interim Report 3-25 November 2003

#

http://news.bbc.co.uk/1/hi/programmes/from_our_own_correspondent/3239732.stm

Georgians topple their president - Damian Grammaticas

http://news.bbc.co.uk/2/hi/europe/3288547.stm   How to stage a revolution – Natalia Antelava

http://news.bbc.co.uk/2/hi/europe/3231670.stm Shevardnadze's resignation hailed

http://news.bbc.co.uk/2/hi/europe/4231653.stm   Saakashvili steps in as PM dies

https://www.cia.gov/library/publications/resources/the-world-factbook/geos/gg.html

www.civil.ge/eng

www.civicvoices.org People Power: How Engaged Citizens Change the World – Voices of Georgian Video Transcript

https://rm.coe.int/168071b015 Report on local elections in Georgia (2 June 2002), Rapporteur: Mr WHITMORE (United Kingdom) Document adopted by the CLRAE Bureau on 5 July 2002

https://edition.cnn.com/2014/03/13/world/europe/2008-georgia-russia-conflict/index.html

www.dw.com/en/changes-ahead-in-georgia/a-17188393 28.10.2013

https://eeas.europa.eu/headquarters/headquarters-homepage_en/23634/EU-Georgia%20relations,%20 factsheet

www.euraisanet.org/departments/insight/articles/
eav121603_pr.shtml

www.globalsecurity.org Georgia's Rose Revolution

http://museum.ge/?lang_id=ENGGEO&sec_id=1

www.nytimes.com/2003/11/15/world/president-of-georgia-
pleads-for-calm-as-protests-grow.html

https://www.osce.org/odihr/elections/55759   Georgian
parliamentary elections marred by confusion over voter
lists, OSCE, 3 November 2003

www.transparency.org

www.ge.undp.org/content/georgia/en/home/countryinfo/

http://www.usip.org/pubs/specialreports/sr167.html

https://en.wikipedia.org/wiki/Baku%E2%80%93Tbilisi%E
2%80%93Ceyhan_pipeline

https://en.wikipedia.org/wiki/Georgia_(country)

https://en.wikipedia.org/wiki/2003_Georgian_
parliamentary_election

https://en.wikipedia.org/wiki/Liberty_Institute_(Georgia)

https://en.wikipedia.org/wiki/Rose_Revolution

https://en.wikipedia.org/wiki/Kmara

Acknowledgements

With thanks

For her beautiful artwork: Jane Yates

For copy editing: Peter Skelton

For their help or encouragement in the writing of the book:
Jules Adair, Ray Brown, Naheed Maalik, Jane Morrow, Tina Murphy, Helen Page and the Jericho Writers.

For their friendship in Georgia and beyond: Siobhan and Chris Nunn, Maia Kipshidze and everyone at the

Figure 27 Jo, Mike, Chris and Siobhan Nunn

British Embassy. Deborah Barnes Jones and Dick Jones. Maka Gvelesiani. Darren Woodcock and Nino Tatishvili.

The feisty ladies of the English Teachers' Association of Georgia. Pam Fahey and all colleagues of the Procuracy Reform Project.

All the Peacekeeping English Project team, including Gochia Rusia in Poti.

Figure 28 PEP team: Lela Abdushelishvili, Ray Brown, Marina Mshvidobadze, Lia Partsvania, Mzia Skhulukhia, Nino Verulashvili, Tamar Shavlakadze, Eka Patsatsia

Alumni friends – too many to mention by name!

Figure 29 Friends from the alumni association

British Council Armenia: Marina Aghekyan, Yulia Boyle and Mikhayil Yesayan.

Figure 30 Marina and Yulia British Council Armenia

Figure 31 Some friends from the British Council in Georgia

British Council Georgia: Katie Gegidze, Vakho Shalibashvili, Anka Vetsko, Luiza Tarashvili, Tamuna Kvachadze, Eka Meskhi, Maya Zedelashvili, Nata Machaladze, Alexander Turiashvili, Nino Korinteli, Gogi Kvachadze, Anuki Tikaradze, Zaza Purtseladze, Kote Vardzelashvili, Rusiko Tkemaladze, Irakli Pitskhelauri, Irene Barnabishvili, Nutsa Kuridze, Maka Khurtsidze, Gogi Razmadze, Maia Darchia, Sophiko Gelashvili, Mari Chichinadze, Irakli Vetsko, Paata Charashvili and Lela Shekiladze.

Biggest thanks to my fellow traveller, Mike.

Figure 32 Mike and Jo

About the Author

Figure 33 Jo in Tbilisi market 2003

Jo Seaman's parents travelled to follow job opportunities and Jo grew up in Nigeria, Northern Ireland, South East London and Australia. This gave her a love of meeting new people and seeing interesting places. Unsurprisingly, she was drawn to an international career. Jo worked for the British Council for almost 30 years, firstly in London and Manchester, with short assignments all over Africa, Asia and the former Soviet Union. She then lived in Egypt, Georgia, Pakistan, Jamaica and France before returning to the UK. She is married. She and her husband live in Dorset, have various rescue pets and are trying to be environmentally friendly to atone for all the flying about. Her travels have proved a rich source for her writing.

Find Jo on Facebook.com@joseamanauthor<mailto:Facebook. com@joseamanauthor> and Instagram@joseamanauthor and Twitter @joseaman4.